# A-Z WALES

| | |
|---|---|
| Key to Map Pages | 2-3 |
| Road Maps | 4-67 |
| Town Plans, Airports & Port Plans | 68-74 |
| Index to Towns and Villages | 75-87 |

## REFERENCE

| | |
|---|---|
| Motorway | **M4** |
| Under Construction | |
| Proposed | |
| Motorway Junctions with Numbers | |
| Unlimited Interchange **4**　Limited Interchange **5** | |
| Motorway Service Area (with fuel station) | SWANSEA Ⓢ |
| with access from one carriageway only | Ⓢ |
| Major Road Service Areas (with fuel station) | BANGOR |
| with 24 hour facilities | Ⓢ |
| Primary Route (with junction number) | A55 |
| Primary Route Destination | **NEATH** |
| Dual Carriageways (A & B Roads) | |
| Class A Road | A48 |
| Class B Road | B4246 |
| Major Roads Under Construction | |
| Major Roads Proposed | |
| Fuel Station | |
| Gradient 1:7 (14%) & Steeper (Ascent in direction of arrow) | |
| Toll | Toll |
| Mileage between Markers | 8 |
| Railway and Station | |
| Level Crossing and Tunnel | |
| River or Canal | |
| County or Unitary Authority Boundary | |
| National Boundary | |
| Built-up Area | |
| Village or Hamlet | |
| Wooded Area | |
| Spot Height in Feet | • 813 |
| Relief Above 400' (122m) | |
| National Grid Reference (Kilometres) | 100 |
| Area Covered by Town Plan | SEE PAGE 68 |

## TOURIST INFORMATION

| | |
|---|---|
| Airport | |
| Airfield | |
| Heliport | |
| Battle Site a | 1066 |
| Castle (ope | |
| Castle with | |
| Cathedral, | |
| Country Park | |
| Ferry (vehicular) | |
| (foot only) | |
| Garden (open to public) | |
| Golf Course　9 Hole　18 Hole | |
| Historic Building (open to public) | |
| Historic Building with Garden (open to public) | |
| Horse Racecourse | |
| Lighthouse | |
| Motor Racing Circuit | |
| Museum, Art Gallery | |
| National Park | |
| National Trust Property　(open) | NT |
| (Restricted Opening) | NT |
| Nature Reserve or Bird Sanctuary | |
| Nature Trail or Forest Walk | |
| Place of Interest | Craft Centre • |
| Picnic Site | |
| Railway, Steam or Narrow Gauge | |
| Theme Park | |
| Tourist Information Centre | |
| Viewpoint　(360 degrees) | |
| (180 degrees) | |
| Visitor Information Centre | |
| Wildlife Park | |
| Windmill | |
| Zoo or Safari Park | |

## SCALE

| | |
|---|---|
| Map Pages 4-67 | |
| 1:158,400 | |
| 2.5 Miles to 1 Inch | |

EDITION 13　2023

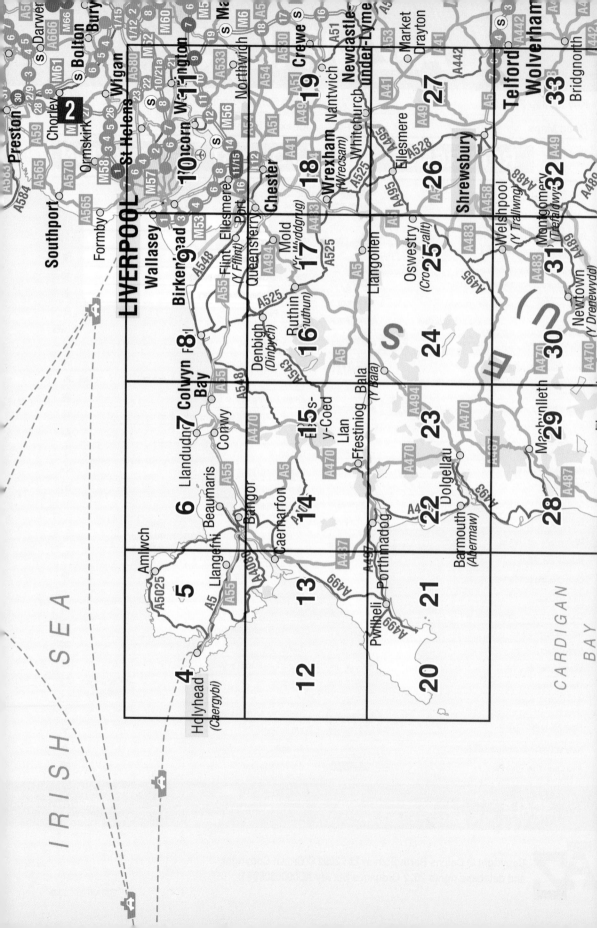

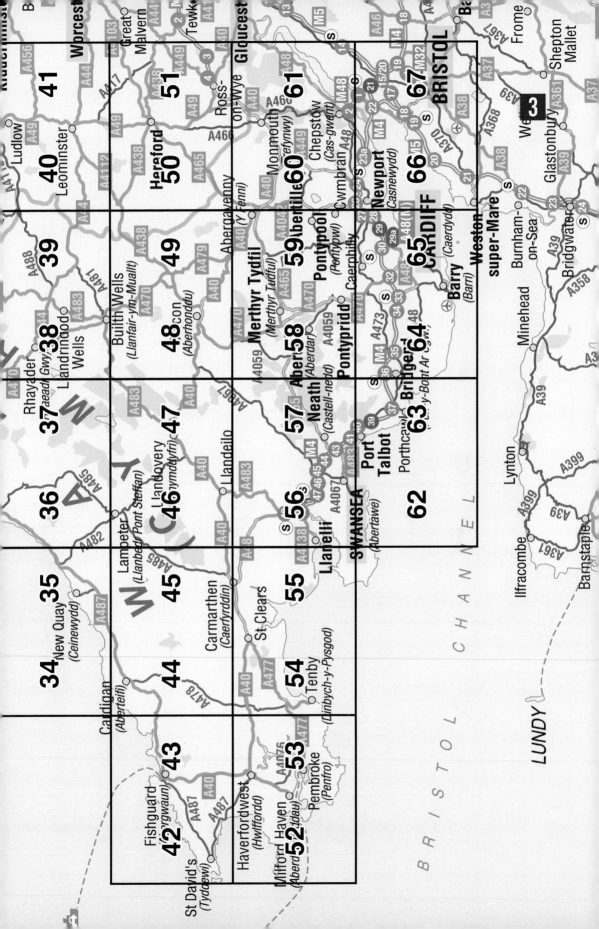

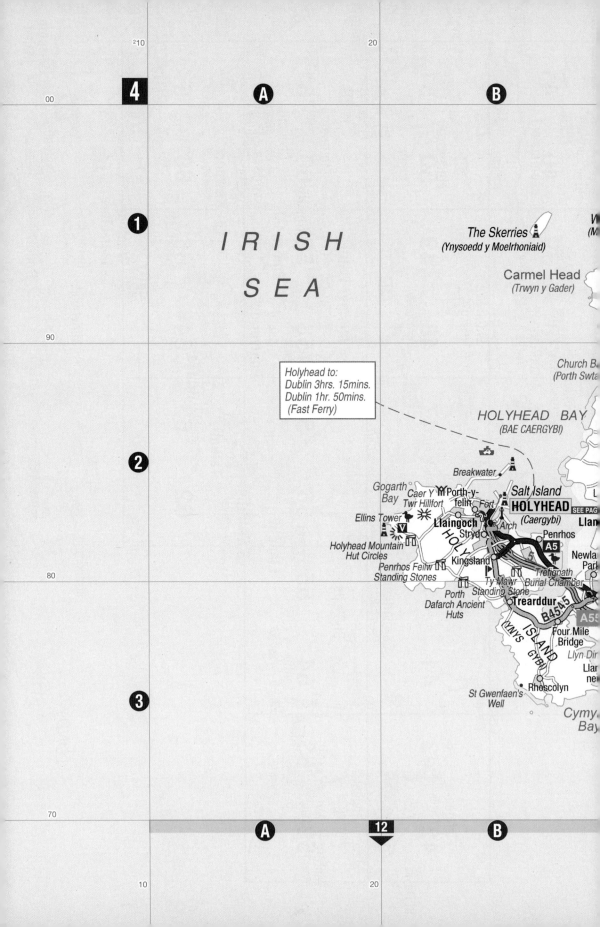

00

❶

*I R I S H*

*S E A*

The Skerries
(Ynysoedd y Moelrhoniaid)

W
(M

Carmel Head
(Trwyn y Gader)

90

Church B.
(Porth Swta

Holyhead to:
Dublin 3hrs. 15mins.
Dublin 1hr. 50mins.
(Fast Ferry)

HOLYHEAD   BAY
(BAE CAERGYBI)

❷

Breakwater

Salt Island

Gogarth
Bay

Caer Y
Twr Hillfort

Porth-y-
felin

Fort

HOLYHEAD
(Caergybi)   SEE PAG

L

Ellins Tower

Llaingoch

Arch

Llan

Strydo

Penrhos

A5

Holyhead Mountain
Hut Circles

Kingsland

Newla
Park

Penrhos Feilw
Standing Stones

Ty Mawr
Standing Stone

Trefignath
Burial Chamber

80

Porth
Dafarch Ancient
Huts

Trearddur

B4545

A55

Four Mile
Bridge

Llyn Dir

ISLAND

Llan
ne

YNYS GYBI

❸

St Gwenfaen's
Well

Rhoscolyn

Cymy
Bay

70

10 20

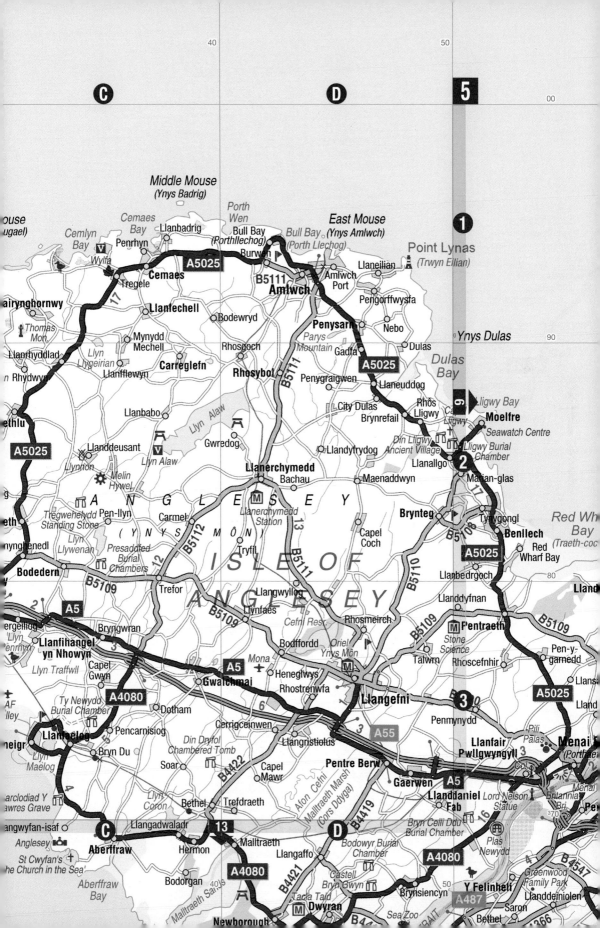

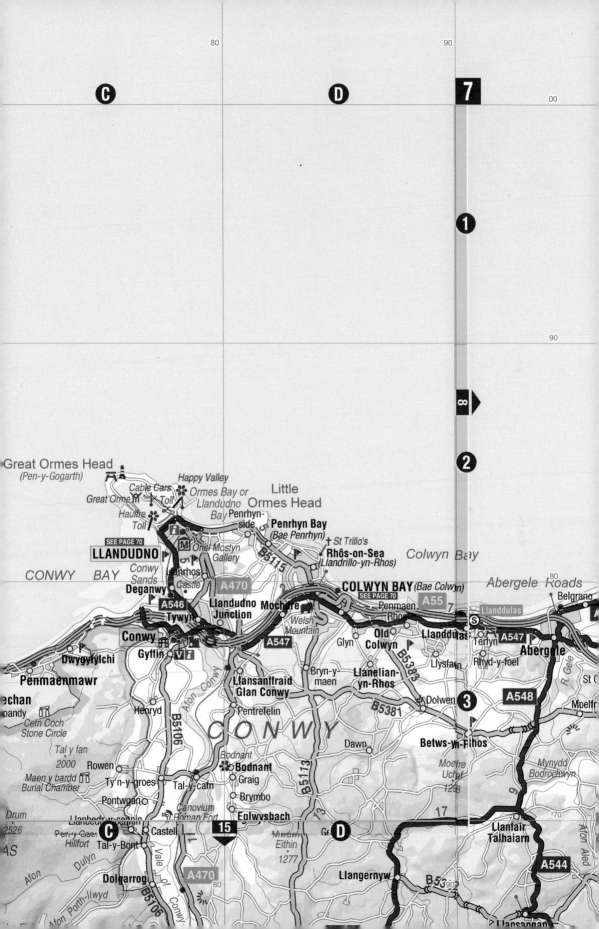

80     90     00

**1**

**8**

**2**

90

**Great Ormes Head**
*(Pen-y-Gogarth)*

Happy Valley

Cable Cars   Ormes Bay or
Great Orme   Toll   Llandudno
    Haulfre   Bay
    Toll

Little
Ormes Head

Penrhyn-
side   **Penrhyn Bay**
    *(Bae Penrhyn)*

St Trillo's

Oriel Mostyn
Gallery

**Rhôs-on-Sea**
*(Llandrillo-yn-Rhos)*

*Colwyn Bay*

SEE PAGE 70
**LLANDUDNO**

*CONWY   BAY*

Conwy
Sands   Llanrhos

Castle

**Deganwy**

A470

**COLWYN BAY** *(Bae Colwyn)*
SEE PAGE 70

*Abergele Roads*

80

Belgrano

A546

**Tywyn**

**Llandudno
Junction**

Mochdre

A547

A55

Penmaen
Rhos

7

Llanddulas

**S**

A547

**Dwygyfylchi**

**Conwy**

Gyffin

Welsh
Mountain

Glyn

Old
Colwyn

Llanddulas

Terfyn

Rhyd-y-foel

**Abergele**

A548

R. Gele

St

Moelfr

**Penmaenmawr**

Bryn-y-
maen

**Llanelian-
yn-Rhos**

Dolwen

Llysfaen

B5383

echan
oandy

Cefn Coch
Stone Circle

Henryd

**Liansanffraid
Glan Conwy**

Pentrefelin

**C O N W Y**

B5381

Dawn

Moefre
Uchaf
1298

**3**

**Betws-yn-Rhos**

Mynydd
Bodrochwyn

Tal y fan
2000

Rowen

Maen y bardd
Burial Chamber

Ty'n-y-groes

Bodnaht
**Bodnant**

Graig

Tal-y-cafn

Brymbo

B5113

370

Drum
2526

Pontwgan

Canovium
Roman Fort

Eglwysbach

17

**Llanfair
Talhaiarn**

AS

Penry Gaer
Hillfort

**C**   Castell
Tal-y-Bont

**15**

Vale of Conwy

Eithin
1277

Ge

**D**

A544

Drum

Afon
Dulyn

**Dolgarrog**

A470

80

**Llangernyw**

B53   902

B5106   Afon Porth-llwyd

**Llansannan**

**A**   **B**

390   00

00

**1**

90

◄ **7**

**2**

Bay

(yn)  † St Trillo's

**Rhôs-on-Sea**
(Llandrillo-yn-Rhos)

Colwyn Bay

SeaQuarium
SC2
**M**

**Prestatyn**  **A548**  SEE PAGE 71

Grona

**A547**

Bryn-llwyr

**Meliden**  **Gwaenys**
(Gallt-Melyd)

Tan-yr-allt

**Kinmel Bay**
(Bae Cinmel)

Abergele  Roads

**RHYL**
SEE PAGE 72

B5119

5

R.
Clwyd

**A547**

**Trelawnyd**

**Dyserth**  **A5**

Boorhyddan
Hall

80

**COLWYN BAY** (Bae Colwyn)
SEE PAGE 70  **A55**

Penmaen-
Rhos

Belgrano  Towyn

**A548**

**Rhuddlan**

2

Marian
Cwm

Rhuallt

B5429

3

Glyn

**Old
Colwyn**

**Llanddulas**

Terfyn

**A547**

**A525**

Cwm

**Llandulas**

S

Rhyd-y-foel

**Abergele**

Llysfaen

**A547**

**A525**

Pengwern

B5429

Llanelian-
yn-Rhos

Bryn-y-
maen

R. Gele

St George

**Bodelwyddan**

† Marble Church

Waen
Goleuogoed

**Treme**

B5381

**3**

**A548**

Moelfre

KINMEL
PARK

S

**Bodelwyddan**

Graig

So

Dawn

Betws-yn-Rhos

Moelfre
Uchaf
1298

B5381  Glascoed

**St Asaph**
(Llan-Elwy)

B5429

Bodfari

R. Elwy

**A525**

**A541**

9

R.

70

17

Mynydd
Bodrochwyn

**CONWY**

Llannefydd

Plas yn
Cefn

**Trefnant**

Bont-newydd

B5429

Gell

**A**

Afon Aled

Dolwen
Resr.

**16**

Cefn
Berain

**B**

Aberwheeler
(Aberchwile)

**A543**

**Llanfair
Talhaiarn**

**A544**

9

B5382

Henllan

Friary
(remains)

R.

**Llangernyw**  B5902

Gwaenynog
Bach

**Denbigh**
(Dinbych)

Llansannan

LIVERPOOL

**C** **D**

BAY

20

30

Liverpool to
Dublin 8hrs.

Liverpool to
Douglas 2hrs. 30mins.
(Fast Ferry, Seasonal)

Birkenhead to:
Belfast 8hrs.
Douglas 4hrs. 15mins.
(Seasonal)

Crosby Channel

Fort Perch Rock
Marine Radio

Hightown
Lady
Green
Little
Crosby
Great Crosby
CROSBY
LITHERLAND
Waterloo
Seaforth
BOOTLE
WALLASEY
New
Brighton
Liscard
Egremont (Kingsway)
Seacombe
Mersey
Tunnel
(Queensway)
Toll
BIRKENHEAD
Bidston
Claughton
Priory
Toxteth
Tranmere
Festival
Rock
Ferry
New
Ferry
Port
Sunlight
Spital
Brombo
BEBINGTON
Brookhurst
Hooton
Chil
Thorn
Willaston
B5151
A540

Ince
Blundell
Lydi
Homer
Green
MAG
Lunt
Thornton
Buckley
Hill
Netherton
Orrell
Kirkd
Eve

Leasowe
Moreton
Meols
Hoylake
Upton
Greasby
Woodchurch
Arrowe
Frankby
Newton
Grange
West
Kirby
Caldy
Thurstaston
Irby
Thingwall
Wirral
Pensby
Barnston
Brimstage
Oxton
Prenton
M53
A551
A5137
Thornton
Hough
Raby
Windle
Hill
B5133

Hilbre
Islands
Lifeboat
Station
Point of Ayr
Talacre
Llawndy
espyr
Picton
Pen-y-
ffordd
Mostyn
Quay
Trelogan
A548
Mostyn
Glan-y-don
Rhewl-Mostyn
Berthengam
Maen Achwyfan
Cross
Dyke
Llyn
Helyg
Lloc
A5026
Greenfield
(Maes-glas)
Whelston
Pant y
Wacco
Gorsedd
Carmel
Pantasaph
Brynford
Holywell
(Treffynnon)
Bagillt
A548
Dolphin
Caerwys
Babell
FLINTSHIRE
Pentre
Halkyn
Ysceifiog
Lixwm
Afon-wen
Ddol
Halkyn
(Helygain)
A5119
Flint
Mountain
Kelsterton
Flint
(Y Fflint)
Oakenholt
CONNAH'S
QUAY
Shotton
Ewloe
(Ew
Higher
Shotton
Queensferry
Sandycroft
Aston
Mancot
Hawarden

HESWALL
Gayton
Parkgate
Gayton
Sands
NESTON
Little
Neston
Ness
Botanic
Burton
Puddington
Shotwick
A548
DANGER AREA
Shotwick
Castle
Garden
City
A494
B5441
B5129

RIVER DEE (AFON DYFRDWY)
ENGLAND
WALES
Holywell
Bank
Basingwerk
Abbey (remains)

Rhosesmor
Northop
A5119
Soughton
(Sychdyn)
New
Brighton Alltami
Rhydymwyn
Llangwyfan
Castell
C
D
Wat's Dyke
Northop
Hall
B5126
17
23
964
18

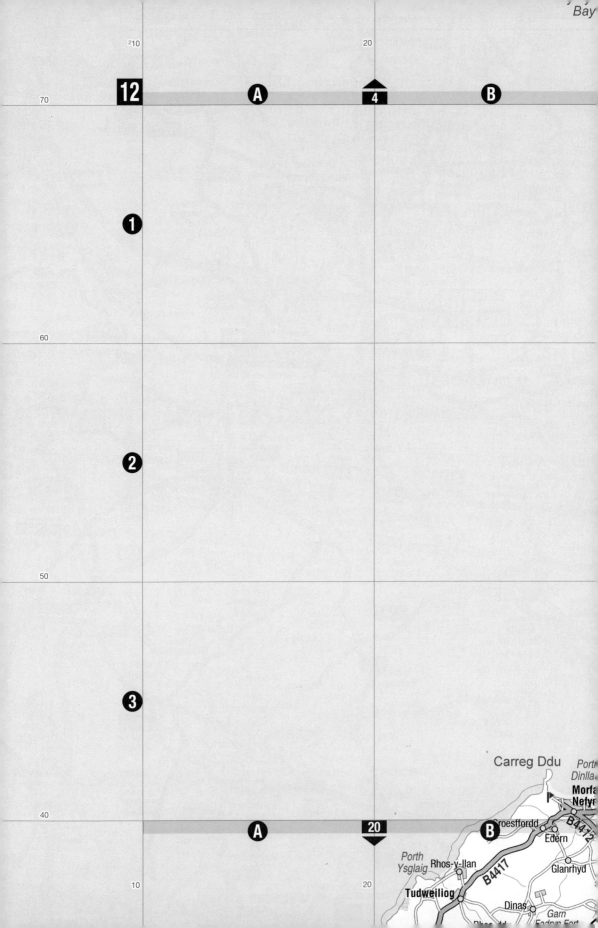

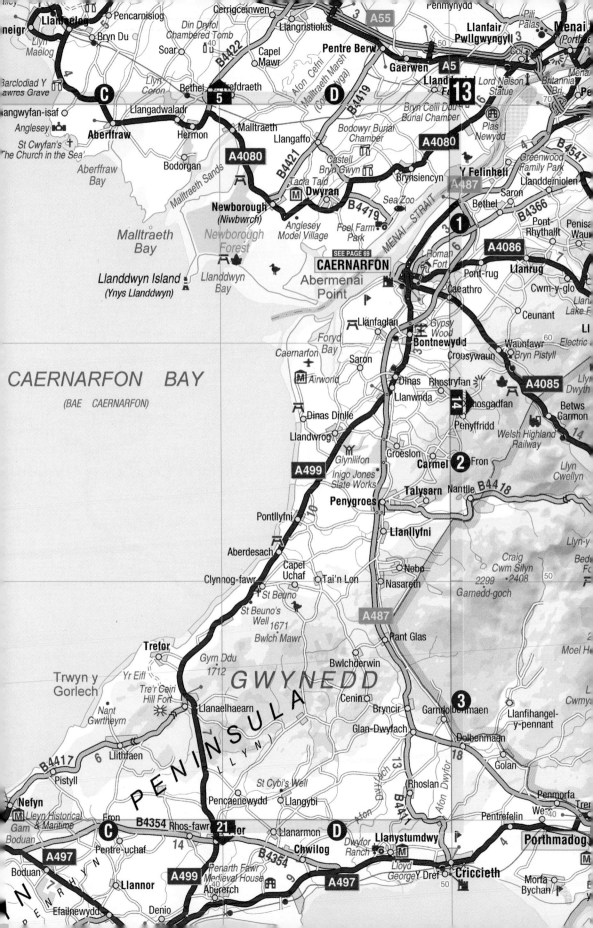

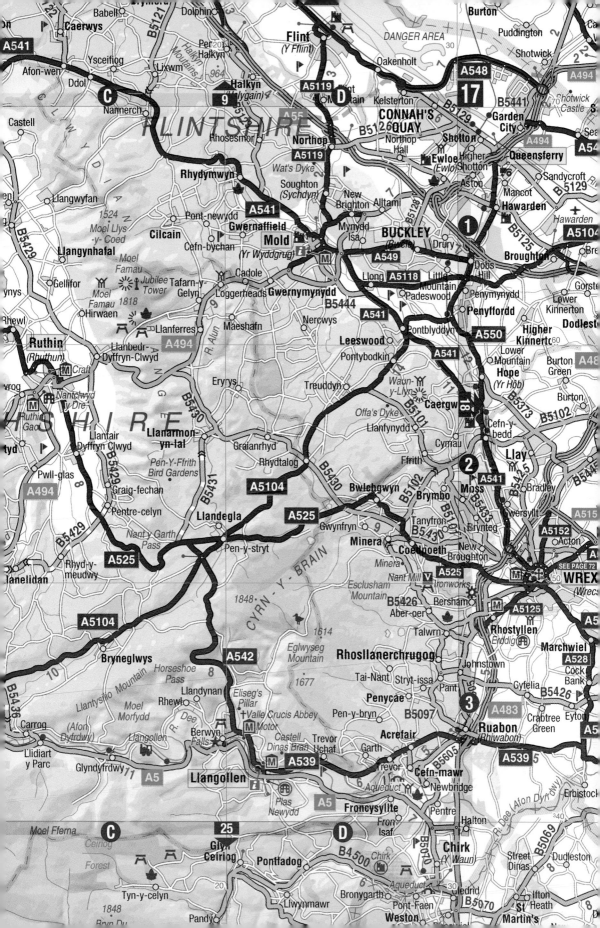

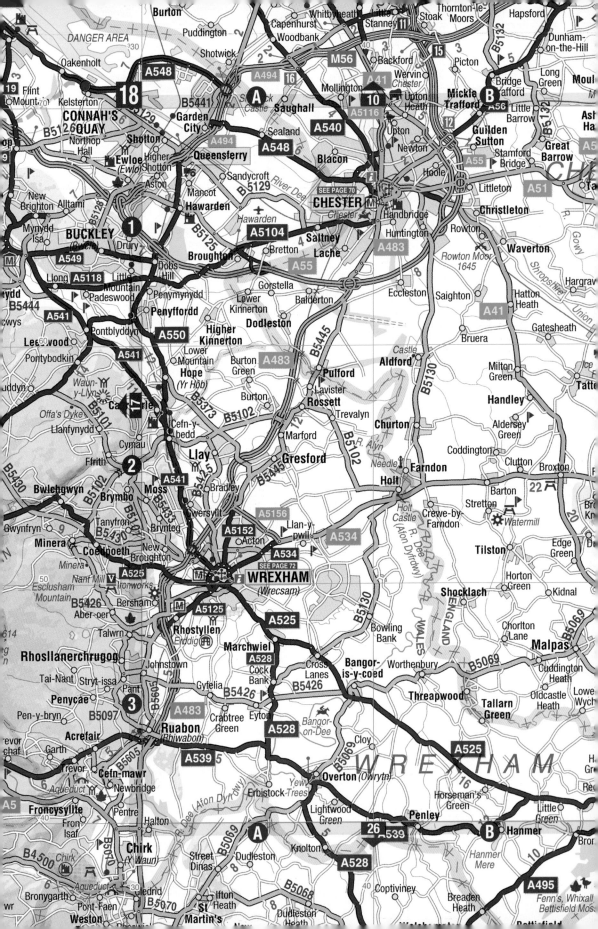

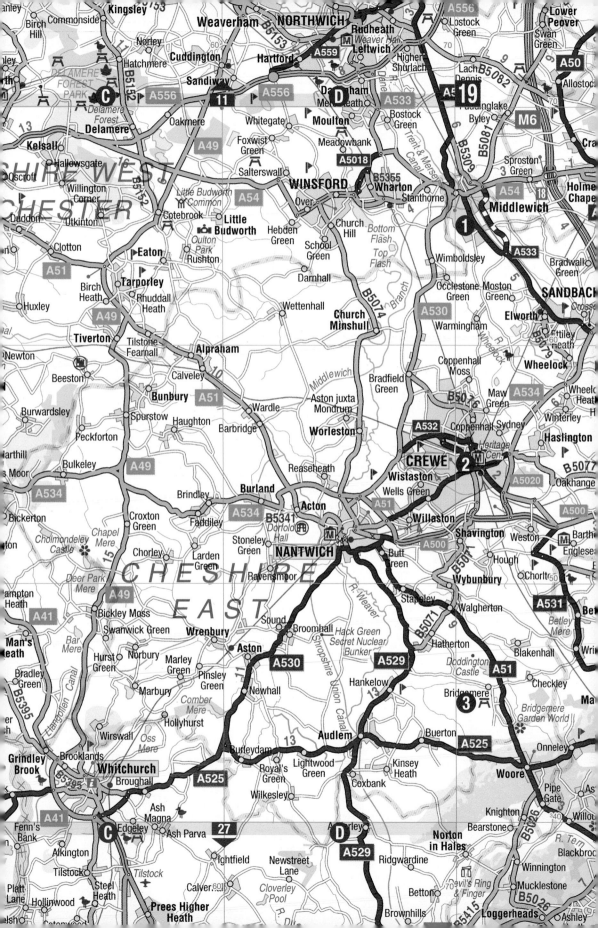

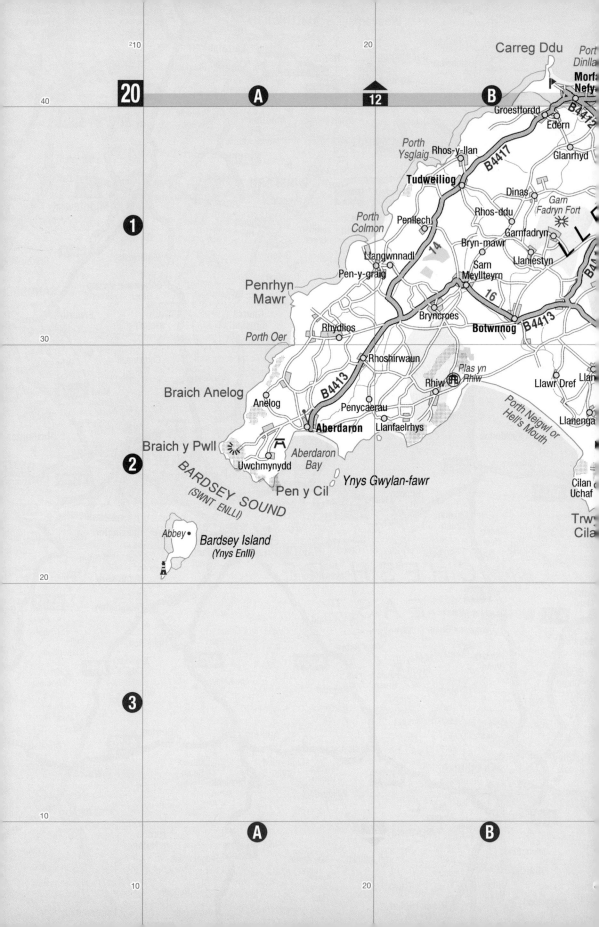

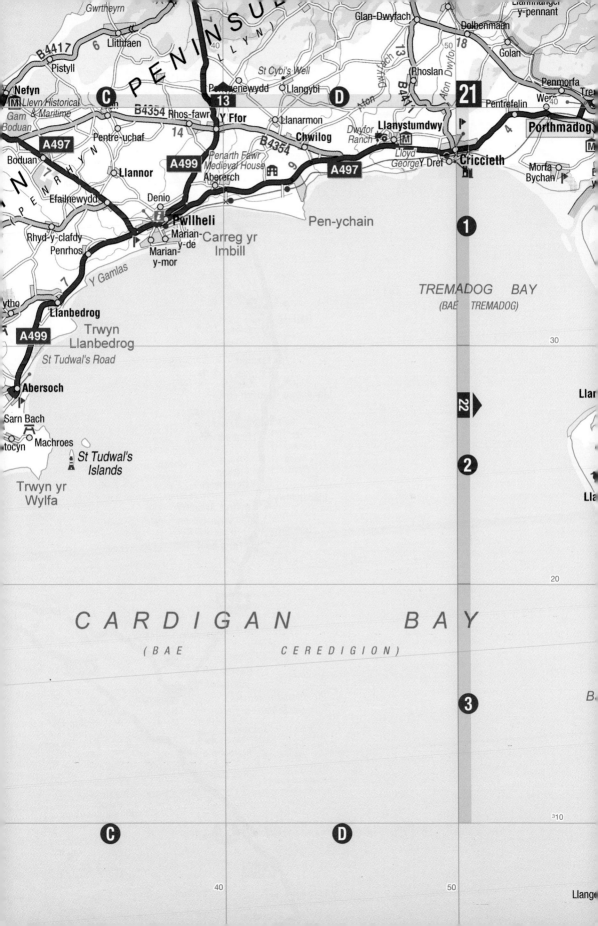

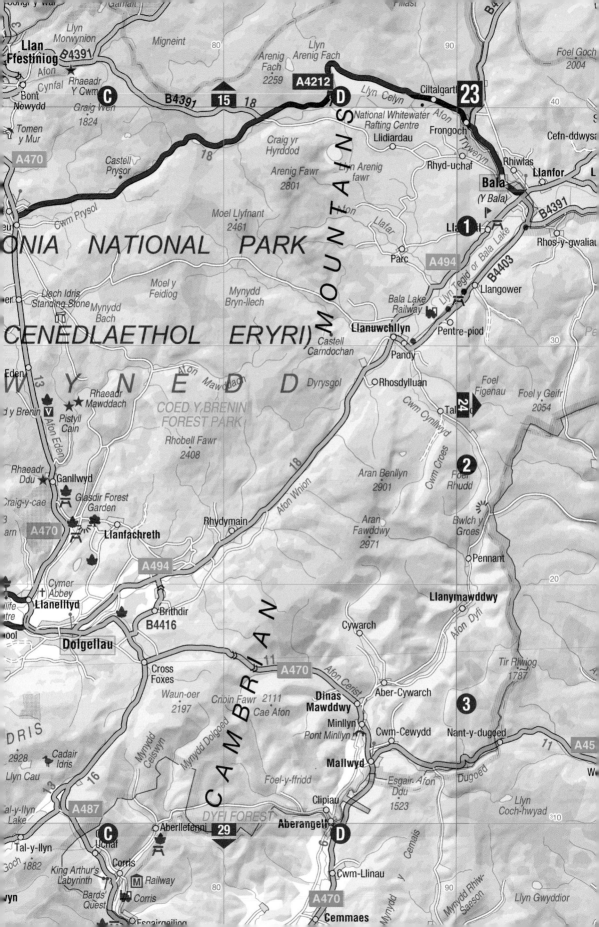

The Bar (Toll)

★ Waterfalls

CADAIR

Fairbourne
Steam Railway
**Fairbourne**
60 Nature
Centre
Friog
20

Mynydd
Pennant
Mary Jones
Monument
(Tyn-y-ddol)

Esgair Berfa

**Llwyngwril**

Llanfihangel-y-pennant

**A493**

Castell
y Bere

Llangelynin

**GWYNEDD**

Dysynni

Aberg

Rhoslefain
Peniarth

B4405

Ⓐ

Llanfendigaid
**Llanegryn**
Dolgoch
Talyllyn
Railway

2076
Torrenhendre

**Tonfanau**
**Bryncrug**
Dolgoch
Falls

Aber
Dysynni
Broad
Water
Pandy

Afon
Dysynni

Rhyd-yr-onen
Trum Gelli

**Tywyn**

Cwrt
11

Ⓜ
Narrow Gauge
Railway
4

Corlan-fraith

**A493**

River

Penhelig

Ⓥℹ
**Aberdovey**
(Aberdyfi)

Dyfi
Furnace
Egl

Snowdonia
National Park

Furnac

Dyfi
Ynyslas
5 B4353

A487

Llancynfelyn
Tre'r-ddol

Tre Taliesin

**Borth**  Ⓜ Station
Animal Kingdom

**Tal-y-bont**

Afon Leri

Upper
Borth
Dol-y-Bont

CERED

B4353

Rhyd-meirionydd
**Llandre**
Bontgoch

B4572  7

9

Ⓑ
**Bow
Street**
Pen-y-garn
Salem
Cwms

Garth

Llangorwen
Penrhyn-coch
Pen-bont
Rhydybeddau

Camera Obscura
National
Library
**A487**
Cefn
Llwyd
Dollwen
Goc

Cliff Railway
**A4159**

Ⓜ ℹ Ⓜ
Comins
Coch
Capel Dewi
Blaen-
geufforddau

**ABERYSTWYTH**
SEE PAGE 68

Waun-Fawr
**Llanbadarn
Fawr**
Afon Rheidol
13 Cwr

The Bar
Southgate
Capel
Bangor
A44

**Penparcau**

Rhydyfelin
Moriah
Capel
Seion
Aberffrwd
Vale of
Rheidol
A41

50
60

**Llanfarian**
Gors
12

Chancery
New Cross
Llanfihangel-y-
Creuddyn

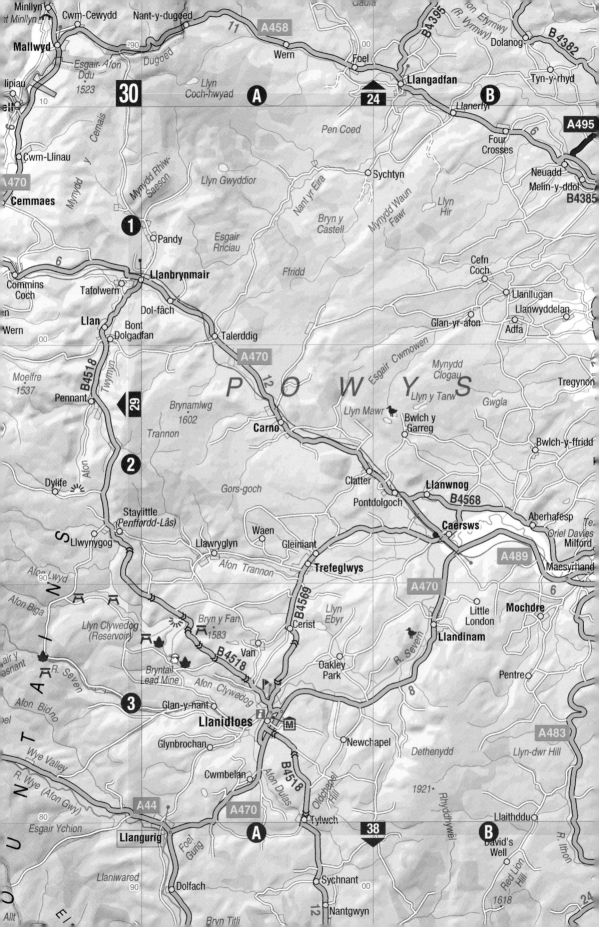

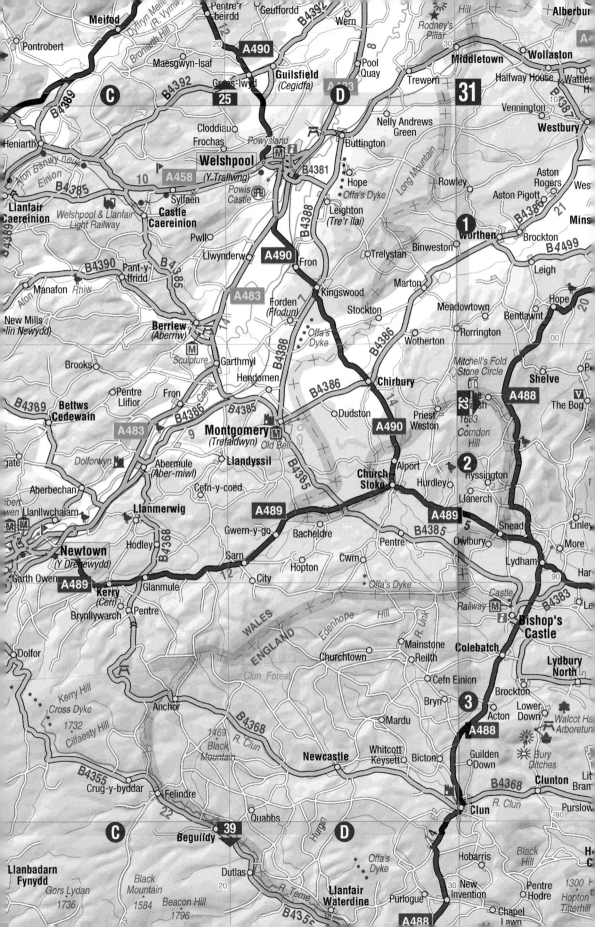

SHREWSBURY
SEE PAGE 72
TELFORD
Oakengates
Donnington
Muxton
Lilyhurst
Sheri

A5112
A5064
A5223
A442
A5
A5061
B4394
B4380
B4379

Uffington
Rodington
Isombridge
Shawbirch
Hortonwood
Trench
Leegomery

Withington
Allscott
Admaston
Hadley

Upton Magna
Walcot
Wrockwardine
Leaton
Wellington
Sunnycroft
Arleston

Preston
Chetton
Uckington
Aston
Cluddley
M54
Old Park
Stafford Park
Redhill

Attingham Park
Norton
B5061
Uppington
Rushton
Lawley
Malinslee
Hollinswood
Haughton

Atcham
Cronkhill
Roman City
Donnington
The Wrekin 1334
Huntington
Dawley
Little Dawley
TELFORD
The Wyke
Shif

Cross Houses
Brompton
Wroxeter
Eyton on Severn
Eaton Constantine
Upper Longwood
Garmston
Little Wenlock
Horsehay
Stirchley
The Hem

Berrington
Bridge
Dryton
Leighton
Darby Houses
Coalbrookdale
Madeley
Brockton
Kemberton

Cantlop
Cound
Harnage
Sheinton
Buildwas
Abbey
Ironbridge
Jackfield
Coalport
Sutton Maddock

Pitchford
Upper Cound
Golding
Cressage
A4169
Farley
Benthall Hall
Benthall
Broseley
China
Tile Tunnel
Norton
Grindle

Acton Burnell
Acton Pigott
Harley
Homer
Wyke
Barrow
Stockton

Frodesley
Ruckley
Kenley
The Bank
Much Wenlock
Priory
Guildhall
Willey
Smithies
Linley
Ewdness
Newton
Stablef

SHIRE
Broome
Chatwall
Church Preen
Hughley
Stretton Westwood
Presthope
Atterley
The Smithies
Colemore Green
Nordley
Allscott

Plaish
Gretton
Longville in the Dale
Brockton
Easthope
B4371
B4378
Callaughton
Muckley
Haughton
Nordley
Astley Abbotts
Bromley
Burcote
Wyken

East Wall
Wilderhope Manor
Shipton
Shipton Hall
Weston
B4368
Astonlane
Aston Eyre
Morville
Tasley
Northgate
Rou
Barr

Rushbury
Stanton Long
Derrington
Ashfield
Upper Netchwood
Lower Netchwood
Monkhopton
The Lye
Underton
Bridgnorth
Cliff Railway
Danesford

Roman Bank
Broadstone
Hungerford
Holdgate
Middleton Priors
Upton Cressett
Chetton
The Down
Oldbury
Knowlesands
Quatford
Mose

Upper Millichope
Ditton Priors
Hillside
Oldfield
Middleton Scriven
Eudon Burnell
Eudon George
Eardington
Glazeley
Chelmarsh
Chelmarsh Resr.
Hampton Loade

Munslow
Broncroft
Tugford
Abdon
Neenton
Lower Faintree
Overton
Sidbury
Sutton
Hampton
Butte

Diddlebury
Heath Chapel
Upper Heath
Cockshutford
Cleobury North
Burwarton
Wrickton
The Highlands
Billingsley
Severn Valley
Highley

Great Sutton
Clee St Margaret
Nordy Bank
Aston Botterell
Chorley
High Green
Woodhill
Netherton
Stanley

Upper Hayton
Stoke St Milborough
Weston Hill
Blackford
Loughton
Stottesdon
Rays Farm
Severn Valley Railway

Hayton's Bent
Hopton Cangeford
Bromdon
Wheathill
Bagginswood
Kinlet
Coppicegate

Cleedownton
Cleestanton
Silvington
Farlow
Oreton
B4363
Buttonbridge

Titterstone Clee Hill 1750
Cleeton St Mary
Crumpsbrook
Catherton
Neen Savage
B4199
B4194
WYRE FOREST

Middleton
Bitterley
Henley
Angelbank
Doddington
Foxwood
Hopton Wafers
Cleobury Mortimer
Buttonoak
Knowles Mill

A4117
A4201

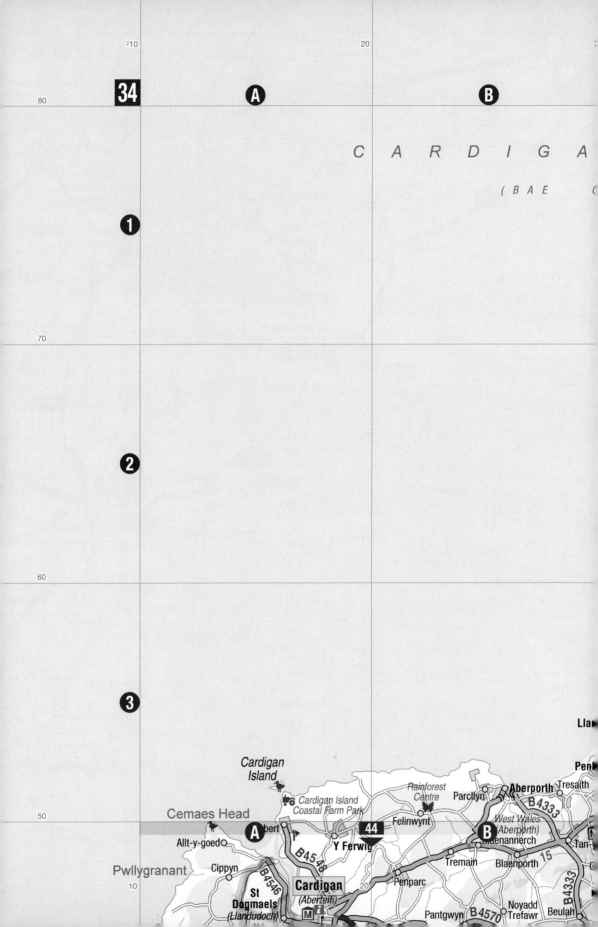

C A R D I G A

( B A E   C

**1**

70

**2**

60

**3**

Lla

Cardigan
Island

Pen

Rainforest
Centre   Parcllyn   **Aberporth**   Tresaith

Cemaes Head    Cardigan Island
Coastal Farm Park     **B4333**

50        **A**   bert    Felinwynt    West Wales
(Aberporth)

Allt-y-goed     **44**    **B**   Blaenannerch   Tan

Pwllygranant     Cippyn     B4548   **Y Ferwig**    Tremain   Blaenporth   15

10     B4546     Penparc    B4333

**Cardigan**
(Aberteifi)

**St**
**Dogmaels**    20    Pantgwyn   B4570   Noyadd
(Llandudoch)      Trefawr   Beulah

40

50

80

**C**

**D**

**1**

Carreg Ti-pw

70

Llanrhystud

**B4337**

Llansantffraid

**36**

**Llan-non**

7

**2**

87

Rhos
Haminiog

Nebo

Aberarth

**B4577**

Cross
Inn

**Aberaeron**

**Pennant**

Monachty

11

Ffos-y-ffin

**A482**

**Ciicennin**

Llanerchaeron

**New Quay**
*(Ceinewydd)*

Marine Wildlife Centre

Llanaeron

60

Newbridge

**B4337**

Llwyncelyn

7

Ciliau
Aeron

8

**Gilfachreda**

8

**Trefilan**

Maen-y-groes

**B43**

**42**

**Llanarth**

Oakford
*(Derwen Gam)*

**B43.39**

Ystrad
Aeron

Talsar

Cwmtudu

4

**B4342**

Geneva

Cross
Inn

New Quay
Honey Farm

Pen-cae

Nanternis

Caerwedros

**A486**

Diheuyd

**Mydroilyn**

**3**

2

Felinfach

Blaen
Celyn

Llwyndafydd

Synod Inn
*(Post-Mawr)*

Ffynnon-oer

ynys-Lochtyn

**CEREDIGION**

**B4337**

anog

Morfa

Pontgarreg

**B4321**

**B4334**

**A487**

Plwmp

**B4338**

Cribyn

**A48**

Brynhoffnant

Pentregat

Gorsgoch

**B4337**

Sarnau

**Talgarreg**

**B4338**

250

**C**

Capel
Cynon

**45**

Bwlch-y-fadfa

**D**

Maestir

**A**

ternal Fire
oes

**A486**

Aber

**Cwrtnewydd**

arthen

**B4334**

Felin
Wnda

Brithdir

Rhydlewis

Ffostrasol

40

Pont-Sian

50

**Llanwnnen**

Pentre-bac

Hawen

**B4577**

11

8

12

Cwmsychpant

Drefach

337

Curlew Weavers
Woollen Mill

**B A Y**

*( R E D I G I O N )*

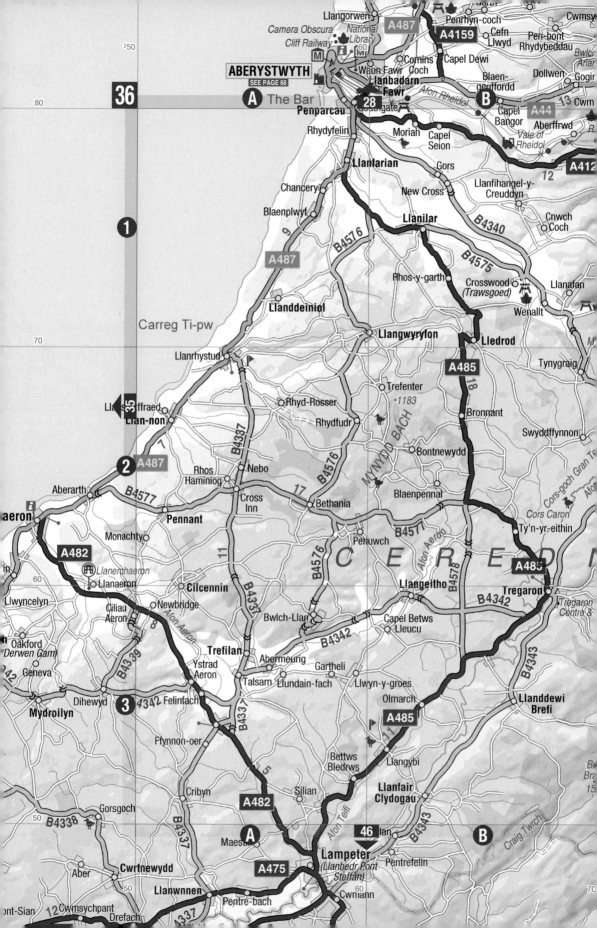

A **The Bar**

**ABERYSTWYTH**
SEE PAGE 68

Llangorwen
Penrhyn-coch
Cefn Llwyd
Pen-bont Rhydybeddau
Cwmsy
A487
A4159
Camera Obscura
Cliff Railway
National Library
Comins Coch
Capel Dewi
Waun-Fawr
Llanbadarn Fawr
Afon Rheidol
Blaen-gefforddd
Dollwen
Gogir
Bwlch Ariar
28
Penparcau
Southgate
Capel Bangor
Aberffrwd
A44
Rhydyfelin
Moriah
Capel Seion
Vale of Rheidol
Cwm
A412
Llanfarian
Gors
Chancery
New Cross
Llanfihangel-y-Creuddyn
Cnwch Coch
Blaenplwyf
Llanilar
B4340
12
B4576
B4575
A487
Rhos-y-garth
Crosswood (Trawsgoed)
Llanafan
Llanddeiniol
Wenallt
Llangwyryfon
Lledrod
Carreg Ti-pw
Llanrhystud
A485
Tynygraig
Trefenter
·1183
MYNYDD BACH
Bronnant
Rhyd-Rosser
Swyddffynnon
Llan-ffraed
35
Llan-non
B4337
Rhydfudr
Bontnewydd
A487
2
Nebo
B4576
Blaenpennal
Aberarth
Rhos Haminiog
Cors-goch Gran Te
B4577
Cross Inn
Bethania
Cors Caron
aeron
Pennant
Afon Aeron
B4577
Ty'n-yr-eithin
Monachty
Penuwch
C E R E D I
A482
17
B4578
Llanerchaeron
B4576
A485
Llwyncelyn
Llanaeron
Ciliau
Cilcennin
Llangeitho
Tregaron
Tregaron Centre &
Oakford (Derwen Gam)
Newbridge
Capel Betws Lleucu
B4342
Geneva
Ciliau Aeron
Bwlch-Llan
B4337
Afon Aeron
8
42
B4339
Trefilan
Abermeurig
Gartheli
Llwyn-y-groes
B4343
Dihewyd
Ystrad Aeron
Llundain-fach
Olmarch
Llanddewi Brefi
Mydroilyn
3
4342
Felinfach
Talsarn
A485
Ffynnon-oer
B4337
5
Bettws Bledrws
Llangybi
Br Bra 15
Cribyn
Silian
Llanfair Clydogau
Gorsgoch
A482
B4338
Maest
46
Ian
B4343
Craig Twrch
Aber
B4337
A475
Lampeter (Llanbedr Pont Steffan)
Pentrefelin
Cwrtnewydd
Cwmsychpant
Llanwnnen
Pentre-bach
Cwmiann
Drefach
ont-Sian
12
337

250
80
70
60
50
1
36

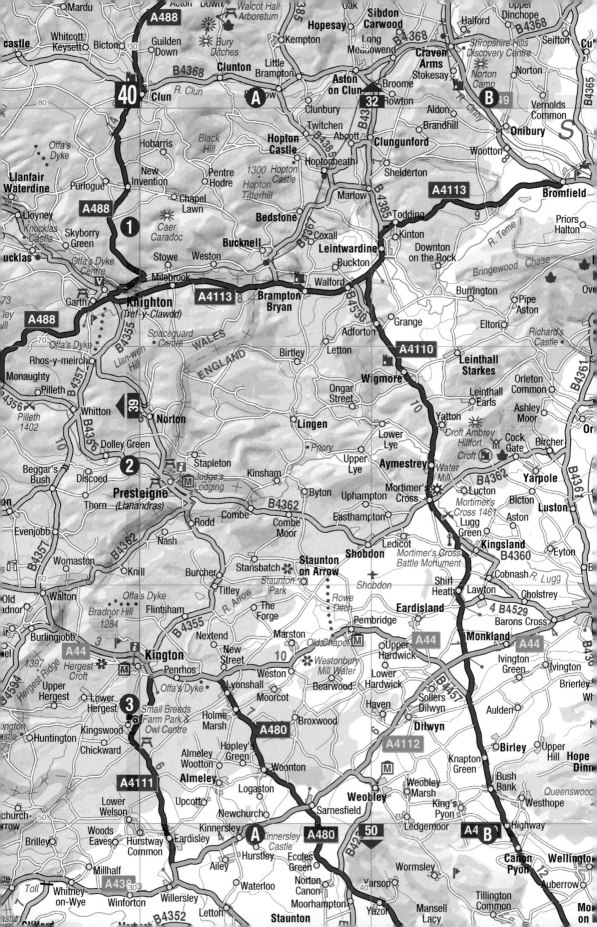

STRUMBLE H

Pen Brush

Ga
Fa

Trefasser

Penbwchdy

Melin
Tregwy

N

Granston

Penclegyr

Abercastle

10

Blue
Lagoon          Porthgain

Trefin          Mathry

Carreg-gwylan-
fach

Llanrhian          Castlem

Penclegyr          Abereiddy   Croes-Goch

Penllechwen

ST
DAVIDS
HEAD

Tretio

A487

Treffynnon

P

Treleddyd-fawr          Rhodiad
-y-Brenin          Carnhedryn          6

R. Solva

Whitesands Bay
(Porth Mawr)

B4583

R. Alun

Caerfarchell

St Davids

Solva
Woollen Mill

Llandeloy

Bishop's
Palace

St Davids
(Tyddewi)          Whitchurch          Hayscastle

Rhosson

i v          Oriel
y-Parc          Solva          Penycwm          Gignog

Ramsey
Island

St Non's
Chapel

Green Scar          Newgale   Wood   16

Roch

Ynys Bery

A487          Simpso
Cross

Rick          B
Head          Simpson

Nolton
Haven          Nolton

70          ST BRIDES BAY   80          Druidston

Herolds

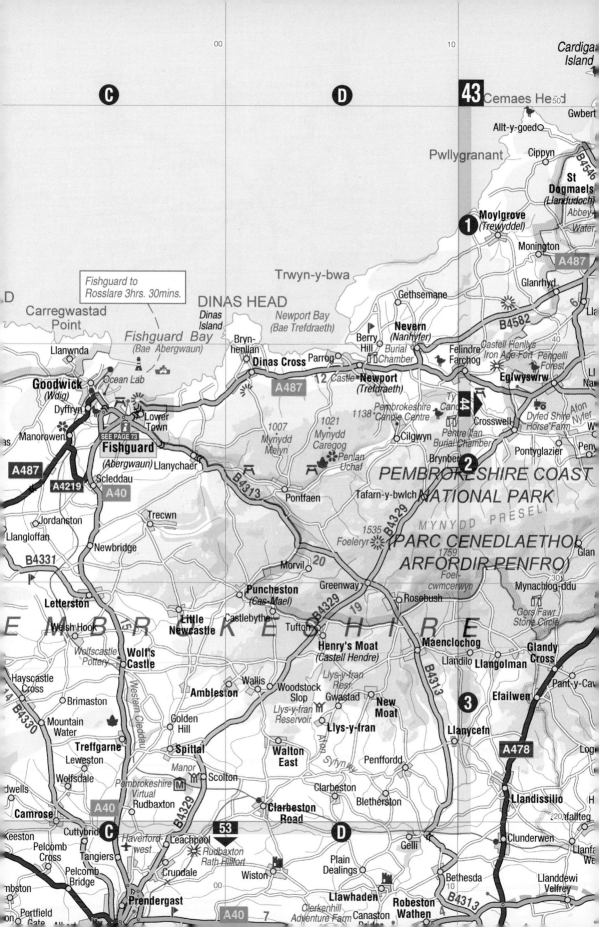

**C** **D** **43** Cemaes Head

Cardigan Island

00  10  50

Gwbert

Allt-y-goed

Cippyn

Pwllygranant

St Dogmaels
(Llandudoch)

B4546

Abbey

**1** Moylgrove
(Trewyddel)

Water

Monington

Glanrhyd

A487

Fishguard to
Rosslare 3hrs. 30mins.

Trwyn-y-bwa

Gethsemane

6

DINAS HEAD

Dinas
Island

Newport Bay
(Bae Trefdraeth)

B4582

40

Carregwastad
Point

Fishguard Bay
(Bae Abergwaun)

Bryn-
henllan

Berry
Hill

Nevern
(Nanhyfer)

Castell Henllys
Iron Age Fort

Llan

Felindre
Farchog

Pengelli
Forest

Llanwnda

Dinas Cross

Parrog

Burial
Chamber

Eglwyswrw

Goodwick
(Wdig)

Ocean Lab

12

Castle

Newport
(Trefdraeth)

Ty
Canol

Afon
Nyfer

Dyfed Shire
Horse Farm

Dyffryn

Lower
Town

Pembrokeshire
Candle Centre

1138

44

Crosswell

Manorowen

SEE PAGE 73

1007
Mynydd
Melyn

1021
Mynydd
Caregog

Cilgwyn

Pentre Ifan
Burial Chamber

Pontyglazier

Peny

A487

Fishguard
(Abergwaun)

Llanychaer

Penlan
Uchaf

Brynberian

**2**

A487

Scleddau

A4219

A40

Pontfaen

Tafarn-y-bwlch

PEMBROKESHIRE COAST
NATIONAL PARK

Jordanston

B4313

MYNYDD PRESELI

Llangloffan

Newbridge

1535
Foeleryr

(PARC CENEDLAETHOL
ARFORDIR PENFRO)

Glan

B4331

Morvil

20

B4329

1759
Foel-
cwmcerwyn

Mynachlog-ddu

Gors Fawr
Stone Circle

Puncheston
(Cas-Mael)

Greenway

Rosebush

Letterston

Castlebythe

Tufton

B4329

19

Maenclochog

Glandy
Cross

Welsh Hook

Little
Newcastle

Henry's Moat
(Castell Hendre)

Llandilo

Llangolman

Wolfscastle
Pottery

Wolf's
Castle

Wallis

Llys-y-fran
Resr.

B4313

Efailwen

Pant-y-Caw

Hayscastle
Cross

Ambleston

Woodstock
Slop

Gwastad

New
Moat

**3**

B4330

Brimaston

Golden
Hill

Llys-y-fran
Reservoir

Llys-y-fran

Llanycefn

A478

Log

Mountain
Water

Spittal

Walton
East

Afon
Syfyny

Penffordd

Treffgarne

Leweston

Manor

Scolton

Clarbeston

Bletherston

Llandissilio

Wolfsdale

Pembrokeshire
Virtual

M

Rudbaxton

Clarbeston
Road

Gelli

Clunderwen

Camrose

A40

**C**

Haverford
west

Leachpool

**53**

**D**

Plain
Dealings

Bethesda

Llanddewi
Velfrey

Keeston

Cuttybridge

Rudbaxton
Rath Hillfort

B4329

Wiston

B4313

Pelcomb
Cross

Tangiers

Crundale

Llawhaden

Robeston
Wathen

Pelcomb
Bridge

Prendergast

A40

7

Clerkenhill
Adventure Farm

Canaston
Bridge

Portfield
Gate

00

Llanfa
We

220

fallteg

10

**PEMBROKESHIRE**

Western Cleddau

15

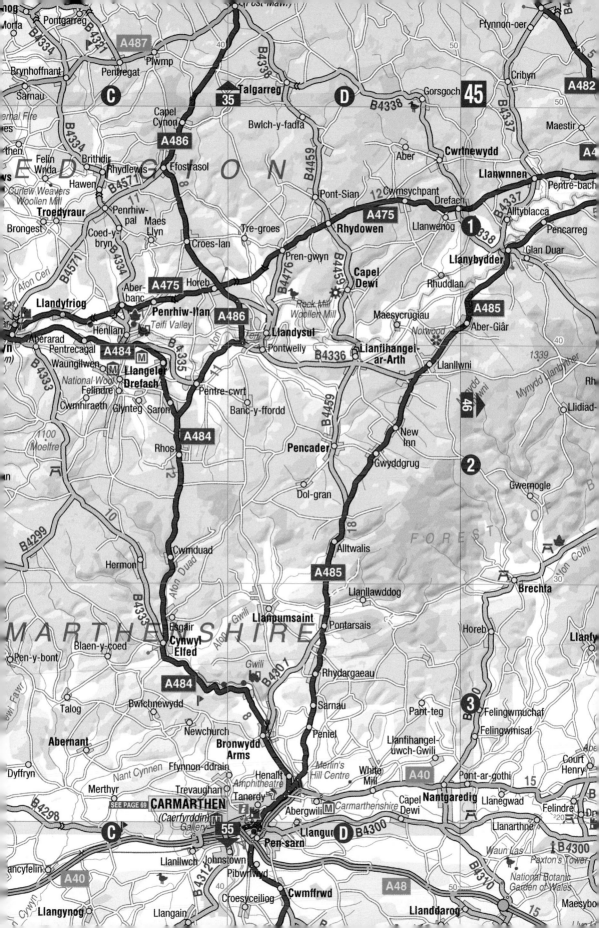

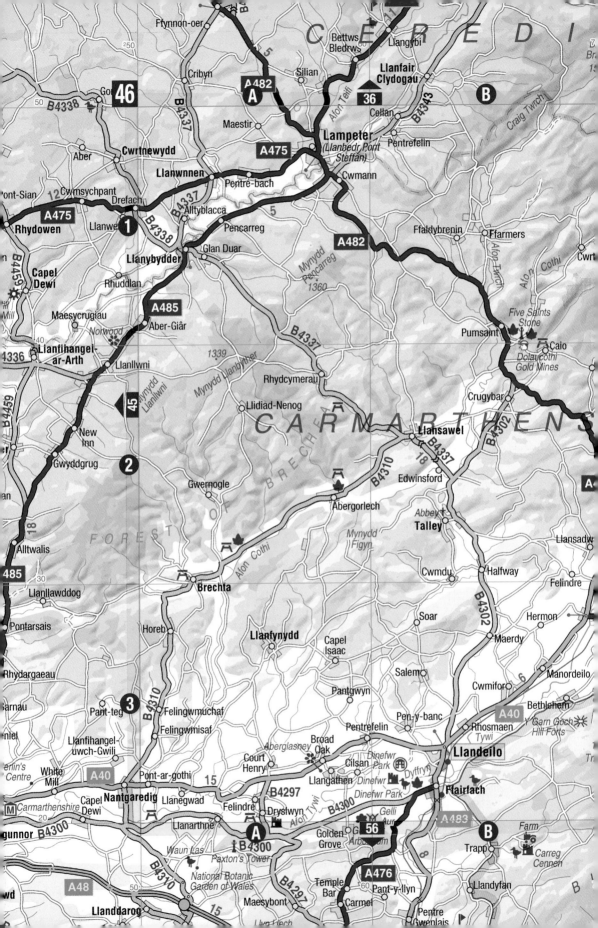

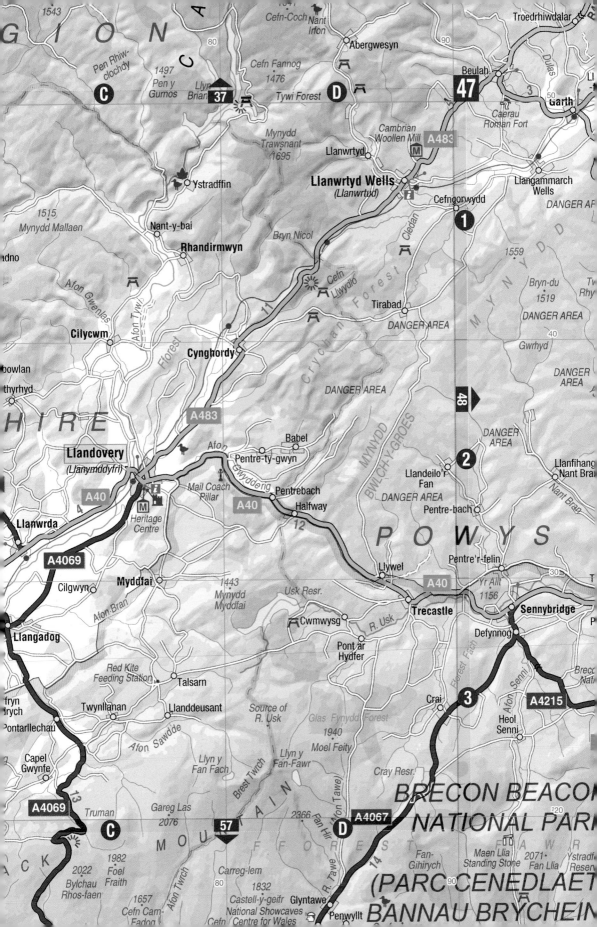

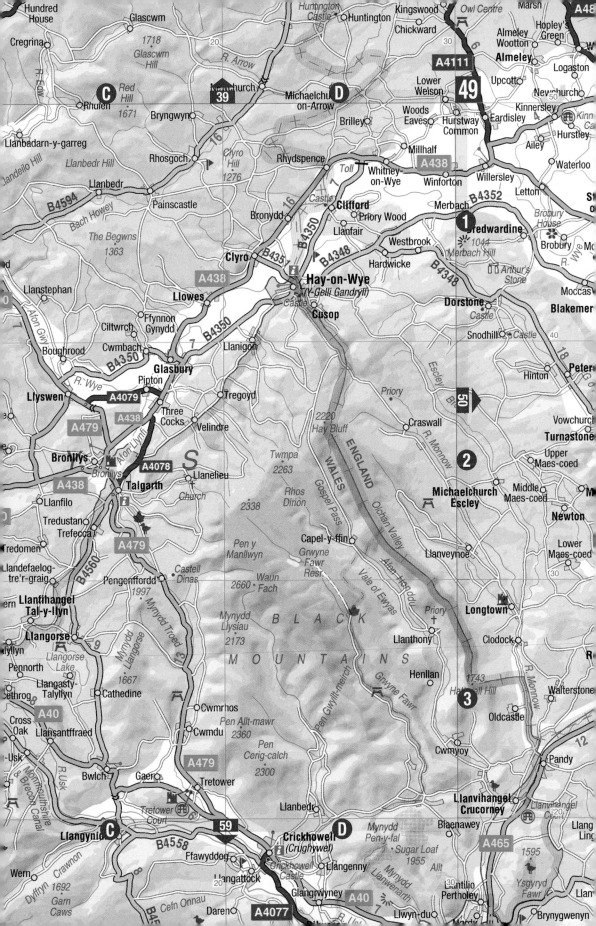

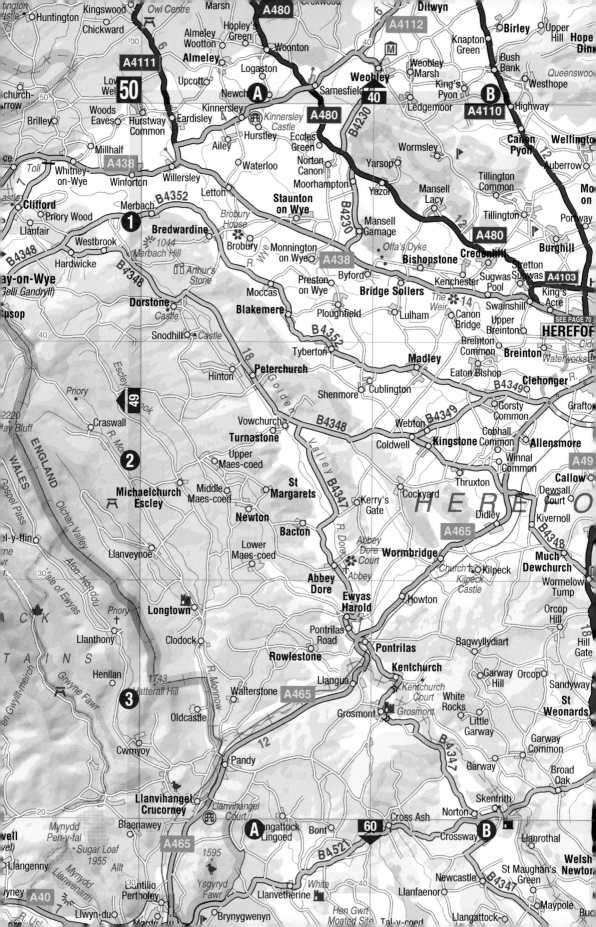

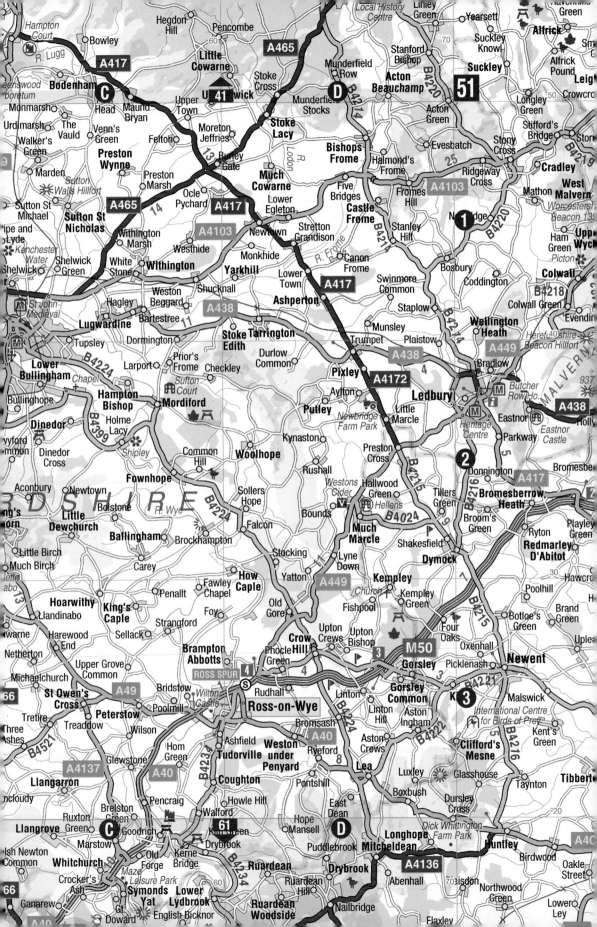

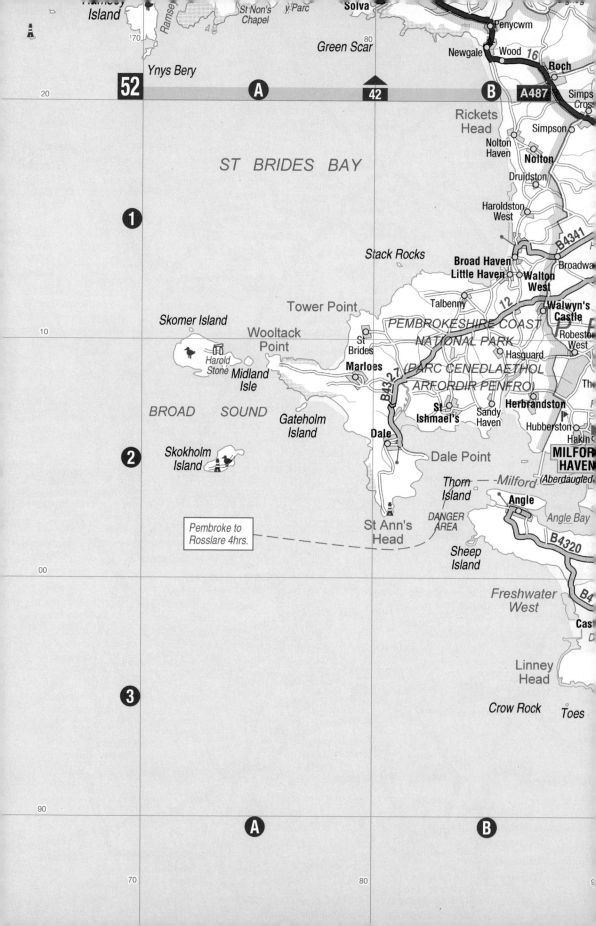

**ST BRIDES BAY**

Ramsey
Island

St Non's
Chapel

y Parc

Solva

Penycwm

Green Scar    80

Newgale    Wood    16

Roch

Ynys Bery

**52**    Ⓐ    42    Ⓑ    **A487**

Simps
Cros

Rickets
Head

Simpson

Nolton
Haven

**Nolton**

Druidston

Haroldston
West

**❶**

Stack Rocks

**Broad Haven**    Broadwa

**Little Haven** ○○ **Walton
West**

Tower Point

Talbenny

**Walwyn's
Castle**

12

Skomer Island

Wooltack
Point

PEMBROKESHIRE COAST

St
Brides

NATIONAL PARK

Robesto
West

Harold
Stone    Midland
Isle

**Marloes**

Hasguard

(PARC CENEDLAETHOL

Th

BROAD    SOUND

Gateholm
Island

ARFORDIR PENFRO)

St
**Ishmael's**    Sandy
Haven

**Herbrandston**

**❷**    Skokholm
Island

**Dale**

Hubberston

Hakin

**MILFOR
HAVEN**

Dale Point

Thorn
Island

-Milford    (Aberdaugled

Pembroke to
Rosslare 4hrs.

St Ann's
Head

DANGER
AREA

**Angle**    Angle Bay

**B4320**

Sheep
Island

Freshwater
West

B4

Cas

**❸**

Linney
Head

Crow Rock    Toes

Ⓐ    Ⓑ

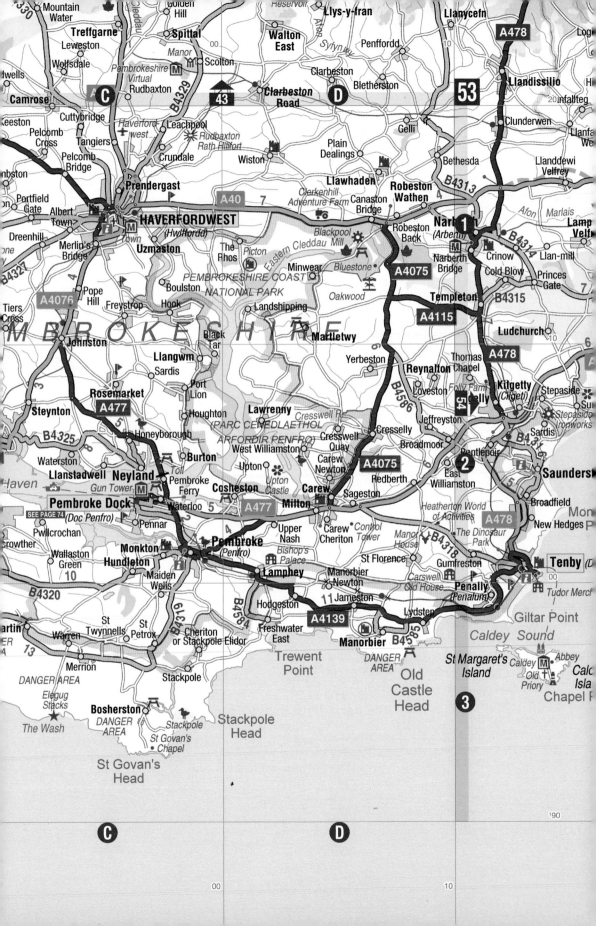

**53**

Mountain
Water

**Treffgarne**
Leweston
Wolfsdale

Golden
Hill
**Spittal**

Llys-y-frân

**Llanycefn**

Manor
Scolton

Pembrokeshire
Virtual
Rudbaxton

**Walton
East**

Penffordd

**Llandissilio**

Clarbeston

nfallteg

**Camrose**
Cuttybridge
Pelcomb
Cross
Pelcomb
Bridge

**C**

Leachpool

**43**

**Clarbeston
Road**

**D**

Bletherston

Gelli

Clunderwen

Llanfa
We

Keeston

Tangiers

Haverford-
west

Rudbaxton
Rath Hillfort
Crundale
Wiston

Plain
Dealings

Bethesda

Llanddewi
Velfrey

Portfield
Gate

Dreenhill

**Prendergast**

**Llawhaden**

Canaston
Bridge

Clerkenhill
Adventure Farm

Albert
Town

**HAVERFORDWEST**
(Hwlffordd)

**Uzmaston**

The
Rhos

Picton

Robeston
Wathen

**Nar**
(Arber)

**1**

**Lamp
Velf**

Narberth
Bridge

Crinow

Llan-mill

Robeston
Back

Merlin's
Bridge

Blackpool
Mill

Cold Blow

Princes
Gate

Minwear

Bluestone

Eastern Cleddau

**PEMBROKESHIRE COAST**

**A4075**

**Templeton**

Pope
Hill

Freystrop

Boulston

Oakwood

**A4115**

**B4315**

Tiers
Cross

**A4076**

Hook

**NATIONAL PARK**

Landshipping

**Ludchurch**

**MBROKESHIRE**

Johnston

Black
Tar

**Marlletwy**

Yerbeston

**Reynalton**

Thomas
Chapel

**A478**

**Llangwm**

Sardis

Port
Lion

Loveston

Folly
Farm

**Kilgetty**
(Cilgeti)

Stepaside

**Rosemarket**

**A477**

Houghton

**Lawrenny**

Cresswell R.

**PARC CENEDLAETHOL**

Cresselly

Jeffreyston

**A4586**

Pantlepoir

Su

Sardis

Stepaside
Ironworks

**Steynton**

Honeyborough

**ARFORDIR PENFRO**

West Williamston

Cresswell
Quay

Broadmoor

**2**

**Saunders**

**B4325**

Waterston

**Burton**

Upton

Carew
Newton

**A4075**

Redberth

East
Williamston

**Llanstadwell**

**Neyland**

Toll

**Coshestón**

Upton
Castle

**Carew**

Sageston

Broadfield

**Pembroke Dock**
(Doc Penfro)

Gun Tower

**M**

Pembroke
Ferry
Waterloo

**A477**

**Milton**

Heatherton World
of Activities

New Hedges

Pennar

Upper
Nash

Carew
Cheriton

Control
Tower

The Dinosaur
Park

Manor
House

**A478**

Mon

Pwllcrochan

**Pembroke**
(Penfro)

**B4318**

**Monkton**

Bishop's
Palace

St Florence

Gumfreston

**Tenby**
(D

Wallaston
Green

**Hundleton**

Maiden
Wells

**Lamphey**

Manorbier
Newton

Carswell
Old House

Penally
(Penalun)

Tudor Merch

**B4320**

Hodgeston

Jameston

Lydsten

Giltar Point

St
Twynnells

St
Petrox

**A4139**

Freshwater
East

**B45**

Caldey Sound

artin

Warren

Cheriton
or Stackpole Elidor

**Manorbier**

DANGER
AREA

St Margaret's
Island

Caldey

Abbey

Cald
Isla

Merrion

**B4584**

Trewent
Point

Old
Castle
Head

Old
Priory

Chapel

DANGER AREA
Elegug
Stacks
The Wash

**Bosherston**

DANGER
AREA

Stackpole

St Govan's
Chapel

Stackpole
Head

**3**

St Govan's
Head

**C**

**D**

00

10

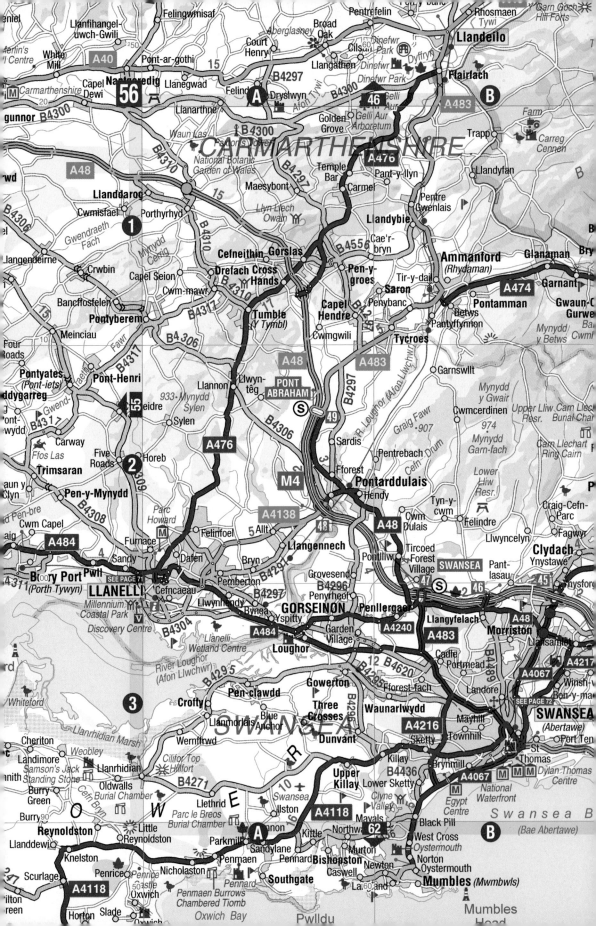

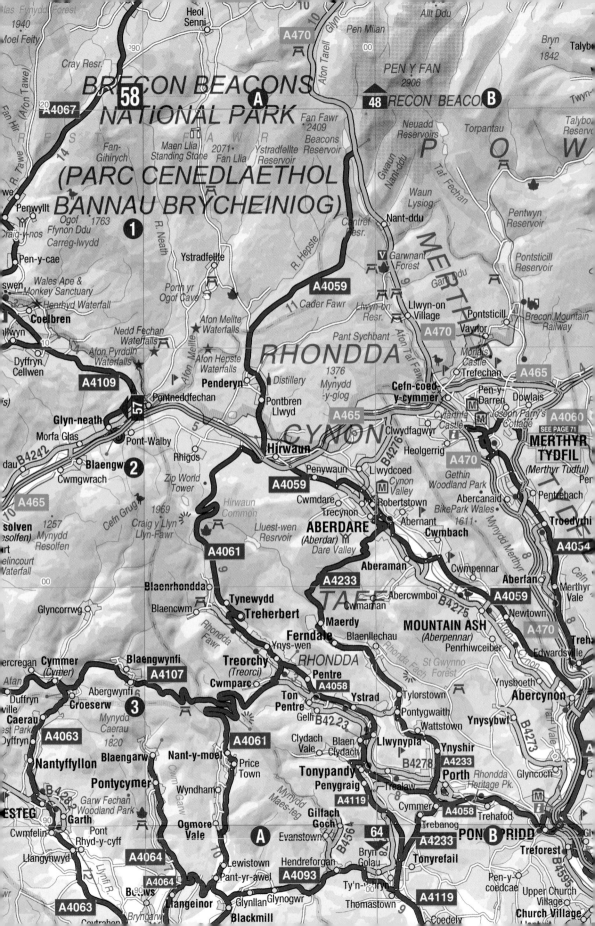

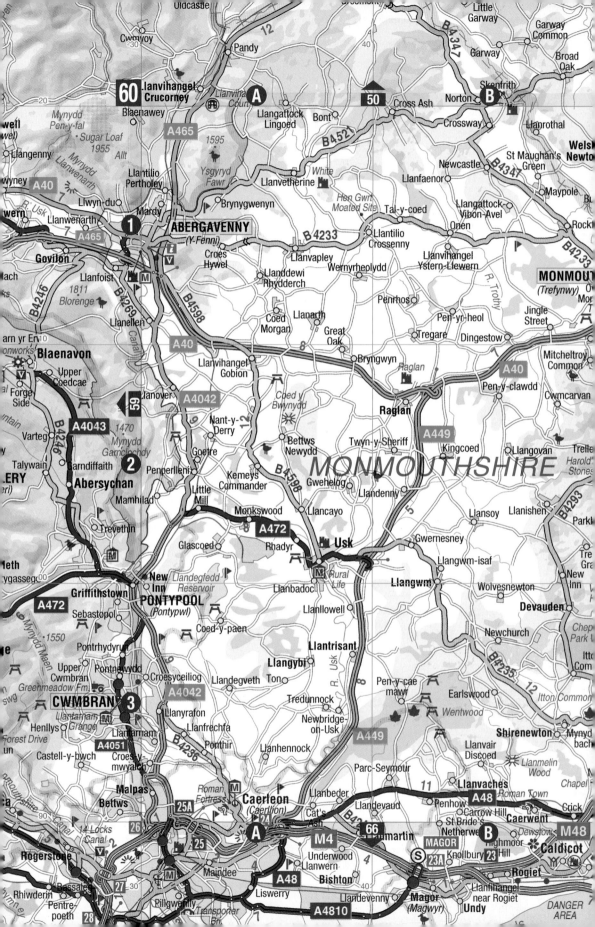

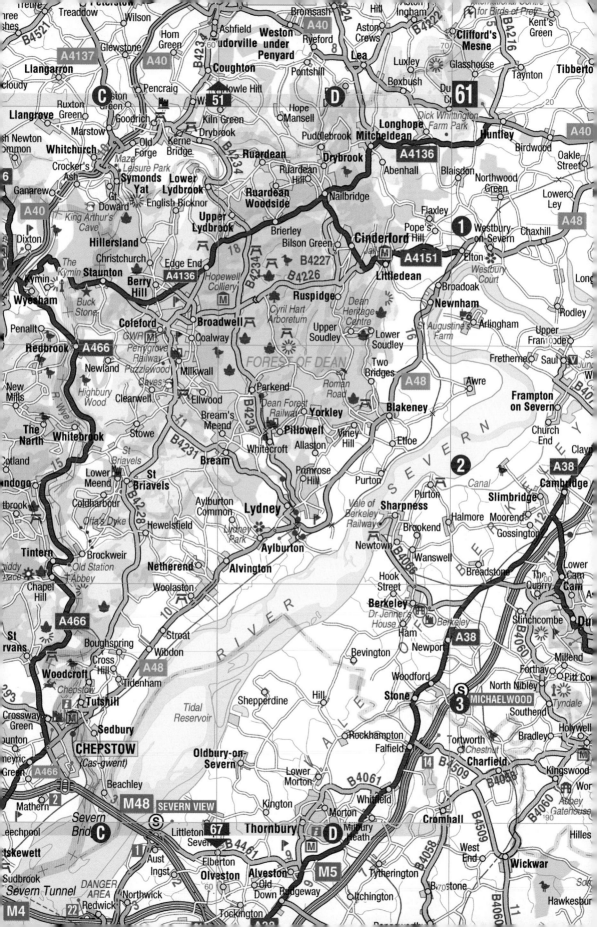

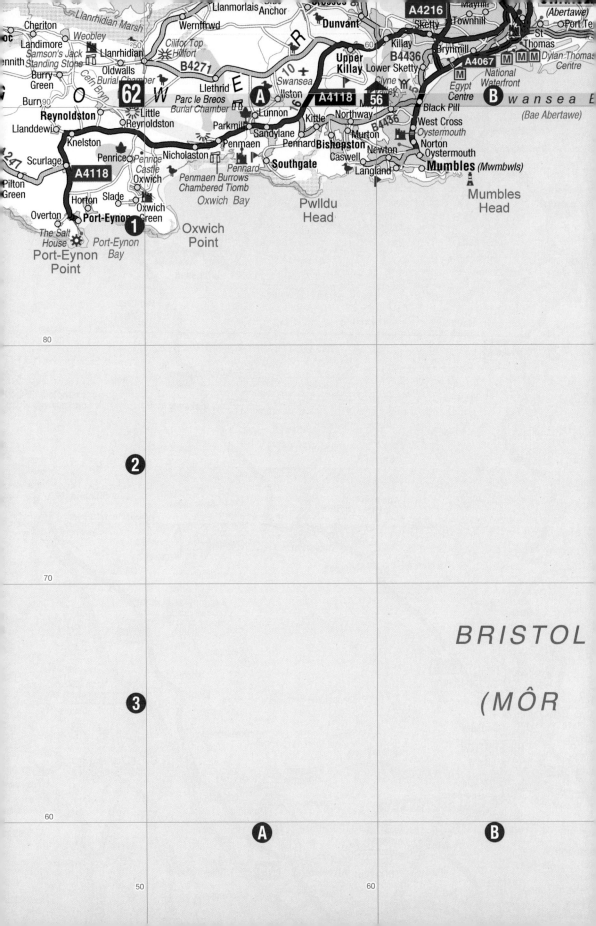

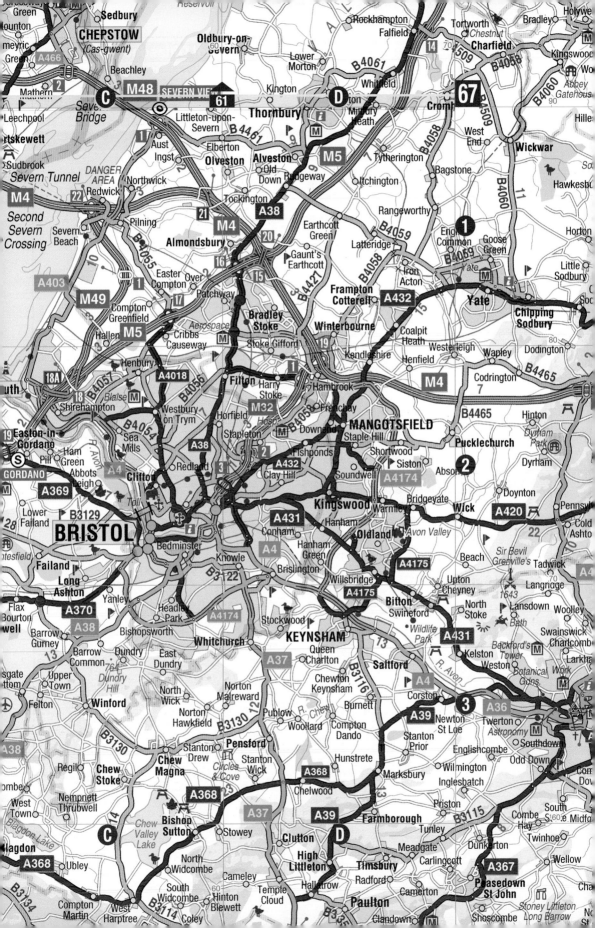

# CITY & TOWN CENTRE PLANS (Cynlluniau Canol Dinasoedd a Threfi)

## Reference to Town Plans (Cyfeiriad at Gynlluniau Trefi)

| | | | |
|---|---|---|---|
| Motorway | M4 | Abbey, Cathedral, Priory etc. | ✝ |
| Motorway Under Construction | | Bus Station | ⬟ |
| Motorway Junctions with Numbers | 4 5 | Car Park (Selection of) | P |
| Unlimited Interchange 4 | | Church | † |
| Limited Interchange 5 | | City Wall | ⊓⊓⊓⊓⊓ |
| Primary Route | A55 | Ferry (vehicular) | |
| Primary Route Junction with Number | 15 | (foot only) | |
| Dual Carriageways | | Golf Course | ⛳9 ⛳18 |
| Class A Road | A48 | Heliport | Ⓗ |
| Class B Road | B4246 | Hospital | H |
| Major Roads Under Construction | | Lighthouse | |
| Major Roads Proposed | | Market | |
| Minor Roads | | National Trust Property (open) | NT |
| Restricted Access | | (restricted opening) | NT |
| Pedestrianized Road & Main Footway | | Park & Ride | P+R |
| One Way Streets | → → | Place of Interest | ■ |
| Fuel Station | ⛽ | Police Station | ▲ |
| Toll | Toll | Post Office | ★ |
| Railway and Station | 🚉 | Shopping Area (Main street and precinct) | |
| Underground / Metro & D.L.R. Station | DLR | Shopmobility | |
| Level Crossing and Tunnel | | Toilet | ▽ |
| Tram Stop and One Way Tram Stop | | Tourist Information Centre | i |
| Built-up Area | | Viewpoint | |
| | | Visitor Information Centre | V |

## ABERYSTWYTH

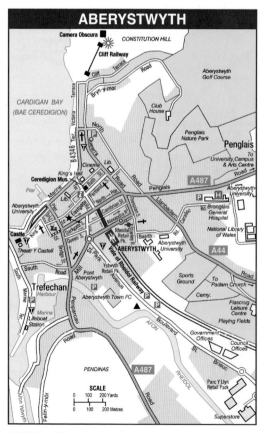

## BANGOR

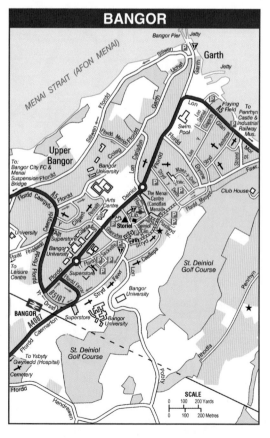

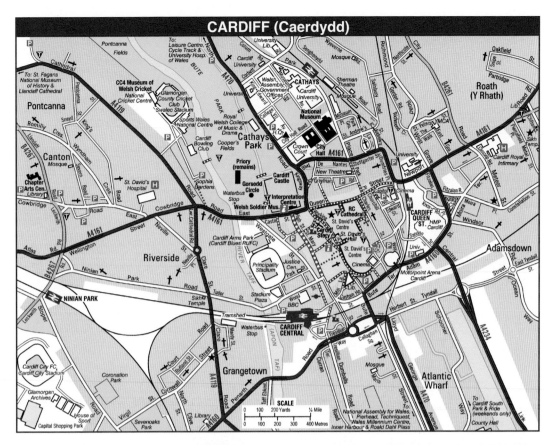

# CARDIFF (Caerdydd)

# CAERNARFON

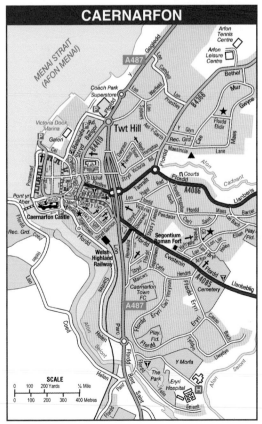

# CARMARTHEN (Caerfyrddin)

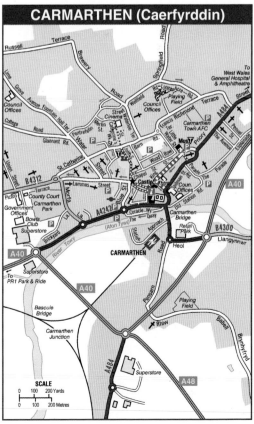

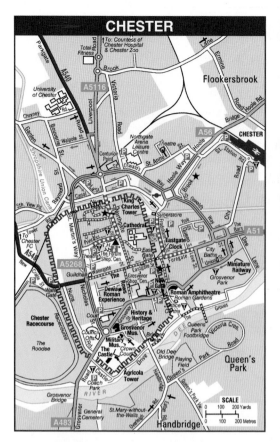

## CHESTER

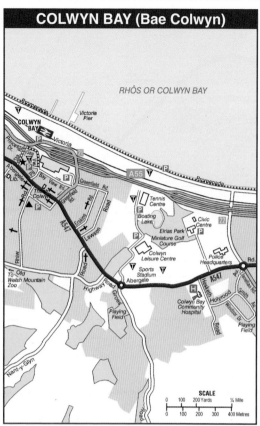

## COLWYN BAY (Bae Colwyn)

RHÔS OR COLWYN BAY

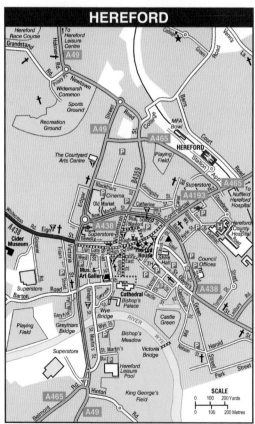

## HEREFORD

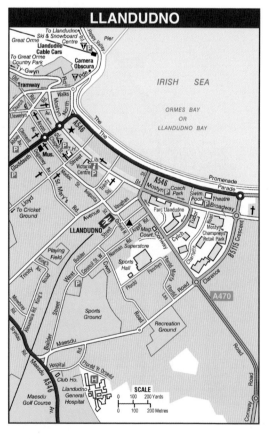

## LLANDUDNO

IRISH SEA

ORMES BAY
OR
LLANDUDNO BAY

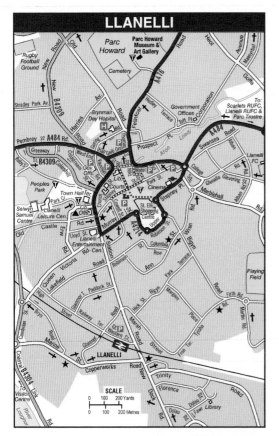

# LLANELLI

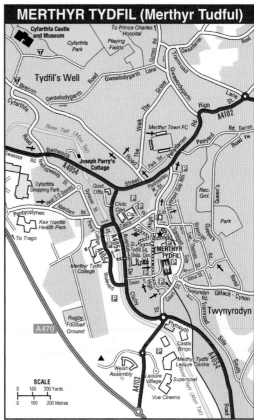

# MERTHYR TYDFIL (Merthyr Tudful)

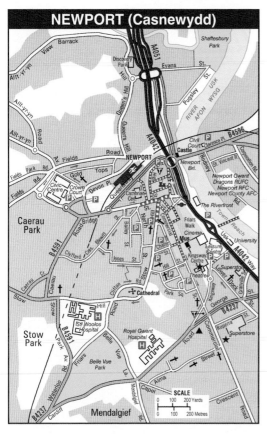

# NEWPORT (Casnewydd)

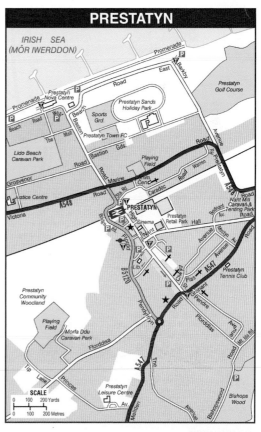

# PRESTATYN

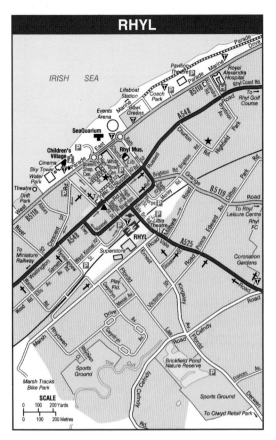

# RHYL

# SHREWSBURY

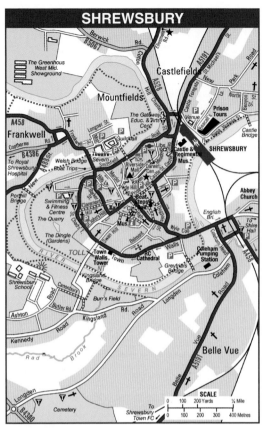

# SWANSEA (Abertawe)

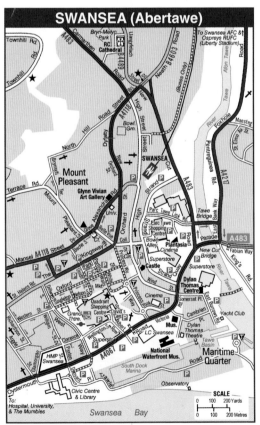

# WREXHAM (Wrecsam)

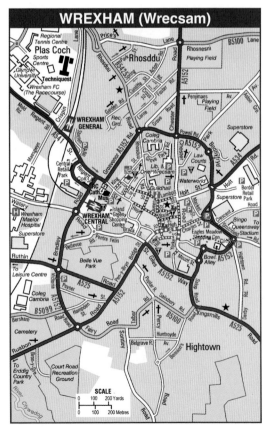

# CARDIFF AIRPORT (Maes Awyr Caerdydd)

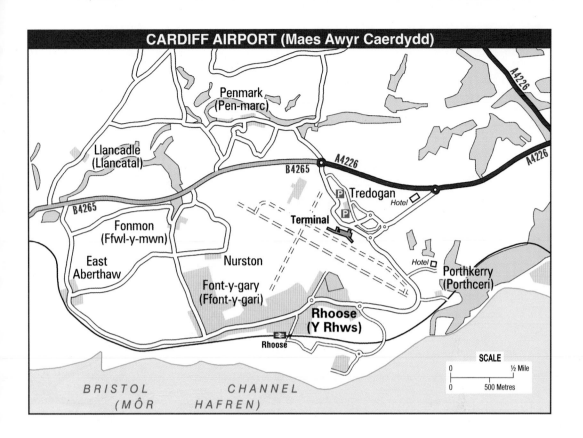

Penmark
(Pen-marc)

Llancadle
(Llancatal)

A4226

B4265

P Tredogan
*Hotel*

Terminal P

Fonmon
(Ffwl-y-mwn)

East
Aberthaw

Nurston

Font-y-gary
(Ffont-y-gari)

*Hotel*
Porthkerry
(Porthceri)

Rhoose
(Y Rhws)

Rhoose

**SCALE**

0 — ½ Mile

0 — 500 Metres

BRISTOL        CHANNEL
(MÔR        HAFREN)

# FISHGUARD (Abergwaun)

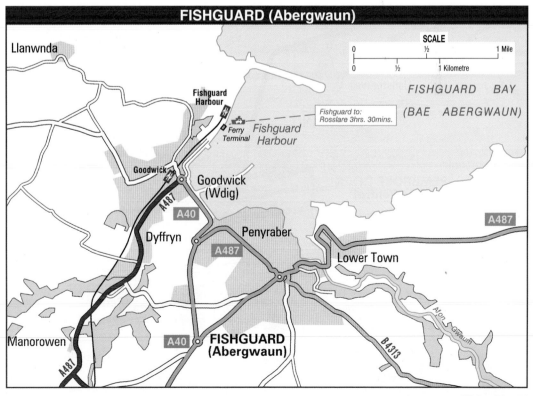

Llanwnda

**SCALE**

0 — ½ — 1 Mile

0 — ½ — 1 Kilometre

FISHGUARD        BAY

(BAE        ABERGWAUN)

Fishguard
Harbour

Fishguard to:
Rosslare 3hrs. 30mins.

Ferry
Terminal        Fishguard
Harbour

Goodwick

Goodwick
(Wdig)

A487

A40

Dyffryn

Penyraber

A487

Lower Town

A487

Manorowen

A40        **FISHGUARD**
(Abergwaun)

B4313

*Afon Gwaun*

A487

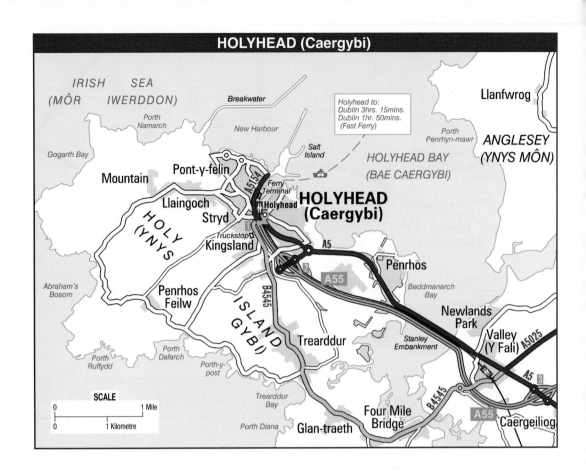

## HOLYHEAD (Caergybi)

IRISH SEA
(MÔR IWERDDON)

Breakwater

Holyhead to:
Dublin 3hrs. 15mins.
Dublin 1hr. 50mins.
(Fast Ferry)

Llanfwrog

Porth
Namarch

New Harbour

Porth
Penrhyn-mawr

ANGLESEY
(YNYS MÔN)

Gogarth Bay

Salt
Island

HOLYHEAD BAY
(BAE CAERGYBI)

Mountain

Pont-y-felin

A5154

Ferry
Terminal

Holyhead

HOLYHEAD
(Caergybi)

Llaingoch

Stryd

A5

Truckstop

Penrhos

Kingsland

A55

Penrhos
Feilw

B4545

Beddmanarch
Bay

Abraham's
Bosom

ISLAND
GYBI)

Trearddur

Stanley
Embankment

Newlands
Park

Valley
(Y Fali)

A5025

HOLY
(YNYS

Porth
Ruffydd

Porth
Dafarch

Porth-y-
post

A5

A55

Caergeiliog

SCALE

0 _____ 1 Mile
0 _____ 1 Kilometre

Trearddur
Bay

Four Mile
Bridge

B4545

Porth Diana

Glan-traeth

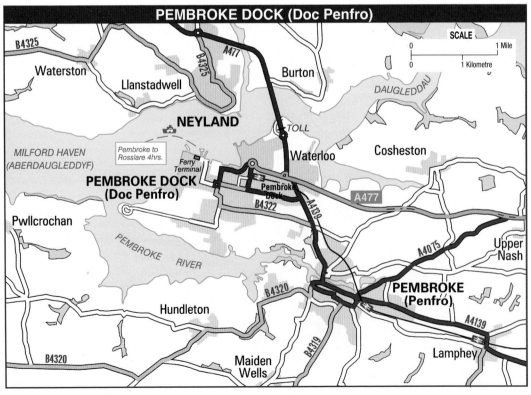

## PEMBROKE DOCK (Doc Penfro)

B4325

SCALE

0 _____ 1 Mile
0 _____ 1 Kilometre

Waterston

Llanstadwell

B4325

A477

Burton

DAUGLEDDAU

NEYLAND

TOLL

MILFORD HAVEN
(ABERDAUGLEDDYF)

Pembroke to
Rosslare 4hrs.

Ferry
Terminal

Waterloo

Cosheston

PEMBROKE DOCK
(Doc Penfro)

Pembroke
Dock

A477

Pwllcrochan

B4322

A4139

PEMBROKE
RIVER

A4075

Upper
Nash

B4320

PEMBROKE
(Penfro)

Hundleton

A4139

B4319

B4320

Lamphey

Maiden
Wells

1. A strict alphabetical order is used e.g. Bishop Sutton follows Bishopstone but precedes Bishopsworth.

2. The map reference given refers to the actual map square in which the town spot or built-up area is located and not to the place name.

3. Only one reference is given although due to page overlaps the place may appear on more than one page.

4. Where two or more places of the same name occur in the same County or Unitary Authority, the nearest large town is also given; e.g. Bethania *Gwyn*.....3C **15** (nr. Blaenau Ffestiniog) indicates that Bethania is located in square 3C on page **15** and is situated near Blaenau Ffestiniog in the County of Gwynedd.

5. Major towns & destinations are shown in bold i.e. **Abertawe** *Swan*.....**72** (3B **56**). Where they appear on a Town Plan a second page reference is given.

## Mynegai i Ddinasoedd, Trefi, Pentrefi, Cymydau a Lleoliadau

1. Glynir yn gaeth wrth drefn y wyddor e.e. mae Bishop Sutton yn dilyn Bishopstone ond yn dod cyn Bishopsworth.

2. Mae'r cyfeirnod map a roddir yn cyfeirio at yr union sgwaryn ar y map lle mae smotyn y dref neu'r ardal adeiliedig ac nid at enw'r lle.

3. Dim ond un cyfeirnod a roddir er ei bod hi'n bosibl i'r lle ymddangos ar fwy nag dudalen oherwydd bod tudalennau'n gorgyffwrdd.

4. Os bydd dau le gyda'r un enw'n digwydd yn yr un Sir neu'r un awdurdod Unedol, rhoddir enw'r dref fawr agosaf hefyd; e.e. Bethania *Gwyn*.....3C **15** (nr. Blaenau Ffestiniog) yn dangos bod Bethania yn sgwaryn 3C ar dudalen **15** a'i bod hi ger Blaenau Ffestiniog yn Gwynedd.

5. Dangosir trefi o bwys mewn print trwm h.y. **Abertawe** *Swan*.....**72** (3B **56**). Rhoddir ail gyfeirnod tudalen pan fyddant yn ymddangos ar Gynllun Tref.

## COUNTIES AND UNITARY AUTHORITIES with the abbreviations used in this index

## Siroedd ac Awdurdodau Unedol gyda'r byrfoddau a ddefnyddir yn y mynegai hwn

| | | | |
|---|---|---|---|
| Bath & N E Somerset : *Bath* | Conwy : *Cnwy* | Merseyside : *Mers* | Somerset : *Som* |
| Blaenau Gwent : *Blae* | Denbighshire : *Den* | Merthyr Tydfil : *Mer T* | South Gloucestershire : *S Glo* |
| Bridgend : *B'end* | Flintshire : *Flin* | Monmouthshire : *Mon* | Staffordshire : *Staf* |
| Bristol : *Bris* | Gloucestershire : *Glos* | Neath Port Talbot : *Neat* | Swansea : *Swan* |
| Caerphilly : *Cphy* | Greater Manchester : *G Man* | Newport : *Newp* | Telford & Wrekin : *Telf* |
| Cardiff : *Card* | Gwynedd : *Gwyn* | North Somerset : *N Som* | Torfaen : *Torf* |
| Carmarthenshire : *Carm* | Halton : *Hal* | Pembrokeshire : *Pemb* | Vale of Glamorgan : *V Glam* |
| Ceredigion : *Cdgn* | Herefordshire : *Here* | Powys : *Powy* | Warrington : *Warr* |
| Cheshire East : *Ches E* | Isle of Anglesey : *IOA* | Rhondda Cynon Taff : *Rhon* | Worcestershire : *Worc* |
| Cheshire West & Chester : *Ches W* | Lancashire : *Lanc* | Shropshire : *Shrp* | Wrexham : *Wrex* |

## INDEX

### A

| | | | |
|---|---|---|---|
| Abberley *Worc*.....2D **41** | Aberdare *Rhon* .....2A **58** | Aber-oer *Wrex*.....3D **17** | Admaston *Telf*.....3D **27** |
| Abberley Common *Worc*.....2D **41** | Aberdaron *Gwyn*.....2A **20** | **Aberpennar** *Rhon*.....3B **58** | Adpar *Cdgn* .....1C **45** |
| Abbey-cwm-hir *Powy*.....1B **38** | **Aberdaugleddau** *Pemb*.....2C **53** | Aberporth *Cdgn* .....3B **34** | Afon-wen *Flin*.....3C **9** |
| Abbey Dore *Here* .....2A **50** | Aberdesach *Gwyn*.....2D **13** | Aberriw *Powy* .....1C **31** | Aigburth *Mers*.....2A **10** |
| Abbots Leigh *N Som* .....2C **67** | Aberdovey *Gwyn*.....2B **28** | Abersoch *Gwyn*.....2C **21** | Ailey *Here* .....1A **50** |
| Abcott *Shrp* .....1A **40** | Aberdulais *Neat*.....2C **57** | Abersychan *Torf* .....2D **59** | Aintree *Mers*.....1A **10** |
| Abdon *Shrp*.....3C **33** | Aberdyfi *Gwyn* .....2B **28** | **Abertawe** *Swan*.....**72** (3B **56**) | Alberbury *Shrp*.....3A **26** |
| Abenhall *Glos*.....1D **61** | Aberedw *Powy* .....1B **48** | Aberteifi *Cdgn* .....1A **44** | Albert Town *Pemb* .....1C **53** |
| Aber *Cdgn* .....1D **45** | Abereiddy *Pemb* .....2A **42** | Aberthin *V Glam*.....2B **64** | Albrighton *Shrp*.....3B **26** |
| Aberaeron *Cdgn*.....2D **35** | Abererch *Gwyn*.....1C **21** | **Abertillery** *Blae*.....2D **59** | Alcaston *Shrp*.....3B **32** |
| Aberafan *Neat*.....3C **57** | Aberfan *Mer T* .....2B **58** | Abertridwr *Cphy*.....1C **65** | Aldersey Green *Ches W* .....2B **18** |
| Aberaman *Rhon*.....2B **58** | Aberffraw *IOA*.....1C **13** | Abertridwr *Powy*.....3B **24** | Alderton *Shrp* .....3B **26** |
| Aberangell *Gwyn*.....3D **23** | Aberffrwd *Cdgn* .....1B **36** | **Abertyleri** *Blae*.....2D **59** | Aldford *Ches W*.....2B **18** |
| Aberarad *Carm* .....2C **45** | Abergarw *B'end*.....1A **64** | Abertysswg *Cphy* .....2C **59** | Aldon *Shrp*.....1B **40** |
| Aberarth *Cdgn* .....2D **35** | Abergarwed *Neat*.....2D **57** | Aber Village *Powy* .....3C **49** | Alfrick *Worc*.....3D **41** |
| Aberavon *Neat*.....3C **57** | **Abergavenny** *Mon*.....1A **60** | Aberwheeler *Den*.....1B **16** | Alfrick Pound *Worc* .....3D **41** |
| Aber-banc *Cdgn* .....1C **45** | Abergele *Cnwy* .....3A **8** | Aberyscir *Powy*.....3A **48** | Alkington *Shrp*.....1C **27** |
| Aberbargoed *Cphy*.....3C **59** | Aber-Giâr *Carm* .....1A **46** | **Aberystwyth** *Cdgn*.....**68** (3A **28**) | Allaston *Glos*.....2D **61** |
| Aberbechan *Powy*.....2C **31** | Abergorlech *Carm*.....2A **46** | **Abram** *G Man* .....1D **11** | Allensmore *Here* .....2B **50** |
| Aberbeeg *Blae*.....2D **59** | Abergwesyn *Powy* .....3D **37** | Abson *S Glo*.....2D **67** | Allerton *Mers*.....2B **10** |
| Aberbowlan *Carm*.....2B **46** | Abergwili *Carm*.....3D **45** | Aconbury *Here*.....2C **51** | Allostock *Ches W*.....3D **11** |
| Aberbran *Powy* .....3A **48** | Abergwynfi *Neat*.....3D **57** | Acrefair *Wrex*.....3D **17** | Allscott *Telf* .....3D **27** |
| Abercanaid *Mer T* .....2B **58** | Abergwyngregyn *Gwyn*.....3B **6** | Acton *Ches E*.....2D **19** | Allscott *Shrp*.....2D **33** |
| Abercarn *Cphy*.....3D **59** | Abergynolwyn *Gwyn* .....1B **28** | Acton *Wrex*.....2A **18** | All Stretton *Shrp* .....2B **32** |
| Abercastle *Pemb* .....2B **42** | Aberhafesp *Powy*.....2B **30** | Acton *Shrp*.....3A **32** | Allt *Carm* .....2A **56** |
| Abercegir *Powy* .....1D **29** | Aberhonddu *Powy*.....3B **48** | Acton Beauchamp *Here*.....3D **41** | Alltami *Flin* .....1D **17** |
| Aberchwiler *Den*.....1B **16** | Aberhosan *Powy*.....2D **29** | Acton Bridge *Ches W*.....3C **11** | Alltmawr *Powy*.....1B **48** |
| Abercraf *Powy*.....1D **57** | Aberkenfig *B'end*.....1D **63** | Acton Burnell *Shrp*.....1C **33** | Alltwalis *Carm* .....2D **45** |
| Abercregan *Neat*.....3D **57** | Aberllefenni *Gwyn*.....1C **29** | Acton Green *Here* .....3D **41** | Alltwen *Neat*.....2C **57** |
| Abercwmboi *Rhon* .....3B **58** | Abermaw *Gwyn* .....3B **22** | Acton Pigott *Shrp*.....1C **33** | Alltyblacca *Cdgn* .....1A **46** |
| Abercych *Pemb* .....1B **44** | Abermeurig *Cdgn*.....3A **36** | Acton Round *Shrp*.....2D **33** | Allt-y-goed *Pemb* .....1A **44** |
| **Abercynon** *Rhon*.....3B **58** | Aber-miwl *Powy*.....2C **31** | Acton Scott *Shrp*.....3B **32** | Almeley *Here* .....3A **40** |
| Aber-Cywarch *Gwyn*.....3D **23** | Abermule *Powy*.....2C **31** | Adderley *Shrp*.....1D **27** | Almeley Wootton *Here* .....3A **40** |
| **Aberdar** *Rhon* .....2A **58** | Abernant *Rhon*.....2B **58** | Adeney *Telf*.....3D **27** | Almington *Staf*.....1D **27** |
| | Abernant *Carm* .....3C **45** | Adfa *Powy* .....1B **30** | Almondsbury *S Glo* .....1D **67** |
| | | Adforton *Here* .....1B **40** | Alport *Powy* .....2D **31** |

Alpraham Ches E....................2C **19**
Alvanley Ches W....................3B **10**
Alveston S Glo.........................1D **67**
Alvington Glos.........................2D **61**
Ambleston Pemb ....................3D **43**
Amlwch IOA.............................1D **5**
Amlwch Port IOA.....................1D **5**
**Ammanford** Carm.................1B **56**
Amroth Pemb ..........................2A **54**
Anchor Shrp.............................3C **31**
Anderton Ches W....................3D **11**
Anelog Gwyn ...........................2A **20**
Anfield Mers............................1A **10**
Angelbank Shrp.......................1C **41**
Angle Pemb.............................2B **52**
Annscroft Shrp.........................1B **32**
Antrobus Ches W....................3D **11**
Appleton Hal............................2C **11**
Appleton Thorn Warr...............2D **11**
Arberth Pemb ..........................1A **54**
Arddleen Powy........................3D **25**
Arddlîn Powy...........................3D **25**
Argoed Cphy...........................3C **59**
Argoed Mill Powy.....................2A **38**
Arleston Telf............................3D **27**
Arley Ches E............................2D **11**
Arlingham Glos........................1D **61**
Arthog Gwyn...........................3B **22**
Ashbrook Shrp.........................2B **32**
Ashfield Here...........................3C **51**
Ashfield Shrp...........................3C **33**
Ashford Bowdler Shrp.............1C **41**
Ashford Carbonel Shrp............1C **41**
Ashley Heath Staf....................1D **27**
Ashley Moor Here....................2B **40**
Ash Magna Shrp......................1C **27**
Ash Parva Shrp.......................1C **27**
Ashperton Here........................1D **51**
Ashton Here.............................2C **41**
Ashton Hayes Ches W.............1C **19**
**Ashton-in-Makerfield**
G Man....................................1C **11**
Asterley Shrp...........................1A **32**
Asterton Shrp...........................2A **32**
Astley G Man...........................1D **11**
Astley Shrp..............................3C **27**
Astley Abbotts Shrp.................2D **33**
Aston Ches W..........................3C **11**
..................................(nr Frodsham)
Aston Here...............................2B **40**
..................................(nr Leominster)
Aston Ches E...........................3D **19**
..................................(nr Nantwich)
Aston Shrp...............................2C **27**
..........................................(nr Wem)
Aston Flin................................1A **18**
Aston Telf................................1D **33**
Aston Staf................................3D **19**
Aston Botterell Shrp................3D **33**
Aston Crews Here....................3D **51**
Aston Eyre Shrp......................2D **33**
Aston Ingham Here..................3D **51**
Aston juxta Mondrum Ches E....2D **19**
Astonlane Shrp........................2D **33**
Aston Munslow Shrp................3C **33**
Aston on Clun Shrp.................3A **32**
Aston Pigott Shrp....................1A **32**
Aston Rogers Shrp..................1A **32**
Atcham Shrp............................1C **33**
**Atherton** G Man....................1D **11**
Atterley Shrp............................2D **33**
Auberrow Here.........................1B **50**
Audlem Ches E........................3D **19**
Aulden Here.............................3B **40**
Aust S Glo...............................1C **67**
Avonmouth Bris........................2C **67**
Awre Glos.................................2D **61**
Aylburton Glos..........................2D **61**
Aylburton Common Glos ..........2D **61**
Aylton Here..............................2D **51**
Aymestrey Here .......................2B **40**

# B

Babbinswood Shrp...................1A **26**
Babel Carm.............................2D **47**
Babell Flin...............................3C **9**
Bachau IOA.............................2D **5**
Bacheldre Powy.......................2D **31**
Bachymbyd Fawr Den.............1B **16**
Backe Carm.............................1B **54**
Backford Ches W.....................3B **10**
Backwell N Som.......................3B **66**
Bacton Here.............................2A **50**
Bae Cinmel Cnwy .....................2A **8**
**Bae Colwyn** Cnwy.............**70** (3D **7**)
Bae Penrhyn Cnwy ..................2D **7**
Bagginswood Shrp...................3D **33**
Bagillt Flin...............................3D **9**
Baglan Neat.............................3C **57**
Bagley Shrp.............................2B **26**
Bagstone S Glo........................1D **67**
Bagwyllydiart Here....................3B **50**
Bala Gwyn..............................1A **24**
Bala, Y Gwyn..........................1A **24**
Balderton Ches W....................1A **18**
Ball Shrp..................................2A **26**
Ballingham Here.......................2C **51**
Bamfurlong G Man...................1C **11**
Bancffosfelen Carm.................1D **55**
Bancycapel Carm.....................1D **55**
Bancyfelin Carm.......................1C **55**
Banc-y-ffordd Carm.................2D **45**
**Bangor** Gwyn.....................**68** (3A **6**)
Bangor-is-y-coed Wrex.............3A **18**
Bangor Service Area Gwyn ......1A **14**
Bank, The Shrp........................2D **33**
Bank Street Worc.....................2D **41**
Banwell N Som........................3A **66**
Barbridge Ches E.....................2D **19**
Barnston Mers..........................2D **9**
Barnton Ches W.......................3D **11**
Barons Cross Here...................3B **40**
**Barri** V Glam.........................3C **65**
Barrow Shrp.............................1D **33**
Barrow Common N Som...........3C **67**
Barrow Gurney N Som.............3C **67**
Barrow Nook Lanc....................1B **10**
Barrow's Green Hal..................2C **11**
**Barry** V Glam.......................3C **65**
Barry Island V Glam................3C **65**
Bartestree Here........................1C **51**
Barton N Som..........................3A **66**
Barton Ches W.........................2B **18**
Baschurch Shrp........................2B **26**
Bassaleg Newp........................1D **65**
Bate Heath Ches E...................3D **11**
**Bath** Bath.............................3D **67**
Battle Powy..............................2B **48**
Battlefield Shrp.........................3C **27**
Bayston Hill Shrp.....................1B **32**
Bayton Worc............................1D **41**
Bayton Common Worc..............1D **41**
Beach V Glam..........................2D **67**
Beachley Glos..........................3C **61**
Bearstone Shrp........................1D **27**
Bearwood Here.........................3A **40**
Beaufort Blae..........................1C **59**
Beaumaris IOA..........................3B **6**
**Bebington** Mers...................2A **10**
Beddau Rhon...........................1B **64**
Beddgelert Gwyn.....................3A **14**
Bedford G Man........................1D **11**
Bedlinog Mer T........................2B **58**
Bedminster Bris........................2C **67**
Bedstone Shrp.........................1A **40**
Bedwas Cphy..........................1C **65**
Bedwellty Cphy........................2C **59**
Beeston Ches W......................2C **19**
Began Card.............................1D **65**
Begelly Pemb..........................2A **54**
Beggar's Bush Powy................2D **39**
Beguildy Powy.........................1C **39**
Belgrano Cnwy.........................3A **8**
Belle Vue Shrp.........................3B **26**
Benllech IOA.............................2A **6**
Benthall Shrp...........................1D **33**
Bentlawnt Shrp........................1A **32**
Berkeley Glos..........................3D **61**
Berriew Powy...........................1C **31**
Berrington Shrp........................1C **33**
Berrington Worc.......................2C **41**
Berrington Green Worc ............2C **41**
Berrow Green Worc.................3D **41**
Berry Hill Glos.........................1C **61**
Berry Hill Pemb........................1D **43**
Bersham Wrex.........................3A **18**
Berthengam Flin.......................3C **9**
Berwyn Den.............................3C **17**
Bethania Gwyn........................3C **15**
..................(nr Blaenau Ffestiniog)
Bethania Gwyn........................2B **14**
..............................(nr Caernarfon)
Bethania Cdgn.........................2A **36**
Bethel Gwyn............................2B **14**
..............................(nr Bala)
Bethel Gwyn............................1A **14**
..............................(nr Caernarfon)
Bethel IOA...............................3C **5**
Bethesda Gwyn........................1B **14**
Bethesda Pemb........................1D **53**
Bethlehem Carm.......................3B **46**
Betley Staf...............................3D **19**
Bettisfield Wrex........................1B **26**
Betton Shrp..............................1D **27**
Betton Strange Shrp ................1C **33**
Bettws B'end............................1A **64**
Bettws Newp............................3D **59**
Bettws Bledrws Cdgn................3A **36**
Bettws Cedewain Powy ...........2C **31**
Bettws Gwerfil Goch Den.........3B **16**
Bettws Ifan Cdgn.....................1C **45**
Bettws Newydd Mon.................2A **60**
Betws Carm.............................1B **56**
Betws Garmon Gwyn................2A **14**
Betws-y-Coed Cnwy.................2C **15**
Betws-yn-Rhos Cnwy................3A **8**
Beulah Powy............................3A **38**
Beulah Cdgn............................1B **44**
Bevington Glos.........................3D **61**
Bickershaw G Man...................1D **11**
Bickerton Ches E.....................2C **19**
Bickley Moss Ches W...............3C **19**
Bicton Shrp..............................3D **31**
Bicton Shrp..............................3B **26**
..............................(nr Bishop's Castle)
Bicton Shrp..............................3B **26**
..............................(nr Shrewsbury)
Bicton Here..............................2B **40**
Bicton Heath Shrp....................3B **26**
Bidston Mers............................2D **9**
Billinge Mers............................1C **11**
Billingsley Shrp........................3D **33**
Bilson Green Glos....................1D **61**
Bings Heath Shrp.....................3C **27**
Binweston Shrp........................1A **32**
Bircher Here............................2B **40**
Birchgrove Card.......................1C **65**
Birchgrove Swan......................3C **57**
Birch Heath Ches W................1C **19**
Birch Hill Ches W.....................3C **11**
Birchwood Warr.......................1D **11**
Birdwood Glos.........................1D **61**
**Birkenhead** Mers.................2A **10**
Birley Here...............................3B **40**
Birtley Here..............................2A **40**
Bishop's Castle Shrp................3A **32**
Bishops Frome Here ................1D **51**
Bishopston Swan.....................1A **62**
Bishopstone Here .....................1B **50**
Bishop Sutton Bath..................3C **67**
Bishopsworth Bris....................3C **67**
Bishton Newp..........................1A **66**
Bitterley Shrp...........................1C **41**
Bitton S Glo.............................3D **67**
Blackbrook Mers......................1C **11**
Blackford Shrp.........................3C **33**
Blackmill B'end........................1A **64**
Blackmoor G Man....................1D **11**
Black Pill Swan........................3B **56**
Blackrock Mon.........................1D **59**
Black Tar Pemb........................2C **53**
Blacktown Newp.......................1D **65**
**Blackwood** Cphy..................3C **59**
Blacon Ches W........................1A **18**
Blaenannerch Cdgn..................1B **44**
Blaenau Dolwyddelan Cnwy......2B **14**
Blaenau Ffestiniog Gwyn .........3C **15**
Blaenavon Torf.........................2D **59**
Blaenawey Mon.......................1D **59**
Blaen Celyn Cdgn....................3C **35**
Blaen Clydach Rhon................3A **58**
Blaencwm Rhon .......................3A **58**
Blaendulais Neat......................2D **57**
Blaenffos Pemb........................2A **44**
Blaengarw B'end......................3A **58**
Blaen-geuffordd Cdgn..............3B **28**
Blaengwrach Neat....................2D **57**
Blaengwynfi Neat.....................3D **57**
Blaenllechau Rhon...................3A **58**
Blaenpennal Cdgn....................2B **36**
Blaenplwyf Cdgn......................1A **36**
Blaenporth Cdgn......................1B **44**
Blaenrhondda Rhon.................2A **58**
Blaenwaun Carm......................3B **44**
Blaen-y-coed Carm..................3C **45**
Blagdon N Som.......................3C **67**
Blaina Blae..............................2D **59**
Blaisdon Glos...........................1D **61**
Blakemere Here........................1A **50**
Blakeney Glos..........................2D **61**
Blakenhall Ches E....................3D **19**
Bleadon N Som........................3A **66**
Bleddfa Powy...........................2D **39**
Bletchley Shrp..........................1D **27**
Bletherston Pemb.....................3D **43**
Bliss Gate Worc.......................1D **41**
Blists Hill Telf...........................1D **33**
Blue Anchor Swan....................3A **56**
Bodedern IOA............................2C **5**
Bodelwyddan Den......................3B **8**
Bodenham Here.......................3C **41**
Bodewryd IOA...........................1C **5**
Bodfari Den...............................3B **8**
Bodffordd IOA...........................3D **5**
Bodnant Cnwy..........................3D **7**
Bodorgan IOA...........................1C **13**
Boduan Gwyn...........................1C **21**
Bog, The Shrp..........................2A **32**
Bold Heath Mers......................2C **11**
Bolstone Here...........................2C **51**
Bomere Heath Shrp..................3B **26**
Boncath Pemb..........................2B **44**
Bont Mon................................1A **60**
Bontddu Gwyn.........................3B **22**
Bont Dolgadfan Powy...............1D **29**
Bont-Faen, Y V Glam...............2A **64**
Bontgoch Cdgn........................3B **28**
Bont Newydd Gwyn..................3C **15**
Bont-newydd Cnwy.....................3B **8**
Bontnewydd Powy....................1D **13**
Bontnewydd Cdgn....................2B **36**
Bontuchel Den..........................2B **16**
Bonvilston V Glam....................2B **64**

Bon-y-maen *Swan*..................3B **56**
Booley *Shrp*...........................2C **27**
Boothstown *G Man* ................1D **11**
**Bootle** *Mers*...........................1A **10**
Boraston *Shrp*.......................1D **41**
Boreton *Shrp*.........................1C **33**
Borth *Cdgn*............................3B **28**
Borth-y-Gest *Gwyn* ...............1A **22**
Bosbury *Here*........................1D **51**
Bosherston *Pemb* .................3C **53**
Bostock Green *Ches W*...........1D **19**
Botloe's Green *Glos* ...............3D **51**
Botwnnog *Gwyn* ...................1B **20**
Boughrood *Powy*...................2C **49**
Boughspring *Glos*..................3C **61**
Bouldon *Shrp*........................3C **33**
Boulston *Pemb* .....................1C **53**
Bounds *Here*.........................2D **51**
Bourton *N Som*......................3A **66**
Bourton *Shrp*.........................2C **33**
Boverton *V Glam*...................3A **64**
Bowdon *G Man*......................2D **11**
Bowley *Here*..........................3C **41**
Bowling Bank *Wrex*................3A **18**
Bow Street *Cdgn*....................3B **28**
Boxbush *Glos*........................3D **51**
Brackla *B'end*........................2A **64**
Bradfield Green *Ches E*...........2D **19**
Bradley *Glos*..........................3D **61**
Bradley *Wrex*.........................2A **18**
Bradley *Ches W*......................3C **11**
Bradley Green *Ches W*.............3C **19**
Bradley Stoke *S Glo*...............1D **67**
Bradlow *Here*.........................2D **51**
Braichmelyn *Gwyn*.................1B **14**
Brampton Abbotts *Here*...........3D **51**
Brampton Bryan *Here* .............1A **40**
Brand Green *Glos*...................3D **51**
Brandhill *Shrp*.......................1B **40**
Bransley *Shrp*........................1D **41**
Bratton *Telf*...........................3D **27**
Breaden Heath *Shrp* ...............1B **26**
Breadstone *Glos* ....................2D **61**
Bream *Glos*............................2D **61**
Bream's Meend *Glos* ..............2D **61**
Brechfa *Carm* ........................2A **46**
Brecon *Powy*..........................3B **48**
Bredenbury *Here*....................3D **41**
Bredwardine *Here*...................1A **50**
Breinton *Here* ........................2B **50**
Breinton Common *Here* ..........2B **50**
Brelston Green *Here* ...............3C **51**
Bretton *Flin*...........................1A **18**
Bridell *Pemb*..........................1A **44**
Bridgemere *Ches E*.................3D **19**
**Bridgend** *B'end*.....................1A **64**
Bridge Sollers *Here*................1B **50**
Bridge Trafford *Ches W* ..........3B **10**
Bridgeyate *S Glo*....................2D **67**
**Bridgnorth** *Shrp*..................2D **33**
Bridstow *Here*........................3C **51**
Brierley *Glos*..........................1D **61**
Brierley *Here*..........................3B **40**
Brilley *Here*............................1D **49**
Brimaston *Pemb*.....................3C **43**
Brimfield *Here* .......................2C **41**
Brimstage *Mers*.....................2A **10**
Brindley *Ches E*......................2C **19**
Bringsty Common *Here*...........3D **41**
Brislington *Bris*......................2D **67**
**Bristol** *Bris*..........................2C **67**
Brithdir *Gwyn*........................3C **23**
Brithdir *Cphy*.........................2C **59**
Brithdir *Cdgn* ........................1C **45**
Briton Ferry *Neat* ...................3C **57**
Broad, The *Here* .....................2B **40**
Broadfield *Pemb* ....................2A **54**
Broad Haven *Pemb*.................1B **52**
Broadheath *Worc*....................2D **41**

Broadlay *Carm*.......................2C **55**
Broadmoor *Pemb*...................2D **53**
Broad Oak *Here* .....................3B **50**
Broadoak *Glos*.......................1D **61**
Broad Oak *Carm*....................3A **46**
Broadstone *Shrp*....................3C **33**
Broadway *Carm*.....................2C **55**
.................................(nr Kidwelly)
Broadway *Carm*......................2B **54**
.............................(nr Laugharne)
Broadway *Pemb* .....................1B **52**
Broadwell *Glos*.......................1C **61**
Brobury *Here* .........................1A **50**
Brockhampton *Here*................2C **51**
Brockley *N Som*......................3B **66**
Brockton *Shrp*........................3A **32**
..........................(nr Bishop's Castle)
Brockton *Shrp*.......................1D **33**
...................................(nr Madeley)
Brockton *Shrp*........................2C **33**
.............................(nr Much Wenlock)
Brockton *Shrp*........................1D **33**
...............................(nr Pontesbury)
Brockton *Telf*.........................3D **27**
Brockweir *Glos* ......................2C **61**
Bromborough *Mers*................2A **10**
Bromdon *Shrp*........................3D **33**
Bromesberrow Heath *Glos* .......2D **51**
Bromfield *Shrp* ......................1B **40**
Bromley *Shrp*.........................2D **33**
Brompton *Shrp* ......................1C **33**
Bromsash *Here*......................3D **51**
Bromyard *Here* .......................3D **41**
Bromyard Downs *Here*............3D **41**
Bronaber *Gwyn*.......................1C **23**
Broncroft *Shrp*.......................3C **33**
Brongest *Cdgn* ......................1C **45**
Brongwyn *Cdgn* .....................1B **44**
Bronington *Wrex*....................1B **26**
Bronllys *Powy*........................2C **49**
Bronnant *Cdgn*......................2B **36**
Bronwydd Arms *Carm*.............3D **45**
Bronydd *Powy* .......................1D **49**
Bronygarth *Shrp* ...................1D **25**
Brook *Carm* ..........................2B **54**
Brookend *Glos*.......................2D **61**
Brookhurst *Mers*....................2A **10**
Brooklands *Shrp*....................3C **19**
Brooks *Powy*..........................2C **31**
Broome *Shrp* .........................2C **33**
.................................(nr Cardington)
Broome *Shrp*.........................3B **32**
..............................(nr Craven Arms)
Broomedge *Warr* ...................2D **11**
Broomhall *Ches E*...................3D **19**
Broom's Green *Glos*................2D **51**
Broseley *Shrp*........................1D **33**
Broughall *Shrp*.......................3C **19**
Broughton *V Glam*..................2A **64**
Broughton *Flin*.......................1A **18**
Brownhill *Shrp*.......................2B **26**
Brownhills *Shrp*.....................1D **27**
Brown Knowl *Ches W* ..............2C **19**
Broxton *Ches W*......................2B **18**
Broxwood *Here*......................3A **40**
Bruera *Ches W* .......................1B **18**
**Brymbo** *Wrex*......................2D **17**
Brymbo *Cnwy*..........................3D **7**
Bryn *Neat*..............................3D **57**
Bryn *Carm* ............................2A **56**
Bryn *Shrp*...............................3D **31**
Bryn *G Man* ...........................1C **11**
Brynamman *Carm*..................1C **57**
Brynberian *Pemb*....................2A **44**
Brynbryddan *Neat*..................3C **57**
Bryncae *Rhon* ........................1A **64**
Bryncethin *B'end* ...................1A **64**
Bryncir *Gwyn*.........................3D **13**
Bryncoch *Neat*.......................3C **57**

Bryncroes *Gwyn* ....................1B **20**
Bryncrug *Gwyn*......................1B **28**
Bryn Du *IOA*............................3C **5**
Bryn Eden *Gwyn*....................2C **23**
Bryn Eglwys *Gwyn*.................1B **14**
Bryneglwys *Den*.....................3C **17**
Brynford *Flin*...........................3C **9**
Bryn Gates *G Man*..................1C **11**
Bryn Golau *Rhon*...................1B **64**
Bryngwran *IOA*........................3C **5**
Bryngwyn *Powy*.....................1C **49**
Bryngwyn *Mon* ......................2A **60**
Bryn-henllan *Pemb*................2D **43**
Brynhoffnant *Cdgn*................3C **35**
Bryn-llwyn *Den*......................2B **8**
Brynllywarch *Powy*................3C **31**
Bryn-mawr *Gwyn*...................1B **20**
**Brynmawr** *Blae*....................1C **59**
Brynmenyn *B'end*..................1A **64**
Brynmill *Swan* .......................3B **56**
Brynna *Rhon*.........................1A **64**
Brynrefail *Gwyn* ....................1A **14**
Brynrefail *IOA*..........................2D **5**
Brynsadler *Rhon*....................1B **64**
Bryn-Saith Marchog *Den* ........2B **16**
Brynsiencyn *IOA* ....................1D **13**
Brynteg *Wrex*.........................2A **18**
Brynteg *IOA*.............................2D **5**
Brynygwenyn *Mon*.................1A **60**
Bryn-y-maen *Cnwy*...................3D **7**
Buckholt *Here*........................1C **61**
Buckland *Here*.......................3C **41**
**Buckley** *Flin*.......................1D **17**
Buckley Hill *Mers*...................1A **10**
Bucklow Hill *Ches E*................2D **11**
Bucknell *Shrp*........................1A **40**
Buckton *Here*.........................1A **40**
Buerton *Ches E*......................3D **19**
Buildwas *Shrp*.......................1D **33**
Builth Road *Powy*...................3B **38**
Builth Wells *Powy*..................3B **38**
Bulkeley *Ches E*.....................2C **19**
Bull Bay *IOA*............................1D **5**
Bullinghope *Here*...................2C **51**
Bunbury *Ches E*.....................2C **19**
Burcher *Here*.........................2A **40**
Burcote *Shrp*.........................2D **33**
Burford *Shrp*..........................2C **41**
Burghill *Here*..........................1B **50**
Burland *Ches E*......................2D **19**
Burleydam *Ches E*.................3D **19**
Burley Gate *Here* ...................1C **51**
Burlingjobb *Powy*..................3D **39**
Burlton *Shrp*..........................2B **26**
Burnett *Bath*..........................3D **67**
Burrington *N Som*..................3B **66**
Burrington *Here*.....................1B **40**
Burry *Swan*............................3D **55**
Burry Green *Swan*..................3D **55**
Burry Port *Carm*....................2D **55**
Burton *Ches W*.......................1C **19**
.....................................(nr Kelsall)
Burton *Ches W*.......................3A **10**
.....................................(nr Neston)
Burton *Wrex* ..........................2A **18**
Burton *Pemb* .........................2C **53**
Burton Green *Wrex*.................2A **18**
Burtonwood *Warr*...................1C **11**
Burwardsley *Ches W*...............2C **19**
Burwarton *Shrp*.....................3D **33**
Burwen *IOA*.............................1D **5**
Bush Bank *Here*.....................3B **40**
Bushmoor *Shrp*.....................3B **32**
Butcombe *N Som*....................3C **67**
Bute Town *Cphy*.....................2C **59**
Butt Green *Ches E*..................2D **19**
Buttington *Powy*....................1D **31**
Buttonbridge *Shrp*.................1D **41**
Buttonoak *Shrp*.....................1D **41**

**Bwcle** *Flin*............................1D **17**
Bwlch *Powy*............................3C **49**
Bwlchderwin *Gwyn*................3D **13**
Bwlchgwyn *Wrex*...................2D **17**
Bwlch-Llan *Cdgn*....................3A **36**
Bwlchnewydd *Carm*................3C **45**
Bwlchtocyn *Gwyn*..................2C **21**
Bwlch-y-cibau *Powy*...............3C **25**
Bwlchyddar *Powy*..................2C **25**
Bwlch-y-fadfa *Cdgn*................1D **45**
Bwlch-y-ffridd *Powy*...............2B **30**
Bwlch y Garreg *Powy*..............2B **30**
Bwlch-y-groes *Pemb* ..............2B **44**
Bwlch-y-sarnau *Powy*.............1B **38**
Byford *Here* ...........................1A **50**
Bylchau *Cnwy*........................1A **16**
Byley *Ches W* .........................1D **19**
Bynea *Carm*...........................3A **56**
Byton *Here*.............................2A **40**

## C

Cadishead *G Man* ...................1D **11**
Cadle *Swan*............................3B **56**
Cadole *Flin* ............................1D **17**
Cadoxton-juxta-Neath *Neat*......3C **57**
Cadwst *Den*............................1B **24**
Caeathro *Gwyn* ......................1A **14**
Caehopkin *Powy*....................1D **57**
Caerau *B'end*..........................3D **57**
Caerau *Card* ..........................2C **65**
Cae'r-bont *Powy*....................1D **57**
Cae'r-bryn *Carm*....................1A **56**
Caerdeon *Gwyn*.....................3B **22**
**Caerdydd** *Card*..............**69** (2C **65**)
Caerfarchell *Pemb* .................3A **42**
**Caerffili** *Cphy*.......................1C **65**
**Caerfyrddin** *Carm*........**69** (1D **55**)
Caergeiliog *IOA*........................3C **5**
Caergwrle *Flin*........................2A **18**
**Caergybi** *IOA*................**74** (2B **4**)
Caerleon *Newp* ......................3A **60**
Caerlleon *Carm*......................3B **44**
Caerllion *Newp*......................3A **60**
**Caernarfon** *Gwyn*..........**69** (1D **13**)
Caernarfon Airport *Gwyn*........2D **13**
**Caerphilly** *Cphy*....................1C **65**
Caersws *Powy*........................2B **30**
Caerwedros *Cdgn* ..................3C **35**
Caerwent *Mon* .......................3B **60**
Caerwys *Flin*............................3C **9**
Caim *IOA*.................................2B **6**
Caio *Carm*..............................2B **46**
Calcott *Shrp*...........................3B **26**
**Caldicot** *Mon* .......................1B **66**
Caldy *Mers*..............................2D **9**
Callaughton *Shrp*...................2D **33**
Callow *Here*............................2B **50**
Callow Hill *Worc*.....................1D **41**
Calveley *Ches E*......................2C **19**
Calverhall *Shrp* .....................1D **27**
Cam *Glos*...............................3D **61**
Cambridge *Glos*....................2D **61**
Cameley *Bath*........................3D **67**
Camerton *Bath* ......................3D **67**
Camrose *Pemb*......................3C **43**
Canaston Bridge *Pemb* ...........1D **53**
Canon Bridge *Here*.................1B **50**
Canon Frome *Here*.................1D **51**
Canon Pyon *Here* ...................1B **50**
Cantlop *Shrp*..........................1C **33**
Canton *Card* ..........................2C **65**
Capel Bangor *Cdgn*................3B **28**
Capel Betws Lleucu *Cdgn*........3B **36**
Capel Coch *IOA*........................2D **5**
Capel Curig *Cnwy*...................2C **15**
Capel Cynon *Cdgn* .................1C **45**
Capel Dewi *Cdgn*...................3B **28**
...........................(nr Aberystwyth)

Capel Dewi *Cdgn* ...................... 1D **45**
................................ (nr Llandysul)
Capel Dewi *Carm* ..................... 3D **45**
Capel Garmon *Cnwy* ................ 2D **15**
Capel Gwyn *IOA* ....................... 3C **5**
Capel Gwynfe *Carm* .................. 3C **47**
Capel Hendre *Carm* ................. 1A **56**
Capel Isaac *Carm* ..................... 3A **46**
Capel Iwan *Carm* ...................... 2B **44**
Capel Llanilltern *Card* ............. 2B **64**
Capel Mawr *IOA* ......................... 3D **5**
Capel Newydd *Pemb* ................ 2B **44**
Capel Seion *Carm* .................... 1A **56**
Capel Seion *Cdgn* ..................... 1B **36**
Capel Uchaf *Gwyn* .................... 3D **13**
Capel-y-ffin *Powy* ..................... 2D **49**
Capenhurst *Ches W* .................. 3A **10**
Cardeston *Shrp* ....................... 3A **26**
**Cardiff** *Card* ................ **69** (2C **65**)
Cardiff Airport *V Glam* ...... **73** (3B **64**)
Cardiff Gate Service Area
*Card* ...................................... 1D **65**
Cardiff Heliport *Card* ............. 2D **65**
Cardiff West Service Area
*Card* ...................................... 1B **64**
Cardigan *Cdgn* ........................ 1A **44**
Cardington *Shrp* ..................... 2C **33**
Carew *Pemb* ............................ 2D **53**
Carew Cheriton *Pemb* ........... 2D **53**
Carew Newton *Pemb* .............. 2D **53**
Carey *Here* ............................... 2C **51**
Carlingcott *Bath* .................... 3D **67**
**Carmarthen** *Carm* ......... **69** (1D **55**)
Carmel *Flin* ............................... 3C **9**
Carmel *Gwyn* ........................... 2D **13**
Carmel *IOA* ............................... 2C **5**
Carmel *Carm* ........................... 1A **56**
Carnhedryn *Pemb* ................... 3B **42**
Carno *Powy* ............................. 2A **30**
Carreglefn *IOA* ........................ 2C **5**
Carrington *G Man* ................... 1D **11**
Carrog *Den* .............................. 3C **17**
Carrog *Cnwy* ........................... 3C **15**
Carrow Hill *Mon* ...................... 3B **60**
Carway *Carm* .......................... 2D **55**
Cascob *Powy* .......................... 2D **39**
**Cas-gwent** *Mon* ................... 3C **61**
Cas-Mael *Pemb* ..................... 3D **43**
**Casnewydd** *Newp* ........ **71** (1A **66**)
Castell *Den* .............................. 1C **17**
Castell *Cnwy* ........................... 1C **15**
Castell Hendre *Pemb* ............. 3D **43**
**Castell-Nedd** *Neat* ............. 3C **57**
Castell Newydd Emlyn *Carm* .... 1C **45**
Castell-y-bwch *Torf* ................ 3D **59**
Castlebythe *Pemb* .................. 3D **43**
Castle Caereinion *Powy* .......... 1C **31**
Castle Frome *Here* .................. 1D **51**
Castlemartin *Pemb* ................. 3C **53**
Castlemorris *Pemb* ................ 2C **43**
Castleton *Newp* ...................... 1D **65**
Caswell *Swan* ......................... 1A **62**
Catbrook *Mon* ......................... 2C **61**
Cathedine *Powy* ...................... 3C **49**
Catherton *Shrp* ...................... 1D **41**
Cat's Ash *Newp* ...................... 3A **60**
Caynham *Shrp* ........................ 1C **41**
Cefn Berain *Cnwy* ................... 1A **16**
Cefn-brith *Cnwy* ...................... 2A **16**
Cefn-bryn-brain *Carm* ............ 1C **57**
Cefn-bychan *Flin* .................... 1C **17**
Cefncaeau *Carm* ..................... 3A **56**
Cefn Canol *Powy* .................... 1D **25**
Cefn Coch *Powy* ...................... 1B **30**
.................... (nr Llanfair Caereinion)
Cefn-coch *Powy* ...................... 2C **25**
......(nr Llanrhaeadr-ym-Mochnant)
Cefn-coed-y-cymmer *Mer T* .... 2B **58**
Cefn Cribwr *B'end* ................... 1D **63**

Cefn-ddwysarn *Gwyn* ............. 1A **24**
Cefn Einion *Shrp* ..................... 3D **31**
Cefneithin *Carm* ..................... 1A **56**
Cefn Glas *B'end* ...................... 1D **63**
Cefngorwydd *Powy* ................. 1A **48**
Cefn Llwyd *Cdgn* ..................... 3B **28**
Cefn-mawr *Wrex* ..................... 3D **17**
Cefn-y-bedd *Flin* ..................... 2A **18**
Cefn-y-coed *Powy* ................... 2C **31**
Cefn-y-pant *Carm* ................... 3A **44**
Cegidfa *Powy* .......................... 3D **25**
Ceinewydd *Cdgn* ..................... 3C **35**
Cellan *Cdgn* ............................ 1B **46**
Cemaes *IOA* ............................. 1C **5**
Cemmaes *Powy* ...................... 1D **29**
Cemmaes Road *Powy* ............. 1D **29**
Cenarth *Cdgn* .......................... 1B **44**
Cenin *Gwyn* ............................. 3D **13**
Centre for Alternative Technology
*Powy* ................................... 1C **29**
Ceri *Powy* ................................ 3C **31**
Cerist *Powy* ............................. 3A **30**
Cerrigceinwen *IOA* ................... 3D **5**
Cerrigydrudion *Cnwy* .............. 3A **16**
Ceunant *Gwyn* ........................ 1A **14**
Chadwick Green *Mers* ............ 1C **11**
Chancery *Cdgn* ....................... 1A **36**
Chapel Hill *Mon* ...................... 2C **61**
Chapel Lawn *Shrp* ................... 1A **40**
Charfield *S Glo* ........................ 3D **61**
Charlcombe *Bath* ................... 3D **67**
Charlton *Telf* ........................... 3C **27**
Chatwall *Shrp* ......................... 2C **33**
Chaxhill *Glos* .......................... 1D **61**
Checkley *Ches E* ..................... 3D **19**
Checkley *Here* ......................... 2C **51**
Chelmarsh *Shrp* ..................... 3D **33**
Chelmick *Shrp* ........................ 2B **32**
Chelvey *N Som* ....................... 3B **66**
Chelwood *Bath* ....................... 3D **67**
Cheney Longville *Shrp* ............ 3B **32**
**Chepstow** *Mon* .................... 3C **61**
Cheswardine *Shrp* .................. 1D **27**
Cheswell *Telf* .......................... 3D **27**
Chetton *Shrp* .......................... 2D **33**
Chetwynd Aston *Telf* .............. 3D **27**
Chew Magna *Bath* ................... 3C **67**
Chew Stoke *Bath* .................... 3C **67**
Chewton Keynsham *Bath* ....... 3D **67**
Chickward *Here* ...................... 3D **39**
Childer Thornton *Ches W* ....... 3A **10**
Child's Ercall *Shrp* ................. 2D **27**
Childwall *Mers* ....................... 2B **10**
Chipnall *Shrp* .......................... 1D **27**
**Chipping Sodbury** *S Glo* ..... 1D **67**
Chirbury *Shrp* ......................... 2D **31**
Chirk *Wrex* .............................. 1D **25**
Cholstrey *Here* ....................... 3B **40**
Chorley *Ches E* ....................... 2C **19**
Chorley *Shrp* ........................... 3D **33**
Chorlton *Ches E* ...................... 2D **19**
Chorlton Lane *Ches W* ............ 3B **18**
Choulton *Shrp* ........................ 3A **32**
Christchurch *Glos* .................. 1C **61**
Christleton *Ches W* ................. 1B **18**
Christon *N Som* ...................... 3A **66**
Church Aston *Telf* ................... 3D **27**
Church End *Glos* ..................... 2D **61**
Church Hill *Ches W* ................. 1D **19**
Churchill *N Som* ...................... 3B **66**
Church Minshull *Ches E* ......... 1D **19**
Church Preen *Shrp* ................. 2C **33**
Church Pulverbatch *Shrp* ....... 1B **32**
Church Stoke *Powy* ................. 2D **31**
Church Stretton *Shrp* .............. 2B **32**

Churchtown *Shrp* .................... 3D **31**
Church Village *Rhon* ............... 1B **64**
Churton *Ches W* ...................... 2B **18**
Chwilog *Gwyn* ......................... 1D **21**
Chwittffordd *Flin* .................... 3C **9**
Cilan Uchaf *Gwyn* ................... 2B **20**
Cilcain *Flin* ............................. 1C **17**
Cilcennin *Cdgn* ....................... 2A **36**
Cilfrew *Neat* ............................ 2C **57**
Cilfynydd *Rhon* ....................... 3B **58**
Cilgerran *Pemb* ...................... 1A **44**
Cilgeti *Pemb* ........................... 2A **54**
Cilgwyn *Carm* ......................... 3C **47**
Cilgwyn *Pemb* ........................ 2D **43**
Ciliau Aeron *Cdgn* .................. 3D **35**
Cilmaengwyn *Neat* .................. 2C **57**
Cilmeri *Powy* ........................... 3B **38**
Cilmery *Powy* .......................... 3B **38**
Cilrhedyn *Pemb* ...................... 2B **44**
Cilsan *Carm* ........................... 3A **46**
Ciltalgarth *Gwyn* ..................... 3D **15**
Ciltwrch *Powy* ......................... 1C **49**
Cilybebyll *Neat* ....................... 2C **57**
Cilycwm *Carm* ........................ 1C **47**
Cimla *Neat* .............................. 3C **57**
**Cinderford** *Glos* .................. 1D **61**
Cippyn *Pemb* .......................... 1A **44**
City *V Glam* .............................. 2A **64**
City *Powy* ................................ 2D **31**
City Dulas *IOA* .......................... 2D **5**
Clapton in Gordano *N Som* ..... 2B **66**
Clarbeston *Pemb* .................... 3D **43**
Clarbeston Road *Pemb* .......... 3D **43**
Clatter *Powy* ........................... 2A **30**
Claughton *Mers* ........................ 2D **9**
Claverham *N Som* ................... 3B **66**
Clawdd-côch *V Glam* ............... 2B **64**
Clawdd-newydd *Den* ............... 2B **16**
Clay Hill *Bris* ........................... 2D **67**
Clearwell *Glos* ........................ 2C **61**
Cleedownton *Shrp* .................. 3C **33**
Cleehill *Shrp* ........................... 1C **41**
Clee St Margaret *Shrp* ............ 3C **33**
Cleestanton *Shrp* ................... 1C **41**
Cleeton St Mary *Shrp* ............. 1D **41**
Cleeve *N Som* .......................... 3B **66**
Clehonger *Here* ...................... 2B **50**
Cleobury Mortimer *Shrp* ........ 1D **41**
Cleobury North *Shrp* .............. 3D **33**
**Clevedon** *N Som* .................. 2B **66**
Clifford *Here* ........................... 1D **49**
Clifford's Mesne *Glos* ............ 3D **51**
Clifton *Bris* ............................. 2C **67**
Clifton Hill *Worc* ..................... 2D **41**
Clifton upon Teme *Worc* ......... 2D **41**
Clipiau *Gwyn* ........................... 3D **23**
Clive *Shrp* ............................... 2C **27**
Clocaenog *Den* ....................... 2B **16**
Clock Face *Mers* ..................... 1C **11**
Cloddiau *Powy* ........................ 1D **31**
Clodock *Here* .......................... 3A **50**
Clotton *Ches W* ....................... 1C **19**
Clows Top *Worc* ...................... 1D **41**
Cloy *Wrex* ............................... 3A **18**
Cluddley *Telf* ........................... 3D **27**
Clun *Shrp* ............................... 3A **32**
Clun, Y *Neat* ........................... 2D **57**
Clunbury *Shrp* ........................ 3A **32**
Clunderwen *Pemb* .................. 1A **54**
Clungunford *Shrp* ................... 1A **40**
Clunton *Shrp* .......................... 3A **32**
Clutton *Bath* ........................... 3D **67**
Clutton *Ches W* ....................... 2B **18**
Clwt-y-bont *Gwyn* ................... 1A **14**
Clwydfagwyr *Mer T* ................. 2B **58**
Clydach *Mon* ........................... 1D **59**
**Clydach** *Swan* ..................... 2B **56**
Clydach Vale *Rhon* .................. 3A **58**
Clydey *Pemb* .......................... 2B **44**

Clyne *Neat* .............................. 2D **57**
Clynnog-fawr *Gwyn* ................. 3D **13**
Clyro *Powy* .............................. 1D **49**
Cnwcau *Pemb* ........................ 1B **44**
Cnwch Coch *Cdgn* .................. 1B **36**
Coalbrookdale *Telf* ................. 1D **33**
Coalbrookvale *Blae* ................ 2C **59**
Coalpit Heath *S Glo* ................ 1D **67**
Coalport *Telf* ........................... 1D **33**
Coalway *Glos* .......................... 1C **61**
Cobhall Common *Here* ........... 2B **50**
Cobnash *Here* ......................... 2B **40**
Cock Bank *Wrex* ...................... 3A **18**
Cock Gate *Here* ...................... 2B **40**
Cockshutford *Shrp* ................. 3C **33**
Cockshutt *Shrp* ...................... 2B **26**
Cockyard *Here* ....................... 2B **50**
Coddington *Ches W* ................ 2B **18**
Coddington *Here* .................... 1D **51**
Codrington *S Glo* .................... 2D **67**
**Coed Duon** *Cphy* ................. 3C **59**
Coedely *Rhon* ......................... 1B **64**
Coedglasson *Powy* ................. 2B **38**
Coedkernew *Newp* .................. 1D **65**
Coed Morgan *Mon* .................. 1A **60**
Coedpoeth *Wrex* ..................... 2D **17**
Coedway *Powy* ........................ 3A **26**
Coed-y-bryn *Cdgn* ................... 1C **45**
Coed-y-paen *Mon* ................... 3A **60**
Coed Ystumgwern *Gwyn* ........ 2A **22**
Coelbren *Powy* ........................ 1D **57**
Cogan *V Glam* ......................... 2C **65**
Coity *B'end* .............................. 1A **64**
Cold Ashton *S Glo* .................. 2D **67**
Cold Blow *Pemb* ..................... 1A **54**
Coldharbour *Glos* ................... 2C **61**
Cold Hatton *Telf* ...................... 2D **27**
Cold Hatton Heath *Telf* ........... 2D **27**
Coldwell *Here* ......................... 2B **50**
Colebatch *Shrp* ...................... 3A **32**
**Coleford** *Glos* ..................... 1C **61**
Colemere *Shrp* ....................... 1B **26**
Colemore Green *Shrp* ............. 2D **33**
Collins Green *Warr* ................. 1C **11**
Collins Green *Worc* ................. 3D **41**
Colwall *Here* ........................... 1D **51**
Colwall Green *Here* ................. 1D **51**
Colwinston *V Glam* ................. 2A **64**
**Colwyn Bay** *Cnwy* ........ **70** (3D **7**)
Combe *Here* ............................ 2A **40**
Combe Hay *Bath* ..................... 3D **67**
Combe Moor *Here* ................... 2A **40**
Comberbach *Ches W* .............. 3D **11**
Comberton *Here* ..................... 2B **40**
Comins Coch *Cdgn* ................. 3B **28**
Comley *Shrp* ........................... 2B **32**
Commins *Powy* ....................... 2C **25**
Commins Coch *Powy* .............. 1D **29**
Common Hill *Here* ................... 2C **51**
Commonside *Ches W* .............. 3C **11**
Compton Dando *Bath* ............. 3D **67**
Compton Greenfield *S Glo* ..... 1C **67**
Compton Martin *Bath* ............ 3C **67**
Condover *Shrp* ........................ 1B **32**
Congl-y-wal *Gwyn* ................... 3C **15**
Congresbury *N Som* ............... 3B **66**
Conham *S Glo* ........................ 2D **67**
**Connah's Quay** *Flin* .............. 3D **9**
Conwy *Cnwy* ............................ 3C **7**
Coppenhall *Ches E* ................. 2D **19**
Coppenhall Moss *Ches E* ....... 2D **19**
Coppicegate *Shrp* ................... 3D **33**
Coptiviney *Shrp* ...................... 1B **26**
Coreley *Shrp* ........................... 1D **41**
Corfton *Shrp* ........................... 3B **32**
Corlannau *Neat* ...................... 3C **57**
Corntown *V Glam* .................... 2A **64**
Corris *Gwyn* ............................ 1C **29**
Corris Uchaf *Gwyn* .................. 1C **29**

Corston *Bath*..........3D **67**
Corwen *Den*..........3B **16**
Cosheston *Pemb*..........2D **53**
Cosmeston *V Glam*..........3C **65**
Cotebrook *Ches W*..........1C **19**
Cotland *Mon*..........2C **61**
Coton Hill *Shrp*..........3B **26**
Cotonwood *Shrp*..........1C **27**
Coughton *Here*..........3C **51**
Cound *Shrp*..........1C **33**
Court Henry *Carm*..........3A **46**
Cowbridge *V Glam*..........2A **64**
Cowslip Green *N Som*..........3B **66**
Coxall *Here*..........1A **40**
Coxbank *Ches E*..........3D **19**
Coychurch *B'end*..........1A **64**
Coytrahen *B'end*..........1D **63**
Crabtree Green *Wrex*..........3A **18**
Cradley *Here*..........1D **51**
Cradoc *Powy*..........2B **48**
Crai *Powy*..........3D **47**
Craig-Cefn-Parc *Swan*..........2B **56**
Craig-llwyn *Shrp*..........2D **25**
Craignant *Shrp*..........1D **25**
Craig-y-Duke *Neat*..........2C **57**
Craig-y-nos *Powy*..........1D **57**
Cranage *Ches E*..........1D **19**
Crank *Mers*..........1C **11**
Craswall *Here*..........2D **49**
Craven Arms *Shrp*..........3B **32**
Crawford *Lanc*..........1B **10**
Creamore Bank *Shrp*..........1C **27**
Credenhill *Here*..........1B **50**
Cregrina *Powy*..........3C **39**
Creigiau *Card*..........1B **64**
Cressage *Shrp*..........1C **33**
Cresselly *Pemb*..........2D **53**
Cresswell Quay *Pemb*..........2D **53**
**Crewe** *Ches E*..........2D **19**
Crewe-by-Farndon *Ches W*..........2B **18**
Crewgreen *Powy*..........3A **26**
Cribbs Causeway *S Glo*..........1C **67**
Cribyn *Cdgn*..........3A **36**
Criccieth *Gwyn*..........1D **21**
Crick *Mon*..........3B **60**
Crickadarn *Powy*..........1B **48**
Crickheath *Shrp*..........2D **25**
Crickhowell *Powy*..........1D **59**
Criftins *Shrp*..........1A **26**
Criggion *Powy*..........3D **25**
Crinow *Pemb*..........1A **54**
Crocker's Ash *Here*..........1C **61**
Croeserw *Neat*..........3D **57**
Croes-Goch *Pemb*..........2B **42**
Croes Hywel *Mon*..........1A **60**
Croes-lan *Cdgn*..........1C **45**
Croesor *Gwyn*..........3B **14**
**Croesoswallt** *Shrp*..........2D **25**
Croesyceiliog *Torf*..........3A **60**
Croesyceiliog *Carm*..........1D **55**
Croes-y-mwyalch *Torf*..........3A **60**
Croesywaun *Gwyn*..........2A **14**
Croft *Warr*..........1D **11**
Crofty *Swan*..........3A **56**
Cromhall *S Glo*..........3D **61**
**Crosby** *Mers*..........1A **10**
Cross Ash *Mon*..........1B **60**
Cross Foxes *Gwyn*..........3C **23**
Crossgates *Powy*..........2B **38**
Cross Hands *Carm*..........1A **56**
Crosshands *Carm*..........3A **44**
Cross Hill *Glos*..........3C **61**
Cross Houses *Shrp*..........1C **33**
Cross Inn *Cdgn*..........2A **36**
..........(nr Aberaeron)
Cross Inn *Cdgn*..........3C **35**
..........(nr New Quay)
Cross Inn *Rhon*..........1B **64**

Crosskeys *Cphy*..........3D **59**
Cross Lane Head *Shrp*..........2D **33**
Cross Lanes *Wrex*..........3A **18**
Crosslanes *Shrp*..........3A **26**
Cross Oak *Powy*..........3C **49**
Crossway *Powy*..........3B **38**
Crossway *Mon*..........1B **60**
Crossway Green *Mon*..........3C **61**
Crosswell *Pemb*..........2A **44**
Crosswood *Cdgn*..........1B **36**
Crow Hill *Here*..........3D **51**
Crowton *Ches W*..........3C **11**
Croxton Green *Ches E*..........2C **19**
Cruckmeole *Shrp*..........1B **32**
Cruckton *Shrp*..........3B **26**
Crudgington *Telf*..........3D **27**
Crug *Powy*..........1C **39**
Crughywel *Powy*..........1D **59**
Crugybar *Carm*..........2B **46**
Crug-y-byddar *Powy*..........3C **31**
Crumlin *Cphy*..........3D **59**
Crumpsbrook *Shrp*..........1D **41**
Crundale *Pemb*..........1C **53**
Crwbin *Carm*..........1D **55**
Crymych *Pemb*..........2A **44**
Crynant *Neat*..........2C **57**
Cublington *Here*..........2A **50**
Cuddington *Ches W*..........3D **11**
Cuddington Heath *Ches W*..........3B **18**
Cuerdley Cross *Warr*..........2C **11**
Culcheth *Warr*..........1D **11**
Culmington *Shrp*..........3B **32**
Cusop *Here*..........1D **49**
Cutiau *Gwyn*..........3B **22**
Cuttybridge *Pemb*..........1C **53**
Cwm *Den*..........3B **8**
Cwm *Blae*..........2C **59**
Cwm *Powy*..........2D **31**
Cwmafan *Neat*..........3C **57**
Cwmaman *Rhon*..........3A **58**
Cwmann *Carm*..........1A **46**
Cwmbach *Rhon*..........2B **58**
Cwmbach *Powy*..........2C **49**
Cwmbach *Carm*..........3B **44**
Cwmbach Llechrhyd *Powy*..........3B **38**
Cwmbelan *Powy*..........3A **30**
**Cwmbran** *Torf*..........3D **59**
Cwmbrwyno *Cdgn*..........3C **29**
Cwm Capel *Carm*..........2D **55**
Cwmcarn *Cphy*..........3D **59**
Cwmcarvan *Mon*..........2B **60**
Cwm-celyn *Blae*..........2D **59**
Cwmcerdinen *Swan*..........2B **56**
Cwm-Cewydd *Gwyn*..........3D **23**
Cwm-cou *Cdgn*..........1B **44**
Cwmcych *Pemb*..........2B **44**
Cwmdare *Rhon*..........2A **58**
Cwmdu *Powy*..........3C **49**
Cwmdu *Carm*..........2B **46**
Cwmduad *Carm*..........2C **45**
Cwm Dulais *Swan*..........2B **56**
Cwmerfyn *Cdgn*..........3B **28**
Cwmfelin *B'end*..........1D **63**
Cwmfelin Boeth *Carm*..........1A **54**
Cwmfelinfach *Cphy*..........3C **59**
Cwmfelin Mynach *Carm*..........3B **44**
Cwmffrwd *Carm*..........1D **55**
Cwmgiedd *Powy*..........1C **57**
Cwmgors *Neat*..........1C **57**
Cwmgwili *Carm*..........1A **56**
Cwmgwrach *Neat*..........2D **57**
Cwmhiraeth *Carm*..........2C **45**
Cwmifor *Carm*..........3B **46**
Cwmisfael *Carm*..........1D **55**
Cwm-Llinau *Powy*..........1D **29**
Cwmllynfell *Neat*..........1C **57**
Cwm-mawr *Carm*..........1A **56**
Cwm-miles *Carm*..........3A **44**
Cwmorgan *Carm*..........2B **44**

Cwmparc *Rhon*..........3A **58**
Cwm Penmachno *Cnwy*..........3C **15**
Cwmpennar *Rhon*..........2B **58**
Cwm Plysgog *Pemb*..........1A **44**
Cwmrhos *Powy*..........3C **49**
Cwmsychpant *Cdgn*..........1D **45**
Cwmsyfiog *Cphy*..........2C **59**
Cwmsymlog *Cdgn*..........3B **28**
Cwmtillery *Blae*..........2D **59**
Cwm-twrch Isaf *Powy*..........2C **57**
Cwm-twrch Uchaf *Powy*..........1C **57**
Cwmwysg *Powy*..........3D **47**
Cwm-y-glo *Gwyn*..........1A **14**
Cwmyoy *Mon*..........3A **50**
Cwmystwyth *Cdgn*..........1C **37**
Cwrt *Gwyn*..........1B **28**
Cwrtnewydd *Cdgn*..........1D **45**
Cwrt-y-Cadno *Carm*..........1B **46**
Cydweli *Carm*..........2D **55**
Cyffylliog *Den*..........2B **16**
Cymau *Flin*..........2D **17**
Cymer *Neat*..........3D **57**
Cymmer *Rhon*..........3B **58**
Cymmer *Neat*..........3D **57**
Cyncoed *Card*..........1C **65**
Cynghordy *Carm*..........2D **47**
Cynheidre *Carm*..........2D **55**
Cynonville *Neat*..........3D **57**
Cynwyd *Den*..........3B **16**
Cynwyl Elfed *Carm*..........3C **45**
Cywarch *Gwyn*..........3D **23**

### D

Dafen *Carm*..........2A **56**
Dale *Pemb*..........2B **52**
Danesford *Shrp*..........2D **33**
Daren *Powy*..........1D **59**
Daresbury *Hal*..........2C **11**
Darliston *Shrp*..........1C **27**
Darnhall *Ches W*..........1D **19**
Darowen *Powy*..........1D **29**
Davenham *Ches W*..........3D **11**
David's Well *Powy*..........1B **38**
Dawley *Telf*..........1D **33**
Dawn *Cnwy*..........3D **7**
Daywall *Shrp*..........1D **25**
Ddol *Flin*..........3C **9**
Ddol Cownwy *Powy*..........3B **24**
Dean Pk. *Shrp*..........2D **41**
Defynnog *Powy*..........3A **48**
Deganwy *Cnwy*..........3C **7**
Deiniolen *Gwyn*..........1A **14**
Delamere *Ches W*..........1C **19**
Denbigh *Den*..........1B **16**
Denio *Gwyn*..........1C **21**
Deri *Cphy*..........2C **59**
Derrington *Shrp*..........2D **33**
Derwen *Den*..........2B **16**
Derwen Gam *Cdgn*..........3D **35**
Derwenlas *Powy*..........2C **29**
Deuddwr *Powy*..........3D **25**
Devauden *Mon*..........3B **60**
Devil's Bridge *Cdgn*..........1C **37**
Dewsall Court *Here*..........2B **50**
Diddlebury *Shrp*..........3C **33**
Didley *Here*..........2B **50**
Dihewyd *Cdgn*..........3D **35**
Dilwyn *Here*..........3B **40**
Dinas *Gwyn*..........2D **13**
..........(nr Caernarfon)
Dinas *Gwyn*..........1A **20**
..........(nr Tudweiliog)
Dinas *Carm*..........2B **44**
Dinas Cross *Pemb*..........2D **43**
Dinas Dinlle *Gwyn*..........2D **13**
Dinas Mawddwy *Gwyn*..........3D **23**
Dinas Powys *V Glam*..........2C **65**
Dinbych *Den*..........1B **16**

Dinbych-y-Pysgod *Pemb*..........2A **54**
Dinedor *Here*..........2C **51**
Dinedor Cross *Here*..........2C **51**
Dingestow *Mon*..........1B **60**
Dingle *Mers*..........2A **10**
Dinmael *Cnwy*..........3B **16**
Dinorwig *Gwyn*..........1A **14**
Discoed *Powy*..........2D **39**
Disserth *Powy*..........3B **38**
Ditton *Hal*..........2B **10**
Ditton Priors *Shrp*..........3D **33**
Dixton *Mon*..........1C **61**
Dobs Hill *Flin*..........1A **18**
Dobson's Bridge *Shrp*..........1B **26**
Docklow *Here*..........3C **41**
Doc Penfro *Pemb*..........**74** (2C **53**)
Doddenham *Worc*..........3D **41**
Doddington *Shrp*..........1D **41**
Dodington *S Glo*..........1D **67**
Dodleston *Ches W*..........1A **18**
Dolanog *Powy*..........3B **24**
Dolau *Rhon*..........1B **64**
Dolau *Powy*..........2C **39**
Dolbenmaen *Gwyn*..........3A **14**
Doley *Staf*..........2D **27**
Dol-fâch *Powy*..........1A **30**
Dolfach *Powy*..........1A **38**
Dolfor *Powy*..........3C **31**
Dolgarrog *Cnwy*..........1C **15**
Dolgellau *Gwyn*..........3C **23**
Dolgoch *Gwyn*..........1B **28**
Dol-gran *Carm*..........2D **45**
Dolhelfa *Powy*..........1A **38**
Dolley Green *Powy*..........2D **39**
Dollwen *Cdgn*..........3B **28**
Dolphin *Flin*..........3C **9**
Dolwen *Cnwy*..........3D **7**
Dolwyddelan *Cnwy*..........2C **15**
Dol-y-Bont *Cdgn*..........3B **28**
Dolyhir *Powy*..........3D **39**
Domgay *Powy*..........3D **25**
Donnington *Here*..........2D **51**
Donnington *Shrp*..........1C **33**
Donnington *Telf*..........3D **27**
Dormington *Here*..........1C **51**
Dorrington *Shrp*..........1B **32**
Dorstone *Here*..........1A **50**
Dotham *IOA*..........3C **5**
Dovaston *Shrp*..........2A **26**
Dowlais *Mer T*..........2B **58**
Down, The *Shrp*..........2D **33**
Downall Green *Mers*..........1C **11**
Downend *S Glo*..........2D **67**
Downton on the Rock *Here*..........1B **40**
Doynton *S Glo*..........2D **67**
Draethen *Cphy*..........1D **65**
Dreenhill *Pemb*..........1C **53**
Dref, Y *Gwyn*..........1D **21**
Drefach *Carm*..........1A **56**
..........(nr Meidrim)
Drefach *Carm*..........2C **45**
..........(nr Newcastle Emlyn)
Drefach *Carm*..........3B **44**
..........(nr Tumble)
Drefach *Cdgn*..........1D **45**
**Drenewydd, Y** *Powy*..........2C **31**
Drope *V Glam*..........2C **65**
Druid *Den*..........3B **16**
Druidston *Pemb*..........1B **52**
Drury *Flin*..........1D **17**
Drybrook *Glos*..........1D **61**
Drybrook *Here*..........1C **61**
Dryslwyn *Carm*..........3A **46**
Dryton *Shrp*..........1C **33**
Duckington *Ches W*..........2B **18**
Duddon *Ches W*..........1C **19**
Dudleston *Shrp*..........1A **26**
Dudleston Heath *Shrp*..........1A **26**
Dudston *Shrp*..........2D **31**

Dudwells *Pemb*......................3C **43**
Duffryn *Neat*.........................3D **57**
Dukestown *Blae*....................2C **59**
Dulas *IOA*.............................2D **5**
Dundry *N Som*......................3C **67**
Dunham-on-the-Hill *Ches W*....3B **10**
Dunham Town *G Man*.............2D **11**
Dunham Woodhouses
   *G Man*............................2D **11**
Dunkerton *Bath*....................3D **67**
Dunvant *Swan*......................3A **56**
Durlow Common *Here*.............2D **51**
**Dursley** *Glos*....................3D **61**
Dursley Cross *Glos*................1D **61**
Dutlas *Powy*.........................1D **39**
Dutton *Ches W*.....................3C **11**
Dwygyfylchi *Cnwy*..................3C **7**
Dwyran *IOA*..........................1D **13**
Dyffryn *B'end*.......................3D **57**
Dyffryn *V Glam*.....................2B **64**
Dyffryn *Carm*........................3C **45**
Dyffryn *Pemb*.......................2C **43**
Dyffryn Ardudwy *Gwyn*..........2A **22**
Dyffryn Castell *Cdgn*..............3C **29**
Dyffryn Ceidrych *Carm*...........3C **47**
Dyffryn Cellwen *Neat*............2D **57**
Dylife *Powy*..........................2D **29**
Dymock *Glos*........................2D **51**
Dyrham *S Glo*.......................2D **67**
Dyserth *Den*.........................3B **8**

**E**

Eardington *Shrp*....................2D **33**
Eardisland *Here*....................3B **40**
Eardisley *Here*......................1A **50**
Eardiston *Shrp*......................2A **26**
Eardiston *Worc*.....................2D **41**
Earlestown *Mers*...................1C **11**
Earlswood *Mon*.....................3B **60**
Earthcott Green *S Glo*............1D **67**
East Aberthaw *V Glam*...........3B **64**
East Clevedon *N Som*............2B **66**
East Dean *Glos*.....................3D **51**
East Dundry *N Som*...............3C **67**
East End *N Som*....................2B **66**
Easter Compton *S Glo*............1C **67**
Eastham *Mers*......................2A **10**
Eastham *Worc*......................2D **41**
Eastham Ferry *Mers*..............2A **10**
Easthampton *Here*.................2B **40**
Easthope *Shrp*......................2C **33**
Eastnor *Here*........................2D **51**
Easton-in-Gordano *N Som*......2C **67**
East Wall *Shrp*......................2C **33**
East Williamston *Pemb*...........2D **53**
Eaton *Shrp*...........................3A **32**
   .......................(nr Bishop's Castle)
Eaton *Shrp*...........................3C **33**
   ..................(nr Church Stretton)
Eaton *Ches W*.......................1C **19**
Eaton Bishop *Here*.................2B **50**
Eaton Constantine *Shrp*..........1C **33**
Eaton upon Tern *Shrp*............2D **27**
**Ebbw Vale** *Blae*..................2C **59**
Ebnal *Ches W*.......................3B **18**
Eccles Green *Here*.................1A **50**
Eccleston *Ches W*..................1B **18**
Eccleston *Mers*.....................1B **10**
Edern *Gwyn*..........................1B **20**
Edge *Shrp*............................1A **32**
Edgebolton *Shrp*...................2C **27**
Edge End *Glos*......................1C **61**
Edge Green *Ches W*...............2B **18**
Edgeley *Shrp*........................3C **19**
Edgmond *Telf*.......................3D **27**
Edgmond Marsh *Telf*..............2D **27**
Edgton *Shrp*.........................3A **32**
Edstaston *Shrp*.....................1C **27**

Edwardsville *Mer T*.................3B **58**
Edwinsford *Carm*...................2B **46**
Edwyn Ralph *Here*.................3D **41**
Efail-fach *Neat*......................3C **57**
Efail Isaf *Rhon*......................1B **64**
Efailnewydd *Gwyn*.................1C **21**
Efail-rhyd *Powy*....................2C **25**
Efailwen *Carm*......................3A **44**
Efenechtyd *Den*....................2C **17**
Eglwysbach *Cnwy*..................3D **7**
Eglwys-Brewis *V Glam*...........3B **64**
Eglwys Fach *Cdgn*.................2B **28**
Eglwyswrw *Pemb*..................2A **44**
Egremont *Mers*.....................1A **10**
Eisingrug *Gwyn*.....................1B **22**
Elan Village *Powy*..................2A **38**
Elberton *S Glo*.......................1D **67**
Ellerdine *Telf*........................2D **27**
Ellerdine Heath *Telf*...............2D **27**
Ellerton *Shrp*........................2D **27**
Ellesmere *Shrp*.....................1B **26**
**Ellesmere Port** *Ches W*.......3B **10**
Ellwood *Glos*........................2C **61**
Elton *Ches W*........................3B **10**
Elton Green *Ches W*...............3B **10**
Elton *Here*............................1B **40**
Elton Green *Ches W*...............3B **10**
Elworth *Ches E*.....................1D **19**
Ely *Card*...............................2C **65**
Enchmarsh *Shrp*...................2C **33**
Engine Common *S Glo*...........1D **67**
Englesea-brook *Ches E*..........2D **19**
English Bicknor *Glos*..............1C **61**
Englishcombe *Bath*................3D **67**
English Frankton *Shrp*............2B **26**
Ensdon *Shrp*.........................3B **26**
Erbistock *Wrex*......................3A **18**
Erwood *Powy*........................1B **48**
Eryrys *Den*...........................2D **17**
Esgair *Carm*..........................3C **45**
   .........................(nr Carmarthen)
Esgair *Carm*..........................1B **54**
   ..............................(nr St Clears)
Esgairgeiliog *Powy*................1C **29**
Etloe *Glos*............................2D **61**
Ettiley Heath *Ches E*..............1D **19**
Eudon Burnell *Shrp*...............3D **33**
Eudon George *Shrp*...............3D **33**
Evanstown *B'end*..................1A **64**
Evendine *Here*......................1D **51**
Evenjobb *Powy*.....................2D **39**
Everton *Mers*........................1A **10**
Evesbatch *Here*.....................1D **51**
Ewdness *Shrp*.......................2D **33**
Ewenny *V Glam*.....................2A **64**
Ewlo *Flin*..............................1D **17**
Ewloe *Flin*............................1D **17**
Ewyas Harold *Here*................3A **50**
Exfords Green *Shrp*................1B **32**
Eye *Here*..............................2B **40**
Eyton *Shrp*...........................3A **32**
   .....................(nr Bishop's Castle)
Eyton *Shrp*...........................4D **...**
   ..........................(nr Shrewsbury)
Eyton *Here*...........................2B **40**
Eyton *Wrex*..........................3A **18**
Eyton on Severn *Shrp*............1C **33**
Eyton upon the Weald Moors
   *Telf*................................3D **27**

**F**

Faddiley *Ches E*....................2C **19**
Fagwyr *Swan*........................2B **56**
Failand *N Som*......................2C **67**
Fairbourne *Gwyn*...................3B **22**
Fairwater *Card*......................2C **65**
Falcon *Here*..........................2D **51**
Falfield *S Glo*........................3D **61**

Fali, Y *IOA*............................3B **4**
Far Forest *Worc*....................1D **41**
Farleigh *N Som*.....................3B **66**
Farley *Shrp*...........................1A **32**
   .............................(nr Shrewsbury)
Farley *Shrp*...........................1D **33**
   ..................................(nr Telford)
Farlow *Shrp*..........................3D **33**
Farmborough *Bath*.................3D **67**
Far Moor *G Man*....................1C **11**
Farndon *Ches W*....................2B **18**
Farnworth *Hal*.......................2C **11**
Fauls *Shrp*............................1C **27**
Fawley Chapel *Here*...............3C **51**
Fazakerley *Mers*...................1A **10**
Fearnhead *Warr*....................1D **11**
Felhampton *Shrp*..................3B **32**
Felindre *Carm*.......................3A **46**
Felindre *Carm*.......................2B **46**
   ............................. (nr Llandeilo)
Felindre *Carm*.......................2B **46**
   ............................(nr Llandovery)
Felindre *Carm*.......................2C **45**
   .................(nr Newcastle Emlyn)
Felindre *Powy*.......................3C **31**
Felindre *Swan*.......................2B **56**
Felindre Farchog *Pemb*..........2A **44**
Felinfach *Powy*......................2B **48**
Felinfach *Cdgn*......................3A **36**
Felinfoel *Carm*......................2A **56**
Felingwmisaf *Carm*................3A **46**
Felingwmuchaf *Carm*.............3A **46**
Felinheli, Y *Gwyn*..................1A **14**
Felin Newydd *Powy*...............1B **30**
   ...................................(nr Newtown)
Felin Newydd *Powy*...............2D **25**
   ...................................(nr Oswestry)
Felin Wnda *Cdgn*..................1C **45**
Felinwynt *Cdgn*.....................3B **34**
Felton *N Som*........................3C **67**
Felton *Here*...........................1C **51**
Felton Butler *Shrp*.................3A **26**
**Fenni, Y** *Mon*....................1A **60**
Fenn's Bank *Wrex*.................1C **27**
**Ferndale** *Rhon*..................3A **58**
Ferryside *Carm*......................1C **55**
Ferwig, Y *Cdgn*......................1A **44**
Ffairfach *Carm*......................3B **46**
Ffair Rhos *Cdgn*....................2C **37**
Ffaldybrenin *Carm*.................1B **46**
Ffarmers *Carm*......................1B **46**
Ffawyddog *Powy*...................1D **59**
**Fflint, Y** *Flin*.....................3D **9**
Ffodun *Powy*.........................1D **31**
Ffont-y-gari *V Glam*...............3B **64**
Ffor, Y *Gwyn*........................1C **21**
Fforest *Carm*........................2A **56**
Fforest-fach *Swan*.................3B **56**
Fforest Goch *Neat*.................2C **57**
Ffostrasol *Cdgn*.....................1C **45**
Ffos-y-ffin *Cdgn*....................2D **35**
Ffrith *Flin*.............................2D **17**
Ffwl-y-mwn *V Glam*...............3B **64**
Ffynnon-ddrain *Carm*.............3D **45**
Ffynnongroyw *Flin*.................2C **9**
Ffynnon Gynydd *Powy*............1C **49**
Ffynnon-oer *Cdgn*..................3A **36**
Filton *S Glo*...........................2D **67**
Fishguard *Pemb*..............**73** (2C **43**)
Fishponds *Bris*......................2D **67**
Fishpool *Glos*........................3D **51**
Fishpools *Powy*.....................2C **39**
Fitz *Shrp*...............................3B **26**
Five Bridges *Here*..................1D **51**
Five Roads *Carm*...................2D **55**
Flax Bourton *N Som*...............3C **67**
Flaxley *Glos*..........................1D **61**
Flemingston *V Glam*..............3B **64**
**Flint** *Flin*...........................3D **9**
Flint Mountain *Flin*.................3D **9**

Flintsham *Here*......................3A **40**
Flixton *G Man*.......................1D **11**
Fochriw *Cphy*........................2C **59**
Foel *Powy*............................3A **24**
Fonmon *V Glam*.....................3B **64**
Font-y-gary *V Glam*................3B **64**
Ford *Shrp*.............................3B **26**
Forden *Powy*.........................1D **31**
Ford Heath *Shrp*....................3B **26**
Forge *Powy*..........................2C **29**
Forge, The *Here*....................3A **40**
Forge Side *Torf*.....................2D **59**
Forthay *Glos*.........................3D **61**
Forton *Shrp*..........................3B **26**
Forton *Staf*...........................2D **27**
Forton Heath *Shrp*.................3B **26**
Four Crosses *Powy*................1B **30**
   ....................................(nr Llanerfyl)
Four Crosses *Powy*................3D **25**
   .............................(nr Llanymynech)
Four Mile Bridge *IOA*.............3B **4**
Four Oaks *Glos*.....................3D **51**
Four Roads *Carm*..................2D **55**
Fowley Common *Warr*............1D **11**
Fownhope *Here*.....................2C **51**
Foxwist Green *Ches W*...........1D **19**
Foxwood *Shrp*......................1D **41**
Foy *Here*..............................3C **51**
Frampton Cotterell *S Glo*........1D **67**
Frampton on Severn *Glos*.......2D **61**
Frandley *Ches W*...................3D **11**
Frankby *Mers*.......................2D **9**
Frank's Bridge *Powy*..............3C **39**
Frankwell *Shrp*......................3B **26**
Frenchay *S Glo*.....................2D **67**
Freshwater East *Pemb*...........3D **53**
Fretherne *Glos*......................2D **61**
Freystrop *Pemb*....................1C **53**
Friog *Gwyn*...........................3B **22**
Frith Common *Worc*...............2D **41**
Frochas *Powy*.......................1C **31**
Frodesley *Shrp*......................1C **33**
Frodsham *Ches W*..................3C **11**
Fromes Hill *Here*....................1D **51**
Fron *Gwyn*............................1C **21**
Fron *Powy*............................2B **38**
   .........................(nr Llandrindod Wells)
Fron *Powy*............................2C **31**
   ...................................(nr Newtown)
Fron *Powy*............................1D **31**
   ...................................(nr Welshpool)
Fron, Y *Gwyn*.......................2A **14**
Froncysyllte *Wrex*.................3D **17**
Frongoch *Gwyn*.....................1A **24**
Fron Isaf *Wrex*.....................3D **17**
Fronoleu *Gwyn*.....................1C **23**
Fuller's Moor *Ches W*.............2B **18**
Furnace *Carm*.......................2A **56**
Furnace *Cdgn*.......................2B **28**

**G**

Gadfa *IOA*............................2D **5**
Gaer *Powy*............................3C **49**
Gaerwen *IOA*........................3D **5**
Gallt Melyd *Den*....................2B **8**
Ganarew *Here*.......................1C **61**
Ganllwyd *Gwyn*.....................2C **23**
Garden City *Flin*....................1A **18**
Garden Village *Swan*..............3A **56**
Garmston *Shrp*......................1D **33**
Garnant *Carm*.......................1B **56**
Garndiffaith *Torf*...................2D **59**
Garndolbenmaen *Gwyn*..........3D **13**
Garnfadryn *Gwyn*..................1B **20**
Garnlydan *Blae*.....................1C **59**
Garnswllt *Swan*....................2A **56**
Garn yr Erw *Torf*...................1D **59**
Garreg *Gwyn*........................3B **14**

Garston *Mers*......................2B **10**
Garswood *Mers*......................1C **11**
Garth *Powy*..........................1A **48**
.........................(nr Builth Wells)
Garth *Powy*..........................1D **39**
.............................(nr Knighton)
Garth *B'end*..........................3D **57**
Garth *Wrex*..........................3D **17**
Garth *Gwyn*..........................1A **22**
Garth *Cdgn*..........................3B **28**
Garthbrengy *Powy*..............2B **48**
Gartheli *Cdgn*......................3A **36**
Garthmyl *Powy*......................2C **31**
Garth Owen *Powy*..................2C **31**
Garth Place *Cphy*..................1C **65**
Garway *Here*........................3B **50**
Garway Common *Here*..............3B **50**
Garway Hill *Here*..................3B **50**
Gateacre *Mers*......................2B **10**
Gatesheath *Ches W*................1B **18**
Gaufron *Powy*......................2A **38**
Gaunt's Earthcott *S Glo*..........1D **67**
Gayton *Mers*..........................2D **9**
Gell *Cnwy*..........................1D **15**
Gelli *Rhon*..........................3A **58**
Gelli *Pemb*..........................1D **53**
Gellifor *Den*..........................1C **17**
**Gelligaer** *Cphy*..................3C **59**
Gelli Gandryll, Y *Powy*..........1D **49**
Gellilydan *Gwyn*..................1B **22**
Gellinudd *Neat*......................2C **57**
Gellywen *Carm*......................3B **44**
Geneva *Cdgn*........................3D **35**
Georgetown *Blae*..................2C **59**
Gerlan *Gwyn*........................1B **14**
Gethsemane *Pemb*................1D **43**
Geuffordd *Powy*....................3D **25**
Gignog *Pemb*........................3B **42**
Gileston *V Glam*....................3B **64**
Gilfach *Cphy*........................3C **59**
Gilfach Goch *Rhon*................1A **64**
Gilfachreda *Cdgn*..................3D **35**
Gillar's Green *Mers*................1B **10**
Gilwern *Mon*........................1D **59**
Gladestry *Powy*....................3D **39**
Glais *Swan*..........................2C **57**
Glanaman *Carm*....................1B **56**
Glan-Conwy *Cnwy*................2D **15**
Glan Duar *Carm*....................1A **46**
Glandwr *Blae*........................2C **59**
Glandwr *Pemb*......................3A **44**
Glan-Dwyfach *Gwyn*..............3D **13**
Glandy Cross *Carm*................3A **44**
Glandyfi *Cdgn*......................2B **28**
Glangrwyney *Powy*................1D **59**
Glanmule *Powy*....................2C **31**
Glan-rhyd *Pemb*....................2A **44**
Glan-rhyd *Powy*....................2C **57**
Glanrhyd *Pemb*....................1A **44**
Glanrhyd *Gwyn*....................1B **20**
Glan-y-don *Flin*....................3C **9**
Glan-y-nant *Powy*................3A **30**
Glan-yr-afon *Gwyn*................3B **16**
Glan-yr-afon *IOA*..................2B **6**
Glan-yr-afon *Powy*................1B **30**
Glan-y-wern *Gwyn*................1B **22**
Glasbury *Powy*......................2C **49**
Glascoed *Den*......................3A **8**
Glascoed *Mon*......................2A **60**
Glascwm *Powy*......................3C **39**
Glasfryn *Cnwy*......................2A **16**
Glasinfryn *Gwyn*..................1A **14**
Glaspwll *Cdgn*......................2C **29**
Glasshouse *Glos*..................3D **51**
Glazebrook *Warr*..................1D **11**
Glazebury *Warr*....................1D **11**
Glazeley *Shrp*......................3D **33**
Gledrid *Shrp*........................1D **25**
Gleiniant *Powy*....................2A **30**

Glewstone *Here*....................3C **51**
Glyn *Cnwy*..........................3D **7**
Glynarthen *Cdgn*..................1C **45**
Glynbrochan *Powy*................3A **30**
Glyn Ceiriog *Wrex*................1D **25**
Glyncoch *Rhon*......................3B **58**
Glyncorrwg *Neat*..................3D **57**
Glyndyfrdwy *Den*..................3C **17**
**Glyn Ebwy** *Blae*................2C **59**
Glynllan *B'end*......................1A **64**
Glyn-neath *Neat*..................2D **57**
Glynogwr *B'end*....................1A **64**
Glyntaff *Rhon*........................1B **64**
Glyntawe *Powy*......................1D **57**
Glynteg *Carm*........................2C **45**
Gobowen *Shrp*......................1A **26**
Godre'r-graig *Neat*................2C **57**
Goetre *Mon*..........................2A **60**
Goginan *Cdgn*......................3B **28**
Golan *Gwyn*..........................3A **14**
**Golborne** *G Man*................1D **11**
Goldcliff *Newp*......................1A **66**
Golden Grove *Carm*..............1A **56**
Golden Hill *Pemb*..................3C **43**
Golding *Shrp*........................1C **33**
Goldstone *Shrp*....................2D **27**
Golfa *Powy*..........................2C **25**
Goodrich *Here*......................1C **61**
Goodwick *Pemb*....................2C **43**
Goose Green *S Glo*................1D **67**
Gors *Cdgn*..........................1B **36**
Gorsedd *Flin*........................3C **9**
**Gorseinon** *Swan*................3A **56**
Gorsgoch *Cdgn*....................3D **35**
Gorslas *Carm*........................1A **56**
Gorsley *Glos*........................3D **51**
Gorsley Common *Here*..........3D **51**
Gorstella *Ches W*..................1A **18**
Gorsty Common *Here*............2B **50**
Gossington *Glos*..................2D **61**
Govilon *Mon*........................1D **59**
Gowerton *Swan*....................3A **56**
Goytre *Neat*..........................1C **63**
Grafton *Worc*........................2C **41**
Grafton *Here*........................2B **50**
Grafton *Shrp*........................3B **26**
Graianrhyd *Den*....................2D **17**
Graig *Den*..........................3B **8**
Graig *Cnwy*..........................3D **7**
Graig *Carm*..........................2D **55**
Graig-fechan *Den*..................2C **17**
Graig Penllyn *V Glam*............2A **64**
Grange *Mers*........................2D **9**
Grange *Here*..........................1B **40**
Grangetown *Card*..................2C **65**
Granston *Pemb*......................2B **42**
Grappenhall *Warr*..................2D **11**
Grassendale *Mers*................2A **10**
Gravelhill *Shrp*......................3B **26**
**Greasby** *Mers*..................2D **9**
Great Barrow *Ches W*............1B **18**
Great Bolas *Telf*....................2D **27**
Great Budworth *Ches W*..........3D **11**
Great Crosby *Mers*................1A **10**
Great Doward *Here*................1C **61**
Great Lyth *Shrp*....................1B **32**
Great Ness *Shrp*....................3A **26**
Great Oak *Mon*......................2A **60**
Great Ryton *Shrp*..................1B **32**
**Great Sankey** *Warr*............2C **11**
Great Sutton *Ches W*..............3A **10**
Great Sutton *Shrp*................3C **33**
Great Witley *Worc*................2D **41**
Great Wytheford *Shrp*............3C **27**
Greenfield *Flin*......................3C **9**
Green Lane *Shrp*..................2D **27**
Greenway *V Glam*..................2B **64**
Greenway *Pemb*....................2D **43**
Greete *Shrp*..........................1C **41**

Grendon Green *Here*..............3C **41**
Gresford *Wrex*......................2A **18**
Gretton *Shrp*........................2C **33**
Griffithstown *Torf*..................3D **59**
Grimpo *Shrp*........................2A **26**
Grindle *Shrp*........................1D **33**
Grindley Brook *Shrp*..............3C **19**
Grinshill *Shrp*......................2C **27**
Groes *Cnwy*..........................1B **16**
Groes *Neat*..........................1C **63**
Groes-faen *Rhon*..................1B **64**
Groesffordd *Powy*................3B **48**
Groesffordd *Gwyn*................1B **20**
Groeslon *Gwyn*......................2D **13**
Groes-lwyd *Powy*..................3D **25**
Groes-wen *Cphy*..................1C **65**
Gronant *Flin*..........................2B **8**
Grosmont *Mon*......................3B **50**
Grovesend *Swan*..................2A **56**
Guilden Down *Shrp*................3A **32**
Guilden Sutton *Ches W*..........1B **18**
Guilsfield *Powy*....................3D **25**
Gumfreston *Pemb*..................2A **54**
Gurnos *Powy*........................2C **57**
Gwaelod-y-garth *Card*............1C **65**
Gwaenynog Bach *Den*............1B **16**
Gwaenysgor *Flin*..................2B **8**
Gwalchmai *IOA*......................3C **5**
Gwastad *Pemb*......................3D **43**
Gwaun-Cae-Gurwen *Neat*......1C **57**
Gwbert *Cdgn*........................1A **44**
Gwehelog *Mon*......................2A **60**
Gwenddwr *Powy*..................1B **48**
Gwernaffield *Flin*..................1D **17**
Gwernesney *Mon*..................2B **60**
Gwernogle *Carm*..................2A **46**
Gwern-y-go *Powy*..................2D **31**
Gwernymynydd *Flin*..............1D **17**
Gwersyllt *Wrex*......................2A **18**
Gwespyr *Flin*........................2C **9**
Gwredog *IOA*........................2D **5**
Gwyddelwern *Den*................3B **16**
Gwyddgrug *Carm*..................2D **45**
Gwynfryn *Wrex*......................2D **17**
Gwystre *Powy*......................2B **38**
Gwytherin *Cnwy*..................1D **15**
Gyfelia *Wrex*........................3A **18**
Gyffin *Cnwy*..........................3C **7**

## H

Habberley *Shrp*....................1B **32**
Hadley *Telf*..........................3D **27**
Hadnall *Shrp*........................2C **27**
Hagley *Here*..........................1C **51**
Hakin *Pemb*..........................2B **52**
Hale *Hal*..............................2B **10**
Hale Bank *Hal*......................2B **10**
Hales *Staf*............................1D **27**
Halewood *Mers*......................2B **10**
Halford *Shrp*........................3B **32**
Halfpenny Furze *Carm*............1B **54**
Halfway *Carm*........................2B **46**
.........................(nr Llandeilo)
Halfway *Carm*......................2D **47**
.......................(nr Llandovery)
Halfway House *Shrp*..............3A **26**
Halkyn *Flin*..........................3D **9**
Hallatrow *Bath*......................3D **67**
Hallen *S Glo*........................1C **67**
Hall Green *Wrex*..................3B **18**
Hallowsgate *Ches W*..............1C **19**
Hallwood Green *Glos*............2D **51**
Halmond's Frome *Here*..........1D **51**
Halmore *Glos*......................2D **61**
Halton *Wrex*........................1A **26**
Halton *Hal*..........................2C **11**
Ham *Glos*............................3D **61**
Hambrook *S Glo*..................2D **67**

Ham Green *N Som*................2C **67**
Ham Green *Here*..................1D **51**
Hamperley *Shrp*....................3B **32**
Hampton *Shrp*......................3D **33**
Hampton Bishop *Here*............2C **51**
Hampton Heath *Ches W*..........3C **19**
Hampton Loade *Shrp*............3D **33**
Handbridge *Ches W*................1B **18**
Handley *Ches W*....................2B **18**
Hanham *S Glo*......................2D **67**
Hanham Green *S Glo*..............2D **67**
Hankelow *Ches E*..................3D **19**
Hanley Child *Worc*................2D **41**
Hanley William *Worc*............2D **41**
Hanmer *Wrex*........................1B **26**
Hanwood *Shrp*......................1B **32**
Hapsford *Ches W*..................3B **10**
Hardwick *Shrp*......................2A **32**
Hardwicke *Here*....................1D **49**
Haresfinch *Mers*..................1C **11**
Harewood End *Here*..............3C **51**
Hargrave *Ches W*..................1B **18**
Harlech *Gwyn*......................1A **22**
Harlescott *Shrp*....................3C **27**
Harley *Shrp*........................1C **33**
Harmer Hill *Shrp*..................2B **26**
Harnage *Shrp*......................1C **33**
Haroldston West *Pemb*..........1B **52**
Harpley *Worc*........................2D **41**
Harry Stoke *S Glo*................2D **67**
Hartford *Ches W*..................3D **11**
Harthill *Ches W*....................2C **19**
Harton *Shrp*........................3B **32**
Hasguard *Pemb*....................2B **52**
Haslington *Ches E*................3D **19**
Haston *Shrp*........................2C **27**
Hatchmere *Ches W*................3C **11**
Hatfield *Here*........................3C **41**
Hatherton *Ches E*..................3D **19**
Hatton *Shrp*........................2B **32**
Hatton *Warr*........................2D **11**
Hatton Heath *Ches W*............1B **18**
Haughton *Shrp*......................2D **33**
.........................(nr Bridgnorth)
Haughton *Shrp*......................2A **26**
.........................(nr Oswestry)
Haughton *Shrp*......................1D **33**
.........................(nr Shifnal)
Haughton *Shrp*......................3C **27**
.........................(nr Shrewsbury)
Haughton *Ches E*..................2C **19**
Haven *Here*..........................3B **40**
**Haverfordwest** *Pemb*..........1C **53**
Haverfordwest Airport *Pemb*..1C **53**
**Hawarden** *Flin*..................1A **18**
Hawarden Airport *Flin*............1A **18**
Hawen *Cdgn*........................1C **45**
Haybridge *Shrp*....................1D **41**
**Haydock** *Mers*..................1C **11**
Hay-on-Wye *Powy*................1D **49**
Hayscastle *Pemb*..................3B **42**
Hayscastle Cross *Pemb*..........3C **43**
Hayton's Bent *Shrp*..............3C **33**
Hazler *Shrp*........................2B **32**
Headley Pk. *Bris*..................3C **67**
Heartsease *Powy*..................2C **39**
Heatley *Warr*........................2D **11**
Hebden Green *Ches W*..........1D **19**
Hebron *Carm*........................3A **44**
Hegdon Hill *Here*..................3C **41**
Helsby *Ches W*......................3B **10**
Helygain *Flin*........................3D **9**
Hem, The *Shrp*....................1D **33**
Henallt *Carm*........................3D **45**
Henbury *Bris*........................2C **67**
Henbury *Ches E*....................3D **19**
Hendomen *Powy*..................2D **31**
Hendre *B'end*......................1A **64**
Hendreforgan *Rhon*..............1A **64**
Hendy *Carm*........................2A **56**

Heneglwys *IOA* .........................3D **5**
Henfeddau Fawr *Pemb* ............2B **44**
Henfield *S Glo* .........................2D **67**
Hengoed *Cphy* .........................3C **59**
Hengoed *Shrp* .........................1D **25**
Heniarth *Powy* .........................1C **31**
Henley *Shrp* .........................3B **32**
.........................(nr Church Stretton)
Henley *Shrp* .........................1C **41**
.........................(nr Ludlow)
Henllan *Den* .........................1B **16**
Henllan *Mon* .........................3D **49**
Henllan *Cdgn* .........................1C **45**
Henllan Amgoed *Carm* ............1A **54**
Henllys *Torf* .........................3D **59**
Henryd *Cnwy* .........................3C **7**
Henry's Moat *Pemb* .........................3D **43**
Heolgerrig *Mer T* .........................2B **58**
Heol Senni *Powy* .........................3A **48**
Heol-y-Cyw *B'end* .........................1A **64**
Herbrandston *Pemb* .........................2B **52**
**Hereford** *Here* .........................**70** (2C **51**)
Hermon *Carm* .........................3B **46**
.........................(nr Llandeilo)
Hermon *Carm* .........................2C **45**
.........................(nr Newcastle Emlyn)
Hermon *IOA* .........................1C **13**
Hermon *Pemb* .........................2B **44**
**Heswall** *Mers* .........................2D **9**
Hewelsfield *Glos* .........................2C **61**
Hewish *N Som* .........................3B **66**
Heyop *Powy* .........................1D **39**
Higford *Shrp* .........................1D **33**
High Ercall *Telf* .........................3C **27**
Higher End *G Man* .........................1C **11**
Higher Kinnerton *Flin* .........................1A **18**
Higher Shotton *Flin* .........................1A **18**
Higher Shurlach *Ches W* .........................3D **11**
Higher Walton *Warr* .........................2C **11**
Higher Whitley *Ches W* .........................2D **11**
Higher Wincham *Ches W* .........................3D **11**
Higher Wych *Ches W* .........................3B **18**
Highgate *Powy* .........................2C **31**
High Green *Shrp* .........................3D **33**
High Hatton *Shrp* .........................2D **27**
Highlands, The *Shrp* .........................3D **33**
High Lane *Worc* .........................2D **41**
High Legh *Ches E* .........................2D **11**
Highley *Shrp* .........................3D **33**
High Littleton *Bath* .........................3D **67**
Highmoor Hill *Mon* .........................1B **66**
Hightown *Mers* .........................1D **9**
Highway *Here* .........................1B **50**
Highwood *Worc* .........................2D **41**
Hill *S Glo* .........................3D **61**
Hillend *Swan* .........................3D **55**
Hillersland *Glos* .........................1C **61**
Hill Gate *Here* .........................3B **50**
Hillside *Worc* .........................2D **41**
Hillside *Shrp* .........................3D **33**
Hindford *Shrp* .........................1A **26**
Hindley Green *G Man* .........................1D **11**
Hinstock *Shrp* .........................2D **27**
Hinton *Here* .........................2A **50**
Hinton *S Glo* .........................2D **67**
Hinton *Shrp* .........................1B **32**
Hinton Blewett *Bath* .........................3C **67**
Hints *Shrp* .........................1D **41**
Hiraeth *Carm* .........................3A **44**
Hirnant *Powy* .........................2B **24**
Hirwaen *Den* .........................1C **17**
Hirwaun *Rhon* .........................2A **58**
Hoarwithy *Here* .........................3C **51**
Hôb, Yr *Flin* .........................2A **18**
Hobarris *Shrp* .........................1A **40**
Hodgeston *Pemb* .........................3D **53**
Hodley *Powy* .........................2C **31**
Hodnet *Shrp* .........................2D **27**
Holdgate *Shrp* .........................3C **33**

Hollinfare *Warr* .........................1D **11**
Hollinswood *Telf* .........................1D **33**
Hollinwood *Shrp* .........................1C **27**
Hollybush *Cphy* .........................2C **59**
Hollyhurst *Shrp* .........................3C **19**
Holme Lacy *Here* .........................2C **51**
Holme Marsh *Here* .........................3A **40**
Holmer *Here* .........................1C **51**
Holt *Wrex* .........................2B **18**
**Holyhead** *IOA* .........................**74** (2B **4**)
Holyhead Breakwater *IOA* .........................2B **4**
Holywell *Flin* .........................3C **9**
Homer *Shrp* .........................1D **33**
Homer Green *Mers* .........................1A **10**
Hom Green *Here* .........................3C **51**
Honeyborough *Pemb* .........................2C **53**
Honnington *Telf* .........................3D **27**
Hoo Green *Ches E* .........................2D **11**
Hook *Pemb* .........................1C **53**
Hook-a-Gate *Shrp* .........................1B **32**
Hookgate *Staf* .........................1D **27**
Hook Street *Glos* .........................3D **61**
Hoole *Ches W* .........................1B **18**
Hooton *Ches W* .........................3A **10**
Hope *Flin* .........................2A **18**
Hope *Powy* .........................1D **31**
Hope *Shrp* .........................1A **32**
Hope Bagot *Shrp* .........................1C **41**
Hope Bowdler *Shrp* .........................2B **32**
Hope Mansell *Here* .........................1D **61**
Hopesay *Shrp* .........................3A **32**
Hope under Dinmore *Here* .........................3C **41**
Hopley's Green *Here* .........................3A **40**
Hopton *Shrp* .........................2A **26**
.........................(nr Oswestry)
Hopton *Shrp* .........................2C **27**
.........................(nr Wem)
Hopton *Shrp* .........................2D **31**
Hopton Cangeford *Shrp* .........................3C **33**
Hopton Castle *Shrp* .........................1A **40**
Hoptonheath *Shrp* .........................1A **40**
Hopton Wafers *Shrp* .........................1D **41**
Horderley *Shrp* .........................3B **32**
Hordley *Shrp* .........................1A **26**
Horeb *Carm* .........................3A **46**
.........................(nr Brechfa)
Horeb *Carm* .........................2D **55**
.........................(nr Llanelli)
Horeb *Cdgn* .........................1C **45**
Horfield *Bris* .........................2C **67**
Horsecastle *N Som* .........................3B **66**
Horsehay *Telf* .........................1D **33**
Horseman's Green *Wrex* .........................3B **18**
Horsham *Worc* .........................3D **41**
Horton *Swan* .........................1A **62**
Horton *Shrp* .........................1B **26**
Horton Green *Ches W* .........................3B **18**
Hortonwood *Telf* .........................3D **27**
Hough *Ches E* .........................2D **19**
Hough Green *Hal* .........................2B **10**
Houghton *Pemb* .........................2C **53**
How Caple *Here* .........................2D **51**
Howey *Powy* .........................3B **38**
Howle *Telf* .........................2D **27**
Howle Hill *Here* .........................3D **51**
Howley *Warr* .........................2D **11**
Howton *Here* .........................3B **50**
**Hoylake** *Mers* .........................2D **9**
Hubberston *Pemb* .........................2B **52**
Hughley *Shrp* .........................2C **33**
Humber *Here* .........................3C **41**
Hundleton *Pemb* .........................2C **53**
Hundred, The *Here* .........................2C **41**
Hundred House *Powy* .........................3C **39**
Hungerford *Shrp* .........................3C **33**
Hungryhatton *Shrp* .........................2D **27**
Hunstrete *Bath* .........................3D **67**
Huntington *Ches W* .........................1B **18**
Huntington *Here* .........................3D **39**

Huntington *Telf* .........................1D **33**
Huntley *Glos* .........................1D **61**
Hunt's Cross *Mers* .........................2B **10**
Hurdley *Powy* .........................2D **31**
Hurst Green *Ches E* .........................3C **19**
Hurstley *Here* .........................1A **50**
Hurstway Common *Here* .........................1A **50**
Hutton *N Som* .........................3A **66**
Huxley *Ches W* .........................1C **19**
**Huyton** *Mers* .........................1B **10**
**Hwlffordd** *Pemb* .........................1C **53**
Hyssington *Powy* .........................2A **32**

## I

Icelton *N Som* .........................3A **66**
Idole *Carm* .........................1D **55**
Ifton Heath *Shrp* .........................1A **26**
Ightfield *Shrp* .........................1C **27**
Ilston *Swan* .........................3A **56**
Ince *Ches W* .........................3B **10**
Ince Blundell *Mers* .........................1A **10**
Inglesbatch *Bath* .........................3D **67**
Ingst *S Glo* .........................1C **67**
Irby *Mers* .........................2D **9**
**Irlam** *G Man* .........................1D **11**
Iron Acton *S Glo* .........................1D **67**
Ironbridge *Telf* .........................1D **33**
Islington *Telf* .........................2D **27**
Isombridge *Telf* .........................3D **27**
Itchington *S Glo* .........................1D **67**
Itton Common *Mon* .........................3B **60**
Ivington *Here* .........................3B **40**
Ivington Green *Here* .........................3B **40**

## J

Jackfield *Shrp* .........................1D **33**
Jameston *Pemb* .........................3D **53**
Jeffreyston *Pemb* .........................2D **53**
Jersey Marine *Neat* .........................3C **57**
Jingle Street *Mon* .........................1B **60**
Johnston *Pemb* .........................1C **53**
Johnstown *Wrex* .........................3A **18**
Johnstown *Carm* .........................1D **55**
Jordanston *Pemb* .........................2C **43**

## K

Keckwick *Hal* .........................2C **11**
Keeston *Pemb* .........................1C **53**
Kelsall *Ches W* .........................1C **19**
Kelsterton *Flin* .........................3D **9**
Kelston *Bath* .........................3D **67**
Kemberton *Shrp* .........................1D **33**
Kemeys Commander *Mon* .........................2A **60**
Kempley *Glos* .........................3D **51**
Kempley Green *Glos* .........................3D **51**
Kempton *Shrp* .........................3A **32**
Kenchester *Here* .........................1B **50**
Kendleshire *S Glo* .........................2D **67**
Kenfig *B'end* .........................1D **63**
Kenfig Hill *B'end* .........................1D **63**
Kenley *Shrp* .........................1C **33**
Kenn *N Som* .........................3B **66**
Kenstone *Shrp* .........................2C **27**
Kentchurch *Here* .........................3B **50**
Kent's Green *Glos* .........................3D **51**
Kenwick *Shrp* .........................1B **26**
Kenyon *Warr* .........................1D **11**
Kerne Bridge *Here* .........................1C **61**
Kerry *Powy* .........................3C **31**
Kerry's Gate *Here* .........................2A **50**
Kewstoke *N Som* .........................3A **66**
**Keynsham** *Bath* .........................3D **67**
Kidnal *Ches W* .........................3B **18**
Kidwelly *Carm* .........................2D **55**
Kilcot *Glos* .........................3D **51**
Kilgetty *Pemb* .........................2A **54**

Kilgetty School (Rail) *Pemb* .........................2A **54**
Killay *Swan* .........................3B **56**
Kiln Green *Here* .........................1D **61**
Kilpeck *Here* .........................2B **50**
Kimbolton *Here* .........................2C **41**
Kingcoed *Mon* .........................2B **60**
King's Acre *Here* .........................1B **50**
King's Caple *Here* .........................3C **51**
Kingsland *Here* .........................2B **40**
Kingsland *IOA* .........................2B **4**
Kingsley *Ches W* .........................3C **11**
Kings Moss *Mers* .........................1C **11**
King's Pyon *Here* .........................3B **40**
King's Thorn *Here* .........................2C **51**
Kingstone *Here* .........................2B **50**
Kingston Seymour *N Som* .........................3B **66**
**Kingswood** *S Glo* .........................2D **67**
Kingswood *Glos* .........................3D **61**
Kingswood *Here* .........................3D **39**
Kingswood *Powy* .........................1D **31**
Kington *S Glo* .........................3D **61**
Kington *Here* .........................3D **39**
Kinlet *Shrp* .........................3D **33**
Kinmel Bay *Cnwy* .........................2A **8**
Kinmel Park Service Area *Den* .........................3A **8**
Kinnerley *Shrp* .........................2A **26**
Kinnersley *Here* .........................1A **50**
Kinnerton *Powy* .........................2D **39**
Kinnerton *Shrp* .........................2A **32**
Kinsey Heath *Ches E* .........................3D **19**
Kinsham *Here* .........................2A **40**
Kinton *Shrp* .........................3A **26**
Kinton *Here* .........................1B **40**
**Kirkby** *Mers* .........................1B **10**
Kirkdale *Mers* .........................1A **10**
Kittle *Swan* .........................1A **62**
Kivernoll *Here* .........................2B **50**
Knapton Green *Here* .........................3B **40**
Knelston *Swan* .........................1A **62**
Knightcott *N Som* .........................3A **66**
Knighton *Staf* .........................2D **27**
.........................(nr Eccleshall)
Knighton *Staf* .........................3D **19**
.........................(nr Woore)
Knighton *Powy* .........................1D **39**
Knighton Common *Worc* .........................1D **41**
Knightwick *Worc* .........................3D **41**
Knill *Here* .........................2D **39**
Knockin *Shrp* .........................2A **26**
Knollbury *Mon* .........................1B **66**
Knolton *Wrex* .........................1A **26**
Knotty Ash *Mers* .........................1B **10**
Knowbury *Shrp* .........................1C **41**
Knowle *Bris* .........................2D **67**
Knowle *Shrp* .........................1C **41**
Knowlesands *Shrp* .........................2D **33**
Knowsley *Mers* .........................1B **10**
Knucklas *Powy* .........................1D **39**
**Knutsford** *Ches E* .........................3D **11**
Kymin *Mon* .........................1C **61**
Kynance *Here* .........................2D **51**
Kynaston *Shrp* .........................2A **26**
Kynnersley *Telf* .........................3D **27**
Kyre Green *Worc* .........................2D **41**
Kyre Pk. *Worc* .........................2D **41**
Kyrewood *Worc* .........................2D **41**

## L

Lach Dennis *Ches W* .........................3D **11**
Lache *Ches W* .........................1A **18**
Lady Green *Mers* .........................1A **10**
Laleston *B'end* .........................1D **63**
Lambston *Pemb* .........................1C **53**
Lampeter *Cdgn* .........................1A **46**
Lampeter Velfrey *Pemb* .........................1A **54**
Lamphey *Pemb* .........................2D **53**
Land Gate *G Man* .........................1C **11**
Landimore *Swan* .........................3D **55**

Landore *Swan* ........................ 3B **56**
Landshipping *Pemb* ................ 1D **53**
Lane Head *G Man* .................. 1D **11**
Langland *Swan* ...................... 1B **62**
Langridge *Bath* ..................... 3D **67**
Lansdown *Bath* ..................... 3D **67**
Larden Green *Ches E* ............. 2C **19**
Larport *Here* ......................... 2C **51**
Latteridge *S Glo* ................... 1D **67**
Laugharne *Carm* ................... 1C **55**
Lavister *Wrex* ....................... 2A **18**
Lawley *Telf* ........................... 1D **33**
Lawrenny *Pemb* .................... 2D **53**
Lawton *Here* ......................... 3B **40**
Laysters Pole *Here* ................ 2C **41**
Lea *Shrp* .............................. 3A **32**
..................... (nr Bishop's Castle)
Lea *Shrp* .............................. 1B **32**
.......................... (nr Shrewsbury)
Lea *Here* .............................. 3D **51**
Leachpool *Pemb* ................... 1C **53**
Leasowe *Mers* ...................... 1D **9**
Leaton *Shrp* ......................... 3B **26**
Leaton *Telf* .......................... 3D **27**
Leckwith *V Glam* .................. 2C **65**
Ledbury *Here* ....................... 2D **51**
Ledgemoor *Here* ................... 3B **40**
Ledicot *Here* ........................ 2B **40**
Ledsham *Ches W* .................. 3A **10**
Lee *Shrp* .............................. 1B **26**
Leebotwood *Shrp* .................. 2B **32**
Lee Brockhurst *Shrp* ............. 2C **27**
Leechpool *Mon* ..................... 1C **67**
Leegomery *Telf* .................... 3D **27**
Leeswood *Flin* ...................... 1D **17**
Leftwich *Ches W* ................... 3D **11**
Leigh *Shrp* ........................... 1A **32**
**Leigh** *G Man* ..................... 1D **11**
Leighton *Powy* ...................... 1D **31**
Leighton *Shrp* ....................... 1D **33**
Leinthall Earls *Here* ............... 2B **40**
Leinthall Starkes *Here* ........... 2B **40**
Leintwardine *Here* ................. 1B **40**
Lem Hill *Shrp* ....................... 1D **41**
**Leominster** *Here* ................ 3B **40**
Letterston *Pemb* .................... 3C **43**
Letton *Here* .......................... 1A **50**
............................... (nr Kington)
Letton *Here* .......................... 1A **40**
.......................... (nr Leintwardine)
Leweston *Pemb* ..................... 3C **43**
Lewistown *B'end* ................... 1A **64**
Libanus *Powy* ....................... 3A **48**
Lightwood Green *Ches E* ........ 3D **19**
Lightwood Green *Wrex* ........... 3A **18**
Lilleshall *Telf* ....................... 3D **27**
Lilyhurst *Shrp* ...................... 3D **27**
Lindridge *Worc* ..................... 2D **41**
Lingen *Here* .......................... 2A **40**
Linley *Shrp* .......................... 2A **32**
..................... (nr Bishop's Castle)
Linley *Shrp* .......................... 2D **33**
........................... (nr Bridgnorth)
Linley Green *Here* ................. 3D **41**
Linton *Here* .......................... 3D **51**
Linton Hill *Here* .................... 3D **51**
Lipley *Shrp* .......................... 1D **27**
Liscard *Mers* ........................ 1A **10**
Lisvane *Card* ........................ 1C **65**
Liswerry *Newp* ...................... 1A **66**
Litchard *B'end* ...................... 1A **64**
**Litherland** *Mers* ................. 1A **10**
Little Barrow *Ches W* ............. 1B **18**
Little Birch *Here* ................... 2C **51**
Little Bolas *Shrp* ................... 2D **27**
Little Bollington *Ches E* ......... 2D **11**
Little Brampton *Shrp* ............. 3A **32**
Little Budworth *Ches W* .......... 1C **19**
Little Cowarne *Here* ............... 3D **41**

Little Crosby *Mers* ................. 1A **10**
Little Dawley *Telf* .................. 1D **33**
Littledean *Glos* ..................... 1D **61**
Little Dewchurch *Here* ........... 2C **51**
Little Drayton *Shrp* ............... 1D **27**
Little Garway *Here* ................. 3B **50**
Little Green *Wrex* .................. 3B **18**
Little Haven *Pemb* ................. 1B **52**
Little Hereford *Here* ............... 2C **41**
Little Hulton *G Man* ............... 1D **11**
Little Leigh *Ches W* ............... 3D **11**
Little London *Powy* ................ 3B **30**
Little Marcle *Here* ................. 2D **51**
Little Mill *Mon* ...................... 2A **60**
Little Mountain *Flin* ............... 1D **17**
Little Ness *Shrp* .................... 3B **26**
Little Newcastle *Pemb* ........... 3C **43**
Little Reynoldston *Swan* ......... 1A **62**
Little Ryton *Shrp* ................... 1B **32**
Little Soudley *Shrp* ................ 2D **27**
Little Stanney *Ches W* ............ 3B **10**
Little Stretton *Shrp* ................ 2B **32**
Little Sutton *Ches W* .............. 3A **10**
Littleton *Ches W* ................... 1B **18**
Littleton-upon-Severn *S Glo*..... 1C **67**
Little Wenlock *Telf* ................ 1D **33**
**Liverpool** *Mers* ................... 1A **10**
Lixwm *Flin* ........................... 3C **9**
Llaingoch *IOA* ....................... 2B **4**
Llaithddu *Powy* ..................... 3B **30**
Llampha *V Glam* .................... 2A **64**
Llan *Powy* ............................ 1D **29**
Llanaber *Gwyn* ...................... 3B **22**
Llanaelhaearn *Gwyn* .............. 3C **13**
Llanaeron *Cdgn* .................... 2D **35**
Llanafan *Cdgn* ...................... 1B **36**
Llanafan-fawr *Powy* ............... 3A **38**
Llanafan-fechan *Powy* ............ 3A **38**
Llanallgo *IOA* ........................ 2D **5**
Llanandras *Powy* ................... 2A **40**
Llananno *Powy* ...................... 1B **38**
Llanarmon *Gwyn* ................... 1D **21**
Llanarmon Dyffryn Ceiriog
     *Wrex* ................................ 1C **25**
Llanarmon-yn-Ial *Den* ............ 2C **17**
Llanarth *Mon* ........................ 1A **60**
Llanarth *Cdgn* ...................... 3D **35**
Llanarthne *Carm* ................... 3A **46**
Llanasa *Flin* ......................... 2C **9**
Llanbabo *IOA* ....................... 2C **5**
Llanbadarn Fawr *Cdgn* ........... 3B **28**
Llanbadarn Fynydd *Powy*........ 1C **39**
Llanbadarn-y-garreg *Powy* ...... 1C **49**
Llanbadoc *Mon* ..................... 2A **60**
Llanbadrig *IOA* ...................... 1C **5**
Llanbeder *Newp* .................... 3A **60**
Llanbedr *Powy* ...................... 3D **49**
........................... (nr Crickhowell)
Llanbedr *Powy* ...................... 1C **49**
.......................... (nr Hay-on-Wye)
Llanbedr *Gwyn* ...................... 2A **22**
Llanbedr Airfield *Gwyn* ........... 2A **22**
Llanbedr-Dyffryn-Clwyd *Den*.... 2C **17**
Llanbedrgoch *IOA* .................. 2A **6**
Llanbedrog *Gwyn* ................... 1C **21**
Llanbedr Pont Steffan *Cdgn* .... 1A **46**
Llanbedr-y-cennin *Cnwy*.......... 1C **15**
Llanberis *Gwyn* ..................... 1A **14**
Llanbethery *V Glam* ............... 3B **64**
Llanbister *Powy* ..................... 1C **39**
Llanblethian *V Glam* .............. 2A **64**
Llanboidy *Carm* ..................... 3B **44**
Llanbradach *Cphy* .................. 3C **59**
Llanbrynmair *Powy* ................ 1D **29**
Llanbydderi *V Glam* ............... 3B **64**
Llancadle *V Glam* .................. 3B **64**
Llancarfan *V Glam* ................. 2B **64**
Llancatal *V Glam* ................... 3B **64**

Llancayo *Mon* ....................... 2A **60**
Llancloudy *Here* .................... 3B **50**
Llancoch *Powy* ...................... 1D **39**
Llancynfelyn *Cdgn* ................. 2B **28**
Llandaff *Card* ....................... 2C **65**
Llandanwg *Gwyn* ................... 2A **22**
Llandarcy *Neat* ..................... 3C **57**
Llandawke *Carm* .................... 1B **54**
Llanddaniel Fab *IOA* .............. 3D **5**
Llanddarog *Carm* ................... 1A **56**
Llanddeiniol *Cdgn* ................. 1A **36**
Llanddeiniolen *Gwyn* .............. 1A **14**
Llandderfel *Gwyn* ................... 1A **24**
Llanddeusant *IOA* .................. 2C **5**
Llanddeusant *Carm* ................ 3C **47**
Llanddew *Powy* ..................... 2B **48**
Llanddewi *Swan* .................... 1A **62**
Llanddewi Brefi *Cdgn* ............ 3B **36**
Llanddewi'r Cwm *Powy* .......... 1B **48**
Llanddewi Rhydderch *Mon* ...... 1A **60**
Llanddewi Velfrey *Pemb* ......... 1A **54**
Llanddewi Ystradenni *Powy*..... 2C **39**
Llanddoged *Cnwy* .................. 1D **15**
Llanddona *IOA* ...................... 3A **6**
Llanddowror *Carm* ................. 1B **54**
Llanddulas *Cnwy* ................... 3A **8**
Llanddulas Service Area *Cnwy*.. 3A **8**
Llanddwywe *Gwyn* ................. 2A **22**
Llanddyfnan *IOA* .................... 3A **6**
Llandecwyn *Gwyn* .................. 1B **22**
Llandefaelog Fach *Powy* ......... 2B **48**
Llandefaelog-tre'r-graig
     *Powy* ............................... 2C **49**
Llandefalle *Powy* ................... 2C **49**
Llandegfan *IOA* ..................... 3A **6**
Llandegla *Den* ...................... 2C **17**
Llandegley *Powy* ................... 2C **39**
Llandegveth *Mon* ................... 3A **60**
Llandeilo *Carm* ..................... 3B **46**
Llandeilo Graban *Powy* ........... 1B **48**
Llandeilo'r Fan *Powy* .............. 2D **47**
Llandeloy *Pemb* ..................... 3B **42**
Llandenny *Mon* ...................... 2B **60**
Llandevaud *Newp* ................... 3B **60**
Llandevenny *Mon* ................... 1B **66**
Llandilo *Pemb* ....................... 3A **44**
Llandinabo *Here* .................... 3C **51**
Llandinam *Powy* .................... 3B **30**
Llandissilio *Pemb* .................. 3A **44**
Llandogo *Mon* ....................... 2C **61**
Llandough *V Glam* .................. 2A **64**
......................... (nr Cowbridge)
Llandough *V Glam* .................. 2C **65**
........................... (nr Penarth)
Llandovery *Carm* ................... 2C **47**
Llandow *V Glam* ..................... 2A **64**
Llandre *Cdgn* ........................ 3B **28**
Llandrillo *Den* ....................... 1B **24**
Llandrillo-yn-Rhos *Cnwy*......... 2D **7**
Llandrindod *Powy* .................. 2B **38**
Llandrindod Wells *Powy*........... 2B **38**
Llandrinio *Powy* ..................... 3D **25**
**Llandudno** *Cnwy*.............**70** (2C **7**)
Llandudno Cable Cars *Cnwy*..... 2C **7**
Llandudno Junction *Cnwy*........ 3C **7**
Llandudoch *Pemb* .................. 1A **44**
Llandw *V Glam* ...................... 2A **64**
Llandwrog *Gwyn* .................... 2D **13**
Llandybie *Carm* ..................... 1B **56**
Llandyfaelog *Carm* ................. 1D **55**
Llandyfan *Carm* ..................... 1B **56**
Llandyfriog *Cdgn* ................... 1C **45**
Llandyfrydog *IOA* ................... 2D **5**
Llandygai *Gwyn* ..................... 3B **6**
Llandygwydd *Cdgn* ................. 1B **44**
Llandynan *Den* ...................... 3C **17**
Llandyrnog *Den* ..................... 1C **17**
Llandysilio *Powy* .................... 3D **25**
Llandyssil *Powy* ..................... 2C **31**

Llandysul *Cdgn* ..................... 1D **45**
Llanedeyrn *Card* .................... 1D **65**
Llaneglwys *Powy* ................... 2B **48**
Llanegryn *Gwyn* ..................... 1B **28**
Llanegwad *Carm* .................... 3A **46**
Llaneilian *IOA* ....................... 1D **5**
Llanelian-yn-Rhos *Cnwy*.......... 3D **7**
Llanelidan *Den* ...................... 2C **17**
Llanelieu *Powy* ...................... 2C **49**
Llanellen *Mon* ....................... 1A **60**
**Llanelli** *Carm* ..............**71** (3A **56**)
Llanelltyd *Gwyn* ..................... 3C **23**
Llanelly *Mon* ......................... 1D **59**
Llanelly Hill *Mon* ................... 1D **59**
Llanelwedd *Powy* ................... 3B **38**
**Llan-Elwy** *Den* ................... 3B **8**
Llanenddwyn *Gwyn* ................ 2A **22**
Llanengan *Gwyn* .................... 2B **20**
Llanerch *Powy* ...................... 2A **32**
Llanerchymedd *IOA* ................ 2D **5**
Llanerfyl *Powy* ...................... 1B **30**
Llaneuddog *IOA* ..................... 2D **5**
Llanfachraeth *IOA* .................. 2C **5**
Llanfachreth *Gwyn* ................. 2C **23**
Llanfaelog *IOA* ...................... 3C **5**
Llanfaelrhys *Gwyn* ................. 2B **20**
Llanfaenor *Mon* ..................... 1B **60**
Llanfaes *Powy* ...................... 3B **48**
Llanfaes *IOA* ........................ 3B **6**
Llanfaethlu *IOA* ..................... 2C **5**
Llanfaglan *Gwyn* .................... 1D **13**
Llanfair *Here* ........................ 1D **49**
Llanfair *Gwyn* ....................... 2A **22**
Llanfair Caereinion *Powy* ........ 1C **31**
Llanfair Clydogau *Cdgn*........... 3B **36**
Llanfair Dyffryn Clwyd *Den* ..... 2C **17**
Llanfairfechan *Cnwy* ............... 3B **6**
Llanfair-Nant-Gwyn *Pemb*........ 2A **44**
Llanfair Pwllgwyngyll *IOA*......... 3A **6**
Llanfair Talhaiarn *Cnwy*........... 3A **8**
Llanfair Waterdine *Shrp* .......... 1D **39**
Llanfair-ym-Muallt *Powy*.......... 3B **38**
Llanfairyneubwll *IOA* ............... 3C **5**
Llanfairynghornwy *IOA*............. 1C **5**
Llanfallteg *Carm* .................... 1A **54**
Llanfallteg West *Carm* ............. 1A **54**
Llanfaredd *Powy* .................... 3B **38**
Llanfarian *Cdgn* ..................... 1A **36**
Llanfechain *Powy* ................... 2C **25**
Llanfechell *IOA* ..................... 1C **5**
Llanfendigaid *Gwyn* ................ 1A **28**
Llanferres *Den* ...................... 1C **17**
Llan Ffestiniog *Gwyn* .............. 3C **15**
Llanfflewyn *IOA* ..................... 2C **5**
Llanfihangel-ar-Arth *Carm*........ 2D **45**
Llanfihangel Glyn Myfyr *Cnwy*.. 3A **16**
Llanfihangel Nant Bran *Powy*... 2A **48**
Llanfihangel-Nant-Melan
     *Powy* ............................... 3C **39**
Llanfihangel near Rogiet *Mon*.. 1B **66**
Llanfihangel Rhydithon *Powy*... 2C **39**
Llanfihangel Tal-y-llyn *Powy*.... 3C **49**
Llanfihangel-uwch-Gwili
     *Carm* ............................... 3D **45**
Llanfihangel-y-Creuddyn
     *Cdgn* ............................... 1B **36**
Llanfihangel-yng-Ngwynfa
     *Powy* ............................... 3B **24**
Llanfihangel yn Nhowyn *IOA*..... 3C **5**
Llanfihangel-y-pennant *Gwyn*.. 3A **14**
........................................ (nr Golan)
Llanfihangel-y-pennant *Gwyn*.. 1B **28**
...................................... (nr Tywyn)
Llanfihangel-y-traethau *Gwyn*.. 1A **22**
Llanfilo *Powy* ........................ 2C **49**
Llanfleiddan *V Glam* ............... 2A **64**
Llanfoist *Mon* ........................ 1D **59**
Llanfor *Gwyn* ........................ 1A **24**
Llanfrechfa *Torf* ..................... 3A **60**

Llanfrothen *Gwyn* ...............3B **14**
Llanfrynach *Powy* ...............3B **48**
Llanfwrog *Den* ...................2C **17**
Llanfwrog *IOA* ......................2C **5**
Llanfyllin *Powy* ...................3C **25**
Llanfynydd *Flin* ...................2D **17**
Llanfynydd *Carm* .................3A **46**
Llanfyrnach *Pemb* ...............2B **44**
Llangadfan *Powy* .................3B **24**
Llangadog *Carm* ..................3C **47**
..........................(nr Llandovery)
Llangadog *Carm* ..................2D **55**
..........................(nr Llanelli)
Llangadwaladr *IOA* ...............1C **13**
Llangadwaladr *Powy* .............1C **25**
Llangaffo *IOA* ......................1D **13**
Llangain *Carm* .....................1C **55**
Llangammarch Wells *Powy* ......1A **48**
Llangan *V Glam* ...................2A **64**
Llangarron *Here* ...................3C **51**
Llangasty-Talyllyn *Powy* .........3C **49**
Llangathen *Carm* ..................3A **46**
Llangattock *Powy* .................1D **59**
Llangattock Lingoed *Mon* ........3A **50**
Llangattock-Vibon-Avel *Mon* ....1B **60**
Llangedwyn *Powy* .................2C **25**
Llangefni *IOA* ........................3D **5**
Llangeinor *B'end* ..................1A **64**
Llangeitho *Cdgn* ...................3B **36**
Llangeler *Carm* .....................2C **45**
Llangelynin *Gwyn* ................1A **28**
Llangendeirne *Carm* ..............1D **55**
Llangennech *Carm* ................2A **56**
Llangennith *Swan* .................3D **55**
Llangenny *Powy* ...................1D **59**
Llangernyw *Cnwy* .................1D **15**
Llangian *Gwyn* .....................2B **20**
Llangiwg *Neat* ......................2C **57**
Llangloffan *Pemb* ..................2C **43**
Llanglydwen *Carm* ................3A **44**
Llangoed *IOA* ........................3B **6**
Llangoedmor *Cdgn* ...............1A **44**
Llangollen *Den* ....................3D **17**
Llangolman *Pemb* .................3A **44**
Llangorse *Powy* ...................3C **49**
Llangorwen *Cdgn* .................3B **28**
Llangovan *Mon* .....................2B **60**
Llangower *Gwyn* ...................1A **24**
Llangranog *Cdgn* ..................3C **35**
Llangristiolus *IOA* ..................3D **5**
Llangrove *Here* .....................1C **61**
Llangua *Mon* ........................3A **50**
Llangunllo *Powy* ...................1D **39**
Llangunnor *Carm* ..................3D **45**
Llangurig *Powy* ....................1A **38**
Llangwm *Cnwy* ....................3A **16**
Llangwm *Mon* .......................2B **60**
Llangwm *Pemb* .....................2C **53**
Llangwm-isaf *Mon* .................2B **60**
Llangwnnadl *Gwyn* ...............1B **20**
Llangwyfan *Den* ...................1C **17**
Llangwyfan-isaf *IOA* ..............1C **13**
Llangwyllog *IOA* .....................3D **5**
Llangwyryfon *Cdgn* ...............1B **36**
Llangybi *Gwyn* .....................3D **13**
Llangybi *Mon* .......................3A **60**
Llangybi *Cdgn* ......................3B **36**
Llangyfelach *Swan* ................3B **56**
Llangynhafal *Den* ..................1C **17**
Llangynidr *Powy* ...................1C **59**
Llangynin *Carm* ....................1B **54**
Llangynog *Carm* ...................1C **55**
Llangynog *Powy* ...................2B **24**
Llangynwyd *B'end* .................1D **63**
Llanhamlach *Powy* .................3B **48**
Llanharan *Rhon* ....................1B **64**
Llanharry *Rhon* .....................1B **64**
Llanhennock *Mon* ..................3A **60**
Llanhilleth *Blae* .....................2D **59**

Llanidloes *Powy* ...................3A **30**
Llaniestyn *Gwyn* ..................1B **20**
Llanigon *Powy* ......................1D **49**
Llanilar *Cdgn* .......................1B **36**
Llanilid *Rhon* .......................1A **64**
Llanilltud Fawr *V Glam* ........**3A 64**
Llanishen *Card* .....................1C **65**
Llanishen *Mon* ......................2B **60**
Llanllawddog *Carm* ................3D **45**
Llanllechid *Gwyn* ..................1B **14**
Llanllowell *Mon* ....................3A **60**
Llanllugan *Powy* ...................1B **30**
Llanllwch *Carm* ....................1C **55**
Llanllwchaiarn *Powy* ..............2C **31**
Llanllwni *Carm* .....................2D **45**
Llanllyfni *Gwyn* ....................2D **13**
Llanmadoc *Swan* ..................3D **55**
Llanmaes *V Glam* ..................3A **64**
Llanmartin *Newp* ...................1A **66**
Llanmerewig *Powy* ................2C **31**
Llanmihangel *V Glam* .............2A **64**
Llan-mill *Pemb* .....................1A **54**
Llanmiloe *Carm* ....................2B **54**
Llanmorlais *Swan* ..................3A **56**
Llannefydd *Cnwy* ....................3A **8**
Llan-non *Cdgn* ......................2A **36**
Llannon *Carm* .......................2A **56**
Llannor *Gwyn* .......................1C **21**
Llanover *Mon* ........................2A **60**
Llanpumsaint *Carm* ...............3D **45**
Llanrhaeadr *Den* ...................1B **16**
Llanrhaeadr-ym-Mochnant
   *Powy* ..............................2C **25**
Llanrhian *Pemb* ....................2B **42**
Llanrhidian *Swan* ..................3D **55**
Llanrhos *Cnwy* ......................2C **7**
Llanrhyddlad *IOA* ...................2C **5**
Llanrhystud *Cdgn* ..................2A **36**
Llanrothal *Here* .....................1B **60**
Llanrug *Gwyn* .......................1A **14**
Llanrumney *Card* ..................1D **65**
Llanrwst *Cnwy* ......................1C **15**
Llansadurnen *Carm* ................1B **54**
Llansadwrn *IOA* ......................3A **6**
Llansadwrn *Carm* ..................2B **46**
Llansaint *Carm* .....................2C **55**
Llansamlet *Swan* ...................3B **56**
Llansanffraid Glan Conwy *Cnwy*.3D **7**
Llansannan *Cnwy* ..................1A **16**
Llansannor *V Glam* ................2A **64**
Llansantffraed *Powy* ..............3C **49**
Llansantffraed *Cdgn* ..............2A **36**
Llansantffraed Cwmdeuddwr
   *Powy* ..............................2A **38**
Llansantffraed-in-Elwel *Powy* ..3B **38**
Llansantffraid-ym-Mechain
   *Powy* ..............................2D **25**
Llansawel *Neat* .....................3C **57**
Llansawel *Carm* ....................2B **46**
Llansilin *Powy* ......................2D **25**
Llansoy *Mon* .........................2B **60**
Llanspyddid *Powy* .................3B **48**
Llanstadwell *Pemb* ................2C **53**
Llansteffan *Carm* ...................1C **55**
Llanstephan *Powy* .................1C **49**
Llantarnam *Torf* ....................3A **60**
Llanteg *Pemb* .......................1A **54**
Llanthony *Mon* ......................3D **49**
Llantilio Crossenny *Mon* ..........1A **60**
Llantilio Pertholey *Mon* ...........1A **60**
Llantood *Pemb* ......................1A **44**
Llantrisant *Rhon* ...................1B **64**
Llantrisant *Mon* ....................3A **60**
Llantrithyd *V Glam* .................2B **64**
Llantwit Fardre *Rhon* ..............1B **64**
Llantwit Major *V Glam* ..........**3A 64**
Llanuwchllyn *Gwyn* ...............1D **23**
Llanvaches *Newp* ...................3B **60**
Llanvair Discoed *Mon* .............3B **60**

Llanvapley *Mon* ....................1A **60**
Llanvetherine *Mon* .................1A **60**
Llanveynoe *Here* ...................2A **50**
Llanvihangel Crucorney *Mon* ....3A **50**
Llanvihangel Gobion *Mon* ........2A **60**
Llanvihangel Ystern-Llewern
   *Mon* ...............................1B **60**
Llanwarne *Here* ....................3C **51**
Llanwddyn *Powy* ...................3B **24**
Llanwenarth *Mon* ..................1D **59**
Llanwenog *Cdgn* ...................1D **45**
Llanwern *Newp* .....................1A **66**
Llanwinio *Carm* ....................3B **44**
Llanwnda *Gwyn* ....................2D **13**
Llanwnda *Pemb* .....................2C **43**
Llanwnnen *Cdgn* ...................1A **46**
Llanwnog *Powy* .....................2B **30**
Llanwrda *Carm* .....................2C **47**
Llanwrin *Powy* ......................1C **29**
Llanwrthwl *Powy* ...................2A **38**
Llanwrtud *Powy* ....................1D **47**
Llanwrtyd *Powy* ....................1D **47**
Llanwrtyd Wells *Powy* .............1D **47**
Llanwyddelan *Powy* ...............1B **30**
Llanyblodwel *Shrp* .................2D **25**
Llanybri *Carm* ......................1C **55**
Llanybydder *Carm* .................1A **46**
Llanycefn *Pemb* ....................3D **43**
Llanychaer *Pemb* ...................2C **43**
Llanycil *Gwyn* .......................1A **24**
Llanymawddwy *Gwyn* .............3A **24**
Llanymddyfri *Carm* ................2C **47**
Llanymynech *Powy* ................2D **25**
Llanynghenedl *IOA* ..................2C **5**
Llanynys *Den* ........................1C **17**
Llan-y-pwll *Wrex* ...................2A **18**
Llanyrafon *Torf* .....................3A **60**
Llanyre *Powy* ........................2B **38**
Llanystumdwy *Gwyn* ..............1D **21**
Llanywern *Powy* ....................3C **49**
Llawhaden *Pemb* ...................1D **53**
Llawndy *Flin* ..........................2C **9**
Llawnt *Shrp* ..........................1D **25**
Llawr Dref *Gwyn* ...................2B **20**
Llawryglyn *Powy* ...................2A **30**
Llay *Wrex* .............................2A **18**
Llechfaen *Powy* .....................3B **48**
Llechryd *Cphy* ......................2C **59**
Llechryd *Cdgn* ......................1B **44**
Llechrydau *Wrex* ....................1D **25**
Lledrod *Cdgn* ........................1B **36**
Llethrid *Swan* .......................3A **56**
Llidiad-Nenog *Carm* ...............2A **46**
Llidiardau *Gwyn* ....................1D **23**
Llidiart y Parc *Den* .................3C **17**
Llithfaen *Gwyn* .....................3C **13**
Lloc *Flin* ..............................3C **9**
Llong *Flin* ...........................1D **17**
Llowes *Powy* ........................1C **49**
Lloyney *Powy* ........................1D **39**
Llundain-fach *Cdgn* ................3A **36**
Llwydcoed *Rhon* ...................2A **58**
Llwyncelyn *Cdgn* ...................3D **35**
Llwyncelyn *Swan* ..................2B **56**
Llwyndafydd *Cdgn* .................3C **35**
Llwynderw *Powy* ...................1D **31**
Llwyn-du *Mon* ......................1D **59**
Llwyngwril *Gwyn* ..................1A **28**
Llwynhendy *Carm* ..................3A **56**
Llwynmawr *Wrex* ...................1D **25**
Llwyn-on Village *Mer T* ...........1B **58**
Llwyn-tÂªg *Carm* ...................2A **56**
Llwyn-y-brain *Carm* ...............1A **54**
Llwynygog *Powy* ...................2D **29**
Llwyn-y-groes *Cdgn* ...............3A **36**
Llwynypia *Rhon* ....................3A **58**
Llynclys *Shrp* .......................2D **25**
Llynfaes *IOA* .........................3D **5**
Llysfaen *Cnwy* ......................3D **7**

Llyswen *Powy* ......................2C **49**
Llysworney *V Glam* ................2A **64**
Llys-y-fran *Pemb* ..................3D **43**
Llywel *Powy* .........................2D **47**
Llywernog *Cdgn* ...................3C **29**
Locking *N Som* .....................3A **66**
Lockleywood *Shrp* .................2D **27**
Logaston *Here* ......................3A **40**
Loggerheads *Den* ..................1C **17**
Loggerheads *Staf* ..................1D **27**
Login *Carm* ..........................3A **44**
Long Ashton *N Som* ...............2C **67**
Longden *Shrp* .......................1B **32**
Longden Common *Shrp* ...........1B **32**
Longdon on Tern *Telf* ..............3D **27**
Longford *Telf* ........................3D **27**
Longford *Shrp* ......................1D **27**
Long Green *Ches W* ................3B **10**
Longhope *Glos* .....................1D **61**
Long Lane *Telf* ......................3D **27**
Longley Green *Worc* ...............3D **41**
Long Meadowend *Shrp* ...........3B **32**
Longnor *Shrp* .......................1B **32**
Longshaw *G Man* ..................1C **11**
Longslow *Shrp* .....................1D **27**
Longtown *Here* .....................3A **50**
Longville in the Dale *Shrp* .......2C **33**
Loppington *Shrp* ...................2B **26**
Lostock Gralam *Ches W* ..........3D **11**
Lostock Green *Ches W* ............3D **11**
Loughor *Swan* ......................3A **56**
Loughton *Shrp* .....................3D **33**
Loveston *Pemb* .....................2D **53**
Lowe *Shrp* ...........................1C **27**
Lower Brynamman *Neat* ..........1C **57**
Lower Bullingham *Here* ...........2C **51**
Lower Cam *Glos* ....................2D **61**
Lower Chapel *Powy* ................2B **48**
Lower Down *Shrp* ..................3A **32**
Lower Egleton *Here* ................1D **51**
Lower Failand *N Som* ..............2C **67**
Lower Faintree *Shrp* ...............3D **33**
Lower Frankton *Shrp* ..............1A **26**
Lower Hardwick *Here* ..............3B **40**
Lower Hayton *Shrp* .................3C **33**
Lower Hergest *Here* ................3D **39**
Lower Hordley *Shrp* ................2A **26**
Lower Kinnerton *Ches W* .........1A **18**
Lower Langford *N Som* ............3B **66**
Lower Ledwyche *Shrp* .............1C **41**
Lower Ley *Glos* .....................1D **61**
Lower Llanfadog *Powy* ............2A **38**
Lower Lydbrook *Glos* ..............1C **61**
Lower Lye *Here* .....................2B **40**
Lower Machen *Newp* ...............1D **65**
Lower Maes-coed *Here* ...........2A **50**
Lower Meend *Glos* .................2C **61**
Lower Morton *S Glo* ................3D **61**
Lower Mountain *Flin* ...............2A **18**
Lower Netchwood *Shrp* ...........2D **33**
Lower Penarth *V Glam* ............3C **65**
Lower Peover *Ches W* .............3D **11**
Lower Sketty *Swan* .................3B **56**
Lower Soudley *Glos* ................1D **61**
Lower Town *Here* ...................1D **51**
Lower Town *Pemb* ..................2C **43**
Lower Walton *Warr* .................2D **11**
Lower Welson *Here* .................3D **39**
Lower Whitley *Ches W* ............3D **11**
Lower Wych *Ches W* ...............3B **18**
Lowton *G Man* ......................1D **11**
Lowton Common *G Man* ..........1D **11**
Lucton *Here* .........................2B **40**
Ludchurch *Pemb* ...................1A **54**
Ludford *Shrp* ........................1C **41**
Ludlow *Shrp* .........................1C **41**
Lugg Green *Here* ...................2B **40**
Lugwardine *Here* ...................1C **51**
Lulham *Here* .........................1B **50**

Lulsgate Bottom *N Som*..........3C **67**
Lulsley *Worc*.............................3D **41**
Lunnon *Swan*...........................1A **62**
Lunt *Mers*.................................1A **10**
Luston *Here*.............................2B **40**
Luxley *Glos*..............................3D **51**
Lydbury North *Shrp*................3A **32**
Lydham *Shrp*...........................2A **32**
Lydney *Glos*............................2D **61**
Lydstep *Pemb*.........................3D **53**
Lye, The *Shrp*.........................2D **33**
Lye Head *Worc*.......................1D **41**
**Lymm** *Warr*..........................2D **11**
Lyneal *Shrp*.............................1B **26**
Lyne Down *Here*.....................2D **51**
Lyonshall *Here*........................3A **40**

## M

Machen *Cphy*..........................1D **65**
Machroes *Gwyn*......................2C **21**
Machynlleth *Powy*..................1C **29**
Madeley *Telf*............................1D **33**
Madley *Here*............................2B **50**
Maenaddwyn *IOA*.......................2D **5**
Maenclochog *Pemb*................3D **43**
Maendy *V Glam*......................2B **64**
Maentwrog *Gwyn*....................3B **14**
Maen-y-groes *Cdgn*................3C **35**
Maerdy *Rhon*...........................3A **58**
Maerdy *Cnwy*..........................3B **16**
Maerdy *Carm*..........................3B **46**
Maes Awyr Caerdydd
  *V Glam*....................**73** (3B **64**)
Maesbrook *Shrp*......................2A **26**
Maesbury *Shrp*........................2A **26**
Maesbury Marsh *Shrp*............2A **26**
Maes-glas *Flin*...........................3C **9**
Maesgwyn-Isaf *Powy*.............3C **25**
Maeshafn *Den*.........................1D **17**
Maes Llyn *Cdgn*......................1C **45**
Maesmynis *Powy*....................1B **48**
**Maesteg** *B'end*...................3D **57**
Maestir *Cdgn*...........................1A **46**
Maesybont *Carm*....................1A **56**
Maesycrugiau *Carm*...............1D **45**
Maesycwmmer *Cphy*..............3C **59**
Maesyrhandir *Powy*................2B **30**
**Maghull** *Mers*....................1A **10**
Magor *Mon*..............................1B **66**
Magor Service Area *Mon*........1B **66**
Magor Services Lorry Park
  *Mon*......................................1B **66**
Magwyr *Mon*...........................1B **66**
Maiden Wells *Pemb*................3C **53**
Maindee *Newp*........................1A **66**
Mainstone *Shrp*......................3D **31**
Malinslee *Telf*..........................1D **33**
Malltraeth *IOA*.........................1D **13**
Mallwyd *Gwyn*........................3D **23**
Malpas *Newp*..........................3A **60**
Malpas *Ches W*......................3B **18**
Malswick *Glos*.........................3D **51**
Mamble *Worc*.........................1D **41**
Mamhilad *Mon*........................2A **60**
Manafon *Powy*........................1C **31**
Mancot *Flin*.............................1A **18**
**Mangotsfield** *S Glo*.............2D **67**
Manley *Ches W*.......................3C **11**
Manmoel *Cphy*.......................2C **59**
Manorbier *Pemb*.....................3D **53**
Manorbier Newton *Pemb*........3D **53**
Manordeilo *Carm*...................3B **46**
Manorowen *Pemb*...................2C **43**
Mansell Gamage *Here*............1A **50**
Mansell Lacy *Here*..................1B **50**
Marbury *Ches E*......................3C **19**
Marchamley *Shrp*....................2C **27**
Marchwiel *Wrex*......................3A **18**

Marcross *V Glam*....................3A **64**
Marden *Here*...........................1C **51**
Mardu *Shrp*.............................3D **31**
Mardy *Mon*.............................1A **60**
Marford *Wrex*..........................2A **18**
Margam *Neat*..........................1C **63**
Marian Cwm *Den*......................3B **8**
Mariandyrys *IOA*........................2B **6**
Marian-glas *IOA*.........................2A **6**
Marian-y-de *Gwyn*..................1C **21**
Marian-y-mor *Gwyn*................1C **21**
Market Drayton *Shrp*...............1D **27**
Markham *Cphy*........................2C **59**
Marksbury *Bath*......................3D **67**
Marley Green *Ches E*..............3C **19**
Marloes *Pemb*.........................2A **52**
Marlow *Here*............................1A **40**
Marros *Carm*...........................2B **54**
Marsh, The *Powy*....................2A **32**
Marsh, The *Shrp*.....................2D **27**
Marshbrook *Shrp*....................3B **32**
Marshfield *Newp*.....................1D **65**
Marsh Green *Telf*....................3D **27**
Marston *Ches W*......................3D **11**
Marston *Here*...........................3A **40**
Marston Stannett *Here*............3C **41**
Marstow *Here*..........................1C **61**
Martinscroft *Warr*....................2D **11**
Martletwy *Pemb*......................1D **53**
Martley *Worc*...........................2D **41**
Marton *Shrp*............................2B **26**
  ......................................(nr Myddle)
Marton *Shrp*............................1D **31**
  .....................................(nr Worthen)
Mathern *Mon*..........................3C **61**
Mathon *Here*...........................1D **51**
Mathry *Pemb*..........................2B **42**
Maund Bryan *Here*.................3C **41**
Mawdlam *B'end*.....................1D **63**
Maw Green *Ches E*.................2D **19**
Mayals *Swan*..........................1B **62**
Mayhill *Swan*..........................3B **56**
Maypole *Mon*..........................1B **60**
Meadgate *Bath*.......................3D **67**
Meadowbank *Ches W*.............1D **19**
Meadow Green *Here*...............3D **41**
Meadowtown *Shrp*..................1A **32**
Medlicott *Shrp*.........................2B **32**
Meeson *Telf*.............................2D **27**
Meidrim *Carm*.........................3B **44**
Meifod *Powy*...........................3C **25**
Meinciau *Carm*........................1D **55**
Meliden *Den*..............................2B **8**
Melinbyrhedyn *Powy*...............2D **29**
Melincourt *Neat*......................2D **57**
Melin-y-coed *Cnwy*.................1D **15**
Melin-y-ddol *Powy*..................1B **30**
Melin-y-wig *Den*......................3B **16**
Melling *Mers*............................1A **10**
Melling Mount *Mers*................1B **10**
Melverley *Shrp*.........................3A **26**
Melverley Green *Shrp*..............3A **26**
Menai Bridge *IOA*......................3A **6**
Menithwood *Worc*...................2D **41**
Meole Brace *Shrp*....................3B **26**
Meols *Mers*................................1D **9**
Merbach *Here*..........................1A **50**
Mere *Ches E*............................2D **11**
Mere Heath *Ches W*................3D **11**
Merlin's Bridge *Pemb*..............1C **53**
Merrington *Shrp*......................2B **26**
Merrion *Pemb*..........................3C **53**
Merthyr *Carm*..........................3C **45**
Merthyr Cynog *Powy*...............2A **48**
Merthyr Dyfan *V Glam*.............2C **65**
Merthyr Mawr *B'end*...............2D **63**
**Merthyr Tudful** *Mer T*....**71** (2B **58**)
**Merthyr Tydfil** *Mer T*.....**71** (2B **58**)
Merthyr Vale *Mer T*.................3B **58**

Michaelchurch *Here*................3C **51**
Michaelchurch Escley *Here*......2A **50**
Michaelchurch-on-Arrow
  *Powy*......................................3D **39**
Michaelston-le-Pit *V Glam*.......2C **65**
Michaelston-y-Fedw *Newp*........1D **65**
Mickle Trafford *Ches W*..........1B **18**
Middlehope *Shrp*.....................3B **32**
Middle Maes-coed *Here*..........2A **50**
Middleton *Here*........................2C **41**
Middleton *Shrp*........................1C **41**
  ..........................................(nr Ludlow)
Middleton *Shrp*........................2A **26**
  .......................................(nr Oswestry)
Middleton *Swan*......................3D **55**
Middleton on the Hill *Here*.......2C **41**
Middleton Priors *Shrp*.............2D **33**
Middleton Scriven *Shrp*..........3D **33**
Middletown *Powy*....................3A **26**
Milbury Heath *S Glo*...............3D **61**
Milebrook *Powy*.......................1A **40**
Miles Hope *Here*.....................2C **41**
Milford *Powy*...........................2B **30**
**Milford Haven** *Pemb*.........2C **53**
Milkwall *Glos*...........................2C **61**
Millend *Glos*............................3D **61**
Mill Green *Shrp*.......................2D **27**
Millhalf *Here*............................1D **49**
Milson *Shrp*.............................1D **41**
Milton *N Som*..........................3A **66**
Milton *Pemb*...........................2D **53**
Milton Green *Ches W*..............2B **18**
Minera *Wrex*............................2D **17**
Minffordd *Gwyn*......................1A **22**
Minllyn *Gwyn*..........................3D **23**
Minsterley *Shrp*.......................1A **32**
Minton *Shrp*............................2B **32**
Minwear *Pemb*........................1D **53**
Miskin *Rhon*............................1B **64**
Mitcheldean *Glos*....................1D **61**
Mitchel Troy *Mon*....................1B **60**
Mitcheltroy Common *Mon*.......2B **60**
Moccas *Here*...........................1A **50**
Mochdre *Cnwy*..........................3D **7**
Mochdre *Powy*........................3B **30**
Moelfre *Cnwy*............................3A **8**
Moelfre *IOA*...............................2A **6**
Moelfre *Powy*..........................2C **25**
Mold *Flin*.................................1D **17**
Mollington *Ches W*..................3A **10**
Mona Airfield *IOA*......................3D **5**
Monachty *Cdgn*......................2A **36**
Monaughty *Powy*....................2D **39**
Monington *Pemb*.....................1A **44**
Monkhide *Here*........................1D **51**
Monkhopton *Shrp*...................2D **33**
Monkland *Here*........................3B **40**
Monknash *V Glam*...................2A **64**
Monkswood *Mon*....................2A **60**
Monkton *Pemb*........................2C **53**
Monmarsh *Here*......................1C **51**
Monmouth *Mon*......................1C **61**
Monnington on Wye *Here*........1A **50**
Montford *Shrp*.........................3B **26**
Montford Bridge *Shrp*.............3B **26**
Montgomery *Powy*..................2D **31**
Moorcot *Here*..........................3A **40**
Moore *Hal*...............................2C **11**
Moorend *Glos*.........................2D **61**
Moorhampton *Here*.................1A **50**
Moortown *Telf*.........................3D **27**
Morda *Shrp*.............................2D **25**
Mordiford *Here*........................2C **51**
More *Shrp*...............................2A **32**
**Moreton** *Mers*......................1D **9**
Moreton *Here*..........................2C **41**
Moreton Corbet *Shrp*..............2C **27**
Moreton Jeffries *Here*.............1D **51**

Moretonmill *Shrp*....................2C **27**
Moreton on Lugg *Here*............1C **51**
Moreton Say *Shrp*...................1D **27**
Morfa *Cdgn*............................3C **35**
Morfa Bach *Carm*...................1C **55**
Morfa Bychan *Gwyn*...............1A **22**
Morfa Glas *Neat*.....................2D **57**
Morfa Nefyn *Gwyn*..................3B **12**
Morganstown *Card*.................1C **65**
Moriah *Cdgn*...........................1B **36**
Morriston *Swan*.......................3B **56**
Mortimer's Cross *Here*............2B **40**
Morton *S Glo*...........................3D **61**
Morton *Shrp*............................2D **25**
Morton *Shrp*............................2D **43**
Morville *Shrp*...........................2D **33**
Mose *Shrp*..............................2D **33**
Moss *Wrex*..............................2A **18**
Moss Bank *Mers*.....................1C **11**
Mossbrow *G Man*...................2D **11**
Mossley Hill *Mers*...................2A **10**
Moss Side *Mers*......................1A **10**
Moston *Shrp*............................2C **27**
Moston Green *Ches E*.............1D **19**
Mostyn *Flin*.................................2C **9**
Mostyn Quay *Flin*.......................2C **9**
Moto *Swan*..............................2B **56**
Mouldsworth *Ches W*..............3C **11**
Moulton *V Glam*......................2B **64**
Moulton *Ches W*......................1D **19**
**Mountain Ash** *Rhon*...........3B **58**
Mountain Water *Pemb*............3C **43**
Mounton *Mon*..........................3C **61**
Moylgrove *Pemb*.....................1A **44**
Much Birch *Here*......................2C **51**
Much Cowarne *Here*................1D **51**
Much Dewchurch *Here*............2B **50**
Much Marcle *Here*...................2D **51**
Much Wenlock *Shrp*................1D **33**
Mucklestone *Staf*....................1D **27**
Muckleton *Shrp*.......................2C **27**
Muckley *Shrp*...........................2D **33**
Mumbles *Swan*........................1B **62**
Munderfield Row *Here*.............3D **41**
Munderfield Stocks *Here*.........3D **41**
Munsley *Here*..........................1D **51**
Munslow *Shrp*.........................3C **33**
Murdishaw *Hal*........................2C **11**
Murton *Swan*...........................1A **62**
Muxton *Telf*.............................3D **27**
Mwmbwls *Swan*......................1B **62**
Myddfai *Carm*.........................2C **47**
Myddle *Shrp*............................2B **26**
Mydroilyn *Cdgn*......................3D **35**
Mynachlog-ddu *Pemb*.............2A **44**
Mynydd-bach *Mon*..................3B **60**
Mynydd Isa *Flin*......................1D **17**
Mynyddislwyn *Cphy*................3C **59**
Mynydd Llandegai *Gwyn*.........1B **14**
Mynydd Mechell *IOA*................1C **5**
Mynydd-y-briw *Powy*..............2C **25**
Mynyddygarreg *Carm*.............2D **55**
Mynytho *Gwyn*........................1C **21**
Mytton *Shrp*............................3B **26**

## N

Nailbridge *Glos*........................1D **61**
**Nailsea** *N Som*....................2B **66**
Nanhyfer *Pemb*.......................2D **43**
Nannerch *Flin*..........................1C **17**
Nant-ddu *Powy*.......................1B **58**
Nanternis *Cdgn*.......................3C **35**
Nantgaredig *Carm*...................3D **45**
Nantgarw *Rhon*.......................1C **65**
Nant Glas *Powy*......................2A **38**
Nantglyn *Den*..........................1B **16**
Nantgwyn *Powy*......................1A **38**
Nantlle *Gwyn*...........................2A **14**

Nantmawr *Shrp* ......................2D **25**
Nantmel *Powy* ......................2B **38**
Nantmor *Gwyn*......................3B **14**
Nant Peris *Gwyn* ..................2B **14**
**Nantwich** *Ches E*................2D **19**
Nant-y-bai *Carm*...................1C **47**
Nant-y-bwch *Blae*..................1C **59**
Nant-y-Derry *Mon*.................2A **60**
Nant-y-dugoed *Powy*............3A **24**
Nant-y-felin *Cnwy*.....................3B **6**
Nantyffyllon *B'end* .................3D **57**
Nantyglo *Blae* ......................1C **59**
Nant-y-meichiaid *Powy*..........3C **25**
Nant-y-moel *B'end*................3A **58**
Nant-y-pandy *Cnwy*.................3B **6**
Narberth *Pemb* ....................1A **54**
Narberth Bridge *Pemb* ...........1A **54**
Narth, The *Mon*....................2C **61**
Nasareth *Gwyn*....................2D **13**
Nash *Here* ...........................2A **40**
Nash *Newp*...........................1A **66**
Nash *Shrp*............................1D **41**
**Neath** *Neat*........................3C **57**
Neath Abbey *Neat*................3C **57**
Nebo *Cnwy*...........................2D **15**
Nebo *Gwyn*...........................2D **13**
Nebo *IOA* ................................1D **5**
Nebo *Cdgn*...........................2A **36**
Neen Savage *Shrp*................1D **41**
Neen Sollars *Shrp*................1D **41**
Neenton *Shrp*.......................3D **33**
Nefyn *Gwyn*...........................3C **13**
Nelly Andrews Green *Powy*......1D **31**
Nelson *Cphy* .........................3C **59**
Nempnett Thrubwell *Bath*......3C **67**
Nercwys *Flin*.........................1D **17**
Ness *Ches W*........................3A **10**
Nesscliffe *Shrp* ....................3A **26**
**Neston** *Ches W*.....................3D **9**
Netherend *Glos*....................2C **61**
Netherton *Here*.....................3C **51**
Netherton *Mers*.....................1A **10**
Netherton *Shrp*.....................3D **33**
Netley *Shrp*...........................1B **32**
Neuadd *Powy* .......................1B **30**
Nevern *Pemb*........................2D **43**
Newborough *IOA*...................1D **13**
Newbridge *Wrex*...................3D **17**
Newbridge *Cphy* ..................3D **59**
Newbridge *Cdgn*..................3A **36**
Newbridge *Pemb* .................2C **43**
Newbridge-on-Usk *Mon*.........3A **60**
Newbridge on Wye *Powy*........3B **38**
New Brighton *Mers*................1A **10**
New Brighton *Flin*..................1D **17**
New Broughton *Wrex*.............2A **18**
Newcastle *B'end*....................1D **63**
Newcastle *Mon*.....................1B **60**
Newcastle *Shrp* ...................3D **31**
Newcastle Emlyn *Carm*...........1C **45**
Newchapel *Pemb*...................2B **44**
Newchapel *Powy* ..................3A **30**
Newchurch *Here*....................3A **40**
Newchurch *Powy*...................3D **39**
Newchurch *Mon* ...................3B **60**
Newchurch *Carm*...................3C **45**
New Cross *Cdgn*...................1B **36**
Newent *Glos*.........................3D **51**
New Ferry *Mers*.....................2A **10**
Newgale *Pemb*......................3B **42**
Newhall *Ches E* ....................3D **19**
New Hedges *Pemb* ..............2A **54**
New Inn *Mon*........................2B **60**
New Inn *Torf*.........................3A **60**
New Inn *Carm*.......................2D **45**
New Invention *Shrp* ..............1D **39**
Newland *Glos* .......................2C **61**
Newlands Pk. *IOA* ...................2B **4**
New Lane End *Warr*...............1D **11**

New Marton *Shrp* ..................1A **26**
New Mills *Mon*......................2C **61**
New Mills *Powy*.....................1B **30**
New Moat *Pemb*....................3D **43**
Newnham *Glos*......................1D **61**
Newnham Bridge *Worc*...........2D **41**
Newport *Glos*........................3D **61**
**Newport** *Newp*................**71** (1A **66**)
Newport *Pemb*......................2D **43**
**Newport** *Telf*......................3D **27**
New Quay *Cdgn*...................3C **35**
New Radnor *Powy*.................2D **39**
New Row *Cdgn*.....................1C **37**
New Street *Here* ...................3A **40**
Newstreet Lane *Shrp*.............1D **27**
Newton *B'end*.......................2D **63**
Newton *Ches W*....................1B **18**
.........................(nr Chester)
Newton *Ches W*....................2C **19**
.......................(nr Tattenhall)
Newton *Here*.........................2A **50**
...................(nr Ewyas Harold)
Newton *Here*.........................3C **41**
.....................(nr Leominster)
Newton *Mers*..........................2D **9**
Newton *Shrp*........................2D **33**
...................(nr Bridgnorth)
Newton *Shrp*........................1B **26**
.........................(nr Wem)
Newton *Swan*.......................1B **62**
Newton Green *Mon*...............3C **61**
**Newton-le-Willows** *Mers*......1C **11**
Newton on the Hill *Shrp*...........2B **26**
Newton St Loe *Bath*..............3D **67**
Newtown *Glos* ......................2D **61**
Newtown *Here*......................2C **51**
.............(nr Little Dewchurch)
Newtown *Here*.......................3C **41**
...............(nr Stretton Grandison)
Newtown *Shrp*......................1B **26**
Newtown *Rhon*......................3B **58**
**Newtown** *Powy*...................2C **31**
New Tredegar *Cphy*...............2C **59**
Nextend *Here*.......................3A **40**
Neyland *Pemb*......................2C **53**
Nib Heath *Shrp*.....................3B **26**
Nicholaston *Swan*..................1A **62**
Niwbwrch *IOA*.......................1D **13**
Nobold *Shrp*.........................3B **26**
Nolton *Pemb*........................1B **52**
Nolton Haven *Pemb*..............1B **52**
No Man's Heath *Ches W*........3C **19**
Noneley *Shrp*.......................2B **26**
Norbridge *Here*.....................1D **51**
Norbury *Ches E*....................3C **19**
Norbury *Shrp*........................2A **32**
Nordley *Shrp*........................2D **33**
Norley *Ches W*......................3C **11**
Norris Green *Mers* ................1A **10**
North Cornelly *B'end*.............1D **63**
North End *N Som*....................3B **66**
North Nibley *Glos*..................3D **61**
Northop *Flin*..........................1D **17**
Northop Hall *Flin*....................1D **17**
North Stoke *Bath*...................3D **67**
Northway *Swan*.....................1A **62**
North Weston *N Som*.............2B **66**
**Northwich** *Ches W*................3D **11**
North Wick *Bath*....................3C **67**
Northwick *S Glo*....................1C **67**
North Widcombe *Bath*...........3C **67**
Northwood *Shrp*....................1B **26**
Northwood Green *Glos*...........1D **61**
Norton *Shrp*...........................3B **32**
.........................(nr Ludlow)
Norton *Shrp*........................1D **33**
.......................(nr Madeley)
Norton *Shrp*........................1C **33**
.....................(nr Shrewsbury)

Norton *Powy*........................2A **40**
Norton *Mon* .........................3B **50**
Norton *Swan*........................1B **62**
Norton *Hal*...........................2C **11**
Norton Canon *Here*................1A **50**
Norton Hawkfield *Bath*...........3C **67**
Norton in Hales *Shrp*.............1D **27**
Norton Malreward *Bath*..........3D **67**
Nottage *B'end*......................2D **63**
Nox *Shrp* .............................3B **26**
Noyadd Trefawr *Cdgn*.............1B **44**
Nurston *V Glam* ...................3B **64**

## O

Oakdale *Cphy* .......................3C **59**
Oakengates *Telf*....................3D **27**
Oakenholt *Flin* .........................3D **9**
Oakford *Cdgn* ......................3D **35**
Oaklands *Powy*......................3B **38**
Oakley Pk. *Powy*....................3A **30**
Oakmere *Ches W*....................1C **19**
Oaks *Shrp*............................1B **32**
Occlestone Green *Ches W*........1D **19**
Ocle Pychard *Here*................1C **51**
Odd Down *Bath* ....................3D **67**
Ogmore *V Glam* ....................2D **63**
Ogmore-by-Sea *V Glam*..........2D **63**
Ogmore Vale *B'end*................3A **58**
Oldbury *Shrp* .......................2D **33**
Oldbury-on-Severn *S Glo*........3D **61**
Oldcastle *Mon*......................3A **50**
Oldcastle Heath *Ches W* ........3B **18**
Old Colwyn *Cnwy*.....................3D **7**
Old Down *S Glo* ...................1D **67**
Oldfield *Shrp*.........................3D **33**
Old Forge *Here* .....................1C **61**
Old Gore *Here*......................3D **51**
Oldland *S Glo*.......................2D **67**
Old Llanberis *Gwyn*...............2B **14**
Oldmixon *N Som*....................3A **66**
Old Pk. *Telf*..........................1D **33**
Old Radnor *Powy*...................3D **39**
Old Sodbury *S Glo*.................1D **67**
Old Swan *Mers*.....................1A **10**
Oldwalls *Swan*......................3D **55**
Oldwood Common *Worc*.........2C **41**
Ollerton *Shrp*........................2D **27**
Olmarch *Cdgn*......................3B **36**
Olveston *S Glo*......................1D **67**
Onen *Mon*............................1B **60**
Ongar Street *Here*.................2A **40**
Onibury *Shrp* .......................1B **40**
Onllwyn *Neat*........................1D **57**
Onneley *Staf*.........................3D **19**
Orcop *Here*...........................3B **50**
Orcop Hill *Here* .....................3B **50**
Oreton *Shrp*..........................3D **33**
Orford *Warr* ..........................1D **11**
Orleton *Here*.........................2B **40**
Orleton *Worc*.........................2D **41**
Orleton Common *Here* ...........2B **40**
Orrell *Mers*...........................1A **10**
Osbaston *Shrp*......................2A **26**
Oscroft *Ches W*.....................1C **19**
**Oswestry** *Shrp*....................2D **25**
Otterspool *Mers*....................2A **10**
Oughtrington *Warr*.................2D **11**
Over *S Glo* ...........................1C **67**
Over *Ches W*.........................1D **19**
Over Monnow *Mon*................1C **61**
Overpool *Ches W* ..................3A **10**
Overton *Shrp*.........................3D **33**
.....................(nr Bridgnorth)
Overton *Shrp* ......................1C **41**
.........................(nr Ludlow)
Overton *Wrex*.......................3A **18**
Overton *Swan*.......................1A **62**
Overton *Ches W*....................3C **11**

Owlbury *Shrp*........................2A **32**
Owrytn *Wrex*.........................3A **18**
Oxenhall *Glos*.......................3D **51**
Oxton *Mers*...........................2A **10**
Oxwich *Swan*........................1A **62**
Oxwich Green *Swan* ..............1A **62**
Oystermouth *Swan* ................1B **62**

## P

Paddington *Warr*....................2D **11**
Paddolgreen *Shrp*..................1C **27**
Padeswood *Flin* ....................1D **17**
Painscastle *Powy*...................1C **49**
Pale *Gwyn* ...........................1A **24**
Palmerstown *V Glam* .............3C **65**
Pandy *Gwyn* ........................1D **23**
.........................(nr Bala)
Pandy *Gwyn* ........................1B **28**
.........................(nr Tywyn)
Pandy *Wrex*..........................1C **25**
Pandy *Mon* ..........................3A **50**
Pandy *Powy*..........................1A **30**
Pandy Tudur *Cnwy*.................1D **15**
Pant *Wrex*.............................3D **17**
Pant *Shrp* ............................2D **25**
Pantasaph *Flin*........................3C **9**
Pant Glas *Gwyn* ...................3D **13**
Pant-glas *Shrp*.......................1D **25**
Pantgwyn *Carm*....................3A **46**
Pantgwyn *Cdgn* ...................1B **44**
Pant-lasau *Swan*....................2B **56**
Pant-pastynog *Den*................1B **16**
Pantperthog *Gwyn* ...............1C **29**
Pant-teg *Carm*......................3D **45**
Pant-y-Caws *Carm*................3A **44**
Pant-y-dwr *Powy*...................1A **38**
Pant-y-ffridd *Powy*.................1C **31**
Pantyffynnon *Carm*...............1B **56**
Pantygasseg *Torf*..................2D **59**
Pant-y-llyn *Carm*...................1B **56**
Pant-yr-awel *B'end*................1A **64**
Pant y Wacco *Flin*...................3C **9**
Parc *Gwyn*...........................1D **23**
Parcllyn *Cdgn* ......................3B **34**
Parc-Seymour *Newp*..............3B **60**
Parkend *Glos*........................2D **61**
Parkgate *Ches W*.....................3D **9**
Park Hill *Mers*.......................1B **10**
Parkhouse *Mon*....................2C **61**
Parkmill *Swan* ......................1A **62**
Parkway *Here* .......................2D **51**
Parr *Mers* ............................1C **11**
Parrog *Pemb*.........................2D **43**
Partington *G Man*..................1D **11**
Patchway *S Glo* ...................1D **67**
Paulton *Bath*.........................3D **67**
Peasedown St John *Bath*........3D **67**
Peasley Cross *Mers*...............1C **11**
Peaton *Shrp*..........................3C **33**
Peckforton *Ches E*.................2C **19**
Pedair-ffordd *Powy*................2C **25**
Pelcomb Bridge *Pemb* ...........1C **53**
Pelcomb Cross *Pemb*............1C **53**
Pemberton *Carm*...................2A **56**
Pembrey *Carm*......................2D **55**
Pembrey Airfield *Carm*...........2D **55**
Pembridge *Here*....................3A **40**
Pembroke *Pemb* ...................2C **53**
Pembroke Dock *Pemb*......**74** (2C **53**)
Pembroke Ferry *Pemb*............2C **53**
Penallt *Here*...........................3C **51**
Penallt *Mon* .........................1C **61**
Penally *Pemb*........................3A **54**
Penalum *Pemb* .....................3A **54**
**Penarth** *V Glam*..................2C **65**
Pen-bont Rhydybeddau *Cdgn*...3B **28**
Penbryn *Cdgn*.......................3B **34**
Pencader *Carm*......................2D **45**

Pen-cae Cdgn........................3D 35
Pencaenewydd Gwyn.............3D 13
Pencaerau Neat.....................3C 57
Pencarnisiog IOA ....................3C 5
Pencarreg Carm......................1A 46
Pencelli Powy.........................3B 48
Pen-clawdd Swan....................3A 56
Pencoed B'end........................1A 64
Pencombe Here.......................3C 41
Pencraig Here.........................3C 51
Pencraig Powy........................2B 24
Penderyn Rhon.......................2A 58
Pendine Carm.........................2B 54
Pendoylan V Glam...................2B 64
Pendre B'end..........................1A 64
Penegoes Powy.......................1C 29
Penffordd Pemb......................3D 43
Penffordd-Lâs Powy.................2D 29
Penfro Pemb...........................2C 53
Pengam Card..........................2D 65
Pengam Cphy.........................3C 59
Pengenffordd Powy..................2C 49
Pengorffwysfa IOA ...................1D 5
Pengwern Den..........................3B 8
Penhelig Gwyn........................2B 28
Penhow Newp.........................3B 60
Peniarth Gwyn........................1B 28
Peniel Carm............................3D 45
Penisa'r Waun Gwyn................1A 14
Penketh Warr...........................2C 11
Penley Wrex............................1B 26
Penllech Gwyn........................1B 20
Penllergaer Swan ...................3B 56
Pen-llyn IOA...........................2C 5
Penmachno Cnwy....................2C 15
Penmaen Swan .......................1A 62
Penmaenmawr Cnwy.................3C 7
Penmaenpool Gwyn.................3B 22
Penmaen Rhos Cnwy................3D 7
Pen-marc V Glam.....................3B 64
Penmark V Glam......................3B 64
Penmon IOA............................2B 6
Penmorfa Gwyn.......................3A 14
Penmynydd IOA ......................3A 6
Pennal Gwyn ..........................1C 29
Pennant Den............................1B 24
Pennant Powy.........................2D 29
Pennant Gwyn.........................2A 24
Pennant Cdgn..........................2A 36
Pennant Melangell Powy...........2B 24
Pennar Pemb...........................2C 53
Pennard Swan .........................1A 62
Pennerley Shrp........................2A 32
Pennington G Man...................1D 11
Pennorth Powy........................3C 49
Pennsylvania S Glo..................2D 67
Penparc Cdgn..........................1B 44
Penparcau Cdgn.......................3A 28
Pen-pedair-heol Cphy...............3C 59
Penperlleni Mon.......................2A 60
Penpont Powy.........................3A 48
Penprysg B'end .......................1A 64
Penrherber Carm......................2B 44
Penrhiw Pemb..........................1B 44
Penrhiwceiber Rhon.................3B 58
Pen-Rhiw-fawr Neat.................1C 57
Penrhiw-llan Cdgn....................1C 45
Penrhiw-pal Cdgn.....................1C 45
Penrhos Here...........................3A 40
Penrhos Gwyn.........................1C 21
Penrhos IOA.............................2B 4
Penrhos Mon ..........................1B 60
Penrhos Powy.........................1D 57
Penrhos Garnedd Gwyn .............3A 6
Penrhyn IOA............................1C 5
Penrhyn Bay Cnwy...................2D 7
Penrhyn-coch Cdgn..................3B 28
Penrhyndeudraeth Gwyn..........1B 22
Penrhyn-side Cnwy...................2D 7

Penrice Swan ..........................1A 62
Pen-sarn Gwyn........................2A 22
Pen-sarn Carm ........................1D 55
Pensax Worc...........................2D 41
Pensby Mers.............................2D 9
Pensford Bath..........................3D 67
Pentir Gwyn............................1A 14
Pentlepoir Pemb......................2A 54
Pentraeth IOA...........................3A 6
Pentre Powy............................2D 31
..........................(nr Church Stoke)
Pentre Powy............................3C 31
.............................................(nr Kerry)
Pentre Powy............................3B 30
................................(nr Mochdre)
Pentre Rhon............................3A 58
Pentre Shrp.............................3A 26
Pentre Wrex............................3D 17
.............................................(nr Chirk)
Pentre Wrex............................1C 25
.......(nr Llanarmon Dyffryn Ceiriog)
Pentre-bach Powy....................2A 48
Pentre-bach Cdgn....................1A 46
Pentrebach Mer T.....................2B 58
Pentrebach Carm.....................2D 47
Pentrebach Swan.....................2B 56
Pentre Berw IOA.......................3D 5
Pentre-bont Cnwy....................2C 15
Pentrecagal Carm.....................1C 45
Pentre-celyn Den......................2C 17
Pentre-clawdd Shrp..................1D 25
Pentreclwydau Neat.................2D 57
Pentre-cwrt Carm.....................2C 45
Pentre Dolau Honddu Powy......1A 48
Pentre-dwr Swan......................3B 56
Pentrefelin Cnwy.......................3D 7
Pentrefelin Gwyn.....................1A 22
Pentrefelin Carm......................3A 46
Pentrefelin Cdgn......................1B 46
Pentrefoelas Cnwy...................2D 15
Pentre Galar Pemb...................2A 44
Pentregat Cdgn........................3C 35
Pentre Gwenlais Carm..............1B 56
Pentre Gwynfryn Gwyn............2A 22
Pentre Halkyn Flin....................3D 9
Pentre Hodre Shrp...................1A 40
Pentre-Llanrhaeadr Den...........1B 16
Pentre Llifior Powy...................2C 31
Pentrellwyn IOA........................2A 6
Pentre-llwyn-llwyd Powy..........3A 38
Pentre-llyn-cymmer Cnwy........2A 16
Pentre Meyrick V Glam............2A 64
Pentre-piod Gwyn....................1D 23
Pentre-poeth Newp..................1D 65
Pentre'r beirdd Powy................3C 25
Pentre'r-felin Powy...................3C 25
Pentre-tafarn-y-fedw Cnwy......1D 15
Pentre-ty-gwyn Carm...............2D 47
Pentre-uchaf Gwyn..................1C 21
Pen-twyn Cphy.......................2D 59
Pentwyn Cphy........................2C 59
Pentwyn Card.........................1D 65
Pentyrch Carm........................1C 65
Pentywyn Carm......................2B 54
Penuwch Cdgn........................2A 36
Penwyllt Powy.........................1D 57
Pen-y-banc Carm....................3B 46
Penybanc Carm.......................1B 56
Pen-y-bont Powy....................2D 25
Pen-y-bont Carm....................3C 45
Penybont Powy.......................2C 39
Pen-y-Bont Ar Ogwr B'end.....1A 64
Penybontfawr Powy................2B 24
Pen-y-bryn Wrex....................3D 17
Pen-y-bryn Pemb....................1A 44
Penybryn Cphy.......................3C 59
Pen-y-cae Powy......................1D 57
Penycae Wrex.........................3D 17
Pen-y-cae mawr Mon.............3B 60

Penycaerau Gwyn...................2A 20
Pen-y-cefn Flin........................3C 9
Pen-y-clawdd Mon.................2B 60
Pen-y-coedcae Rhon...............1B 64
Penycwm Pemb......................3B 42
Pen-y-Darren Mer T................2B 58
Pen-y-fai B'end.......................1D 63
Pen-y-ffordd Flin.....................2C 9
Penyffordd Flin........................1A 18
Penyffridd Gwyn.....................2A 14
Pen-y-garn Cdgn....................3B 28
Pen-y-garnedd IOA..................3A 6
Pen-y-garnedd Powy...............2C 25
Pen-y-graig Gwyn...................1B 20
Penygraig Rhon......................3A 58
Penygraigwen IOA..................2D 5
Pen-y-groes Carm..................1A 56
Penygroes Gwyn.....................2D 13
Penygroes Pemb.....................2A 44
Pen-y-Mynydd Carm..............2D 55
Penymynydd Flin....................1A 18
Pen-yr-heol Mon....................1B 60
Penyrheol Cphy......................1C 65
Penyrheol Swan......................3A 56
Penysarn IOA..........................1D 5
Pen-y-stryt Den.......................2C 17
Penywaun Rhon......................2A 58
Peplow Shrp...........................2D 27
Perthy Shrp.............................1A 26
Peterchurch Here.....................2A 50
Peterstone Wentlooge Newp....1D 65
Peterston-super-Ely V Glam.....2B 64
Peterstow Here........................3C 51
Petton Shrp.............................2D 27
Phocle Green Here...................3D 51
Pibwrlwyd Carm......................1D 55
Picklenash Glos......................3D 51
Picklescott Shrp......................2B 32
Pickmere Ches E.....................3D 11
Pickstock Telf..........................2D 27
Picton Ches W........................3B 10
Picton Flin..............................2C 9
Pie Corner Here.......................2D 41
Pill N Som...............................2C 67
Pill, The Mon..........................1B 66
Pilleth Powy............................2D 39
Pillgwenlly Newp....................1A 66
Pillowell Glos..........................2D 61
Pilning S Glo...........................1C 67
Pilton Green Swan...................1A 62
Pinged Carm...........................2D 55
Pinsley Green Ches E...............3C 19
Pipe and Lyde Here.................1C 51
Pipe Aston Here......................1B 40
Pipe Gate Shrp........................3D 19
Pipton Powy...........................2C 49
Pistyll Gwyn...........................3C 13
Pitchford Shrp.........................1C 33
Pitt Court Glos.........................3D 61
Pitton Swan............................3D 55
Pixley Here.............................2D 51
Plain Dealings Pemb...............1D 53
Plaish Shrp..............................2C 33
Plaistow Here..........................2D 51
Plas yn Cefn Den......................3B 8
Platt Bridge G Man.................1D 11
Platt Lane Shrp.......................1C 22
Plealey Shrp...........................1B 32
Ploughfield Here......................1A 50
Plowden Shrp.........................3A 32
Ploxgreen Shrp.......................1A 32
Plumley Ches E.......................3D 11
Plwmp Cdgn...........................3C 35
Ponde Powy............................2C 49
Pont Abraham Service Area
      Carm.................................2A 56
Pontamman Carm....................1B 56
Pontantwn Carm.....................1D 55
Pontardawe Neat....................2C 57

Pontarddulais Swan................2A 56
Pontarfynach Cdgn..................1C 37
Pont-ar-gothi Carm..................3A 46
Pont ar Hydfer Powy...............3D 47
Pontarllechau Carm.................3C 47
Pontarsais Carm......................3D 45
Pontblyddyn Flin.....................1D 17
Pontbren Llwyd Rhon..............2A 58
Pont-Cyfyng Cnwy..................2C 15
Pontdolgoch Powy..................2B 30
Ponterwyd Cdgn......................3C 29
Pontesbury Shrp......................1B 32
Pontesford Shrp......................1B 32
Pontfadog Wrex......................1D 25
Pont-Faen Shrp.......................1D 25
Pont-faen Powy.......................2A 48
Pontfaen Pemb........................2D 43
Pontgarreg Cdgn.....................3C 35
Pont-Henri Carm.....................2D 55
Ponthir Torf............................3A 60
Ponthirwaun Cdgn..................1B 44
Pont-iets Carm........................2D 55
Pont Kemys Cvn & Camping Pk.
      Mon .................................2A 60
Pontllanfraith Cphy..................3C 59
Pontlliw Swan.........................2B 56
Pont Llogel Powy.....................3B 24
Pontllyfni Gwyn......................2D 13
Pontlottyn Cphy......................2C 59
Pontneddfechan Powy.............2A 58
Pont-newydd Flin....................1C 17
Pont-newydd Carm..................2D 55
Pontnewydd Torf....................3D 59
Pont Pen-y-benglog Gwyn......1B 14
Pontrhydfendigaid Cdgn..........2C 37
Pont Rhyd-y-cyff B'end...........1D 63
Pontrhydyfen Neat..................3C 57
Pont-rhyd-y-groes Cdgn.........1C 37
Pontrhydyrun Torf...................3D 59
Pont-Rhythallt Gwyn...............1A 14
Pontrilas Here.........................3A 50
Pontrilas Road Here.................3A 50
Pontrobert Powy......................3C 25
Pont-rug Gwyn........................1A 14
Pontshill Here..........................3D 51
Pont-Sian Cdgn.......................1D 45
Pontsticill Mer T......................1B 58
Pont-Walby Neat.....................2D 57
Pontwelly Carm.......................2D 45
Pontwgan Cnwy........................3C 7
Pontyates Carm.......................2D 55
Pontyberem Carm....................1A 56
Pontybodkin Flin......................2D 17
Pontyclun Rhon.......................1B 64
Pontycymer B'end...................3A 58
Pontyglazier Pemb...................2A 44
Pontygwaith Rhon...................3B 58
Pont-y-pant Cnwy....................2C 15
Pontypool Torf........................3D 59
Pontypridd Rhon.....................1B 64
Pontypwl Torf.........................3D 59
Pontywaun Cphy.....................3D 59
Pool Head Here.......................3C 41
Poolhill Glos............................3D 51
Poolmill Here..........................3C 51
Pool Quay Powy......................3D 25
Pope Hill Pemb.......................1C 53
Pope's Hill Glos.......................1D 61
Portbury N Som......................2C 67
Port-Eynon Swan....................1A 62
Portfield Gate Pemb................1C 53
Porth Rhon.............................3B 58
Porthaethwy IOA......................3A 6
Porthcawl B'end......................2D 63
Porthceri V Glam.....................3B 64
Porthgain Pemb.......................2B 42
Porthill Shrp............................3B 26
Porthkerry V Glam...................3B 64
Porthllechog IOA......................1D 5

Porthmadog *Gwyn* ...................1A **22**
Porth Tywyn *Carm* ..................2D **55**
Porth-y-felin *IOA* .......................2B **4**
Porthyrhyd *Carm* ....................1A **56**
.............................(nr Carmarthen)
Porthyrhyd *Carm* .....................2C **47**
...........................(nr Llandovery)
Porth-y-waen *Shrp* ..................2D **25**
**Portishead** *N Som* .................2B **66**
Port Lion *Pemb* .......................2C **53**
Portmead *Swan* .......................3B **56**
Portmeirion *Gwyn* ...................1A **22**
Portskewett *Mon* ......................1C **67**
Port Sunlight *Mers* ...................2A **10**
**Port Talbot** *Neat* ...................1C **63**
Port Tennant *Swan* ..................3B **56**
Portway *Here* ...........................1B **50**
Post-Mawr *Cdgn* ......................3D **35**
Pound Bank *Worc* ....................1D **41**
Poynton *Telf* ............................3C **27**
Poynton Green *Telf* ..................3C **27**
Prees *Shrp* ..............................1C **27**
Prees Green *Shrp* ....................1C **27**
Prees Higher Heath *Shrp* .........1C **27**
Prendergast *Pemb* ..................1C **53**
Pren-gwyn *Cdgn* .....................1D **45**
Prenteg *Gwyn* .........................3A **14**
Prenton *Mers* ..........................2A **10**
**Prescot** *Mers* .......................1B **10**
Prescott *Shrp* ..........................2B **26**
**Prestatyn** *Den* .............**71 (2B 8)**
Presteigne *Powy* .....................2A **40**
Presthope *Shrp* .......................2C **33**
Preston *Shrp* ...........................3C **27**
Preston Brockhurst *Shrp* .........2C **27**
Preston Brook *Hal* ...................2C **11**
Preston Cross *Glos* .................2D **51**
Preston Gubbals *Shrp* .............3B **26**
Preston Marsh *Here* ................1C **51**
Preston on the Hill *Hal* .............2C **11**
Preston on Wye *Here* ...............1A **50**
Preston upon the Weald Moors
   *Telf* ....................................3D **27**
Preston Wynne *Here* ...............1C **51**
Price Town *B'end* ....................3A **58**
Priest Weston *Shrp* ..................2D **31**
Primrose Hill *Glos* ...................2D **61**
Princes Gate *Pemb* ................1A **54**
Prion *Den* ...............................1B **16**
Prior's Frome *Here* ..................2C **51**
Priors Halton *Shrp* ..................1B **40**
Priorslee *Telf* ..........................3D **27**
Priory Wood *Here* ...................1D **49**
Priston *Bath* ............................3D **67**
Publow *Bath* ...........................3D **67**
Pucklechurch *S Glo* ................2D **67**
Puddinglake *Ches W* ..............1D **19**
Puddington *Ches W* ................3A **10**
Puddlebrook *Glos* ...................1D **61**
Pudleston *Here* .......................3C **41**
Puleston *Telf* ..........................2D **27**
Pulford *Ches W* ......................2A **18**
Pulley *Shrp* .............................1B **32**
Pulverbatch *Shrp* ....................1B **32**
Pumsaint *Carm* .......................1B **46**
Puncheston *Pemb* ...................3D **43**
Purlogue *Shrp* ........................1D **39**
Purslow *Shrp* ..........................3A **32**
Purton *Glos* ............................2D **61**
.................................(nr Lydney)
Purton *Glos* ............................2D **61**
...............................(nr Sharpness)
Putley *Here* .............................2D **51**
Puxton *N Som* .........................3B **66**
Pwll *Carm* ...............................2D **55**
Pwll *Powy* ...............................1C **31**
Pwllcrochan *Pemb* ..................2C **53**
Pwll-glas *Den* ..........................2C **17**
Pwllgloyw *Powy* .......................2B **48**

Pwllheli *Gwyn* ..........................1C **21**
Pwllmeyric *Mon* .......................3C **61**
Pwlltrap *Carm* ..........................1B **54**
Pwll-y-glaw *Neat* ......................3C **57**
Pye Corner *Newp* .....................1A **66**
**Pyle** *B'end* ..........................1D **63**

### Q

Quabbs *Shrp* ...........................3D **31**
Quarry, The *Glos* ......................3D **61**
Quatford *Shrp* ..........................2D **33**
Quatt *Shrp* ...............................3D **33**
Queen Charlton *Bath* ...............3D **67**
Queensferry *Flin* ......................1A **18**
Quina Brook *Shrp* ....................1C **27**

### R

Raby *Mers* ...............................3A **10**
Rachub *Gwyn* ..........................1B **14**
Radford *Bath* ...........................3D **67**
Radyr *Card* ..............................1C **65**
RAF Valley *IOA* ..........................3C **5**
Ragdon *Shrp* ...........................2B **32**
Raglan *Mon* .............................2B **60**
Rainford *Mers* ..........................1B **10**
Rainford Junction *Mers* ............1B **10**
Rainhill *Mers* ...........................1B **10**
Rangeworthy *S Glo* ..................1D **67**
Rassau *Blae* ............................1C **59**
Ratlinghope *Shrp* .....................2B **32**
Ravenhills Green *Worc* .............3D **41**
Ravensmoor *Ches E* ................2D **19**
Reaseheath *Ches E* .................2D **19**
Redberth *Pemb* ........................2D **53**
Redbrook *Glos* .........................2C **61**
Redbrook *Wrex* ........................3C **19**
Redcliffe Bay *N Som* ................2B **66**
Redhill *N Som* ..........................3C **67**
Redhill *Shrp* .............................3D **27**
Redland *Bris* ............................2C **67**
Redmarley D'Abitot *Glos* ..........2D **51**
Rednal *Shrp* .............................2A **26**
Red Roses *Carm* ......................1B **54**
Red Wharf Bay *IOA* ....................2A **6**
Redwick *S Glo* .........................1C **67**
Redwick *Newp* .........................1B **66**
Regil *N Som* .............................3C **67**
Reilth *Shrp* ...............................3D **31**
Resolfen *Neat* ..........................2D **57**
Resolven *Neat* .........................2D **57**
Reynalton *Pemb* .......................2D **53**
Reynoldston *Swan* ...................1A **62**
Rhadyr *Mon* .............................2A **60**
Rhaeadr Gwy *Powy* ..................2A **38**
Rhandirmwyn *Carm* ..................1C **47**
Rhayader *Powy* ........................2A **38**
Rhewl *Den* ...............................3C **17**
.............................(nr Llangollen)
Rhewl *Den* ...............................1C **17**
..................................(nr Ruthin)
Rhewl *Shrp* ..............................1A **26**
Rhewl-Mostyn *Flin* .....................2C **9**
Rhigos *Rhon* ...........................2A **58**
Rhiw *Gwyn* ..............................2B **20**
Rhiwabon *Wrex* .......................3A **18**
Rhiwbina *Card* .........................1C **65**
Rhiwbryfdir *Gwyn* .....................3B **14**
Rhiwderin *Newp* .......................1D **65**
Rhiwlas *Gwyn* .........................1A **24**
....................................(nr Bala)
Rhiwlas *Gwyn* .........................1A **14**
.................................(nr Bangor)
Rhiwlas *Powy* ..........................1C **25**
Rhodiad-y-Brenin *Pemb* ...........3A **42**
Rhondda *Rhon* ........................3A **58**
Rhoose *V Glam* ........................3B **64**
Rhos *Carm* ..............................2C **45**

Rhos *Neat* ...............................2C **57**
Rhos, The *Pemb* ......................1D **53**
Rhosaman *Carm* ......................1C **57**
Rhoscefnhir *IOA* .........................3A **6**
Rhoscolyn *IOA* ...........................3B **4**
Rhos Common *Powy* ................3D **25**
Rhoscrowther *Pemb* ................2C **53**
Rhos-ddu *Gwyn* .......................1B **20**
Rhosdylluan *Gwyn* ...................2D **23**
Rhosesmor *Flin* .......................1D **17**
Rhos-fawr *Gwyn* ......................1C **21**
Rhosgadfan *Gwyn* ...................2A **14**
Rhosgoch *Powy* .......................1C **49**
Rhosgoch *IOA* ...........................2D **5**
Rhos Haminiog *Cdgn* ...............2A **36**
Rhos-hill *Pemb* ........................1A **44**
Rhoshirwaun *Gwyn* ..................2A **20**
Rhoslan *Gwyn* .........................3D **13**
Rhoslefain *Gwyn* ......................1A **28**
**Rhosllanerchrugog** *Wrex* .......3D **17**
Rhôs Lligwy *IOA* .........................2D **5**
Rhosmaen *Carm* ......................3B **46**
Rhosmeirch *IOA* .........................3D **5**
Rhosneigr *IOA* ...........................3C **5**
Rhôs-on-Sea *Cnwy* ....................2D **7**
Rhossili *Swan* ..........................3D **55**
Rhosson *Pemb* ........................3A **42**
Rhostrenwfa *IOA* ........................3D **5**
Rhostryfan *Gwyn* .....................2D **13**
Rhostyllen *Wrex* .......................3A **18**
Rhoswiel *Shrp* .........................1D **25**
Rhosybol *IOA* .............................2D **5**
Rhos-y-brithdir *Powy* ...............2C **25**
Rhos-y-garth *Cdgn* ..................1B **36**
Rhos-y-gwaliau *Gwyn* ..............1A **24**
Rhos-y-llan *Gwyn* ....................1B **20**
Rhos-y-meirch *Powy* ................2D **39**
Rhualt *Den* ..............................3B **8**
Rhuddall Heath *Ches W* ...........1C **19**
Rhuddlan *Den* ..........................3B **8**
Rhuddlan *Cdgn* ........................1D **45**
Rhulen *Powy* ...........................1C **49**
Rhuthun *Den* ...........................2C **17**
Rhws, Y *V Glam* .......................3B **64**
Rhyd *Gwyn* .............................3B **14**
**Rhydaman** *Carm* ..................1B **56**
Rhydargaeau *Carm* ..................3D **45**
Rhydcymerau *Carm* .................2A **46**
Rhyd-Ddu *Gwyn* ......................2A **14**
Rhydding *Neat* .........................3C **57**
Rhydfudr *Cdgn* ........................2A **36**
Rhydlanfair *Cnwy* ....................2D **15**
Rhydlewis *Cdgn* .......................1C **45**
Rhydlios *Gwyn* .........................1A **20**
Rhydlydan *Cnwy* ......................2D **15**
Rhyd-meirionydd *Cdgn* ............3B **28**
Rhydowen *Cdgn* ......................1D **45**
Rhyd-Rosser *Cdgn* ..................2A **36**
Rhydspence *Here* .....................1D **49**
Rhydtalog *Flin* ..........................2D **17**
Rhyd-uchaf *Gwyn* ....................1A **24**
Rhydwyn *IOA* .............................2C **5**
Rhyd-y-clafdy *Gwyn* .................1C **21**
Rhydycroesau *Powy* .................1D **25**
Rhydyfelin *Rhon* .......................1B **64**
Rhydyfelin *Cdgn* ......................1A **36**
Rhyd-y-foel *Cnwy* ......................3A **8**
Rhyd-y-fro *Neat* .......................2C **57**
Rhydymain *Gwyn* .....................2D **23**
Rhyd-y-meudwy *Den* ................2C **17**
Rhydymwyn *Flin* .......................1D **17**
Rhyd-yr-onen *Gwyn* .................1B **28**
Rhyd-y-sarn *Gwyn* ...................3B **14**
**Rhyl** *Den* ......................**72 (2B 8)**
Rhymney *Cphy* .........................2C **59**
Rhymni *Cphy* ...........................2C **59**
Richards Castle *Here* ...............2B **40**
Rickford *N Som* ........................3B **66**
Ridgebourne *Powy* ...................2B **38**

Ridgeway Cross *Here* ...............1D **51**
Ridgwardine *Shrp* .....................1D **27**
Risbury *Here* ............................3C **41**
**Risca** *Cphy* .........................3D **59**
Risley *Warr* ..............................1D **11**
Roath *Card* ..............................2C **65**
Robertstown *Rhon* ....................2A **58**
Robeston Back *Pemb* ...............1D **53**
Robeston Wathen *Pemb* ...........1D **53**
Robeston West *Pemb* ...............2B **52**
Roch *Pemb* ..............................3B **42**
Rock *Worc* ..............................1D **41**
Rock Ferry *Mers* .......................2A **10**
Rockfield *Mon* ..........................1B **60**
Rockgreen *Shrp* .......................1C **41**
Rockhampton *S Glo* .................3D **61**
Rodd *Here* ...............................2A **40**
Roden *Telf* ...............................3C **27**
Rodington *Telf* ..........................3C **27**
Rodington Heath *Telf* ................3C **27**
Rodley *Glos* .............................1D **61**
Rodway *Telf* .............................3D **27**
Rogerstone *Newp* .....................1D **65**
Rogiet *Mon* ..............................1B **66**
Roman Bank *Shrp* ....................2C **33**
Romers Common *Worc* .............2C **41**
Rorrington *Shrp* ........................1A **32**
Rosebush *Pemb* .......................3D **43**
Rosehill *Shrp* ...........................1D **27**
...............................(nr Market Drayton)
Rosehill *Shrp* ...........................3B **26**
...............................(nr Shrewsbury)
Rosemarket *Pemb* ...................2C **53**
Rossett *Wrex* ...........................2A **18**
**Ross-on-Wye** *Here* ...............3D **51**
Rostherne *Ches E* ....................2D **11**
Roughton *Shrp* .........................2D **33**
Round Oak *Shrp* ......................3A **32**
Rowberrow *Som* .......................3B **66**
Rowen *Cnwy* ............................3C **7**
Rowlestone *Here* ......................3A **50**
Rowley *Shrp* ............................1A **32**
Rowton *Shrp* ............................3B **32**
...............................(nr Ludlow)
Rowton *Shrp* ............................3A **26**
...............................(nr Shrewsbury)
Rowton *Ches W* .......................1B **18**
Rowton *Telf* .............................3D **27**
Royal Oak *Lanc* .......................1B **10**
Royal's Green *Ches E* ..............3D **19**
Ruabon *Wrex* ..........................3A **18**
Ruardean *Glos* .........................1D **61**
Ruardean Hill *Glos* ...................1D **61**
Ruardean Woodside *Glos* .........1D **61**
Ruckley *Shrp* ...........................1C **33**
Rudbaxton *Pemb* .....................3C **43**
Rudgeway *S Glo* ......................1D **67**
Rudhall *Here* ............................3D **51**
Rudheath *Ches W* ....................3D **11**
Rudry *Cphy* .............................2D **65**
Rumney *Card* ...........................2D **65**
**Runcorn** *Hal* .......................2C **11**
Rushall *Here* ............................2D **51**
Rushbury *Shrp* .........................2C **33**
Rushton *Ches W* ......................1C **19**
Rushton *Shrp* ...........................1D **33**
Ruspidge *Glos* .........................1D **61**
Ruthin *V Glam* .........................2A **64**
Ruthin *Den* ..............................2C **17**
Ruxton Green *Here* ...................1C **61**
Ruyton-XI-Towns *Shrp* ..............2A **26**
Ryeford *Here* ............................3D **51**
Ryton *Glos* ..............................2D **51**

### S

Sageston *Pemb* .......................2D **53**
Saighton *Ches W* .....................1B **18**
Sain Dunwyd *V Glam* ...............3A **64**

Sain Hilari *V Glam*....................2B **64**
St Andrews Major *V Glam*........2C **65**
St Arvans *Mon*.......................3C **61**
**St Asaph** *Den*.............................3B **8**
Sain Tathan *V Glam*.................3B **64**
St Athan *V Glam*.....................3B **64**
St Athan Airfield *V Glam*..........3B **64**
St Briavels *Glos*.......................2C **61**
St Brides *Pemb*.......................1A **52**
St Brides Major *V Glam*............2D **63**
St Bride's Netherwent *Mon*......1B **66**
St Bride's-super-Ely *V Glam*....2B **64**
St Brides Wentlooge *Newp*.....1D **65**
St Clears *Carm*........................1B **54**
**St Davids** *Pemb*.....................3A **42**
St Davids Airfield *Pemb*...........3A **42**
St Dogmaels *Pemb*.................1A **44**
St Donat's *V Glam*...................3A **64**
St Fagans *Card*.......................2C **65**
St Florence *Pemb*...................2D **53**
St George *Cnwy*........................3A **8**
St George's *N Som*.................3A **66**
St Georges *V Glam*..................2B **64**
St Harmon *Powy*.....................1A **38**
**St Helens** *Mers*.....................1C **11**
St Hilary *V Glam*.....................2B **64**
St Illtyd *Blae*..........................2D **59**
St Ishmael *Carm*.....................2C **55**
St Ishmael's *Pemb*..................2B **52**
St Lythans *V Glam*..................2C **65**
St Margarets *Here*..................2A **50**
St Martin's *Shrp*.....................1A **26**
St Mary Church *V Glam*...........2B **64**
St Mary Hill *V Glam*.................2A **64**
St Maughan's Green *Mon*........1B **60**
St Mellons *Card*......................1D **65**
St Michaels *Worc*....................2C **41**
St Nicholas *V Glam*.................2B **64**
St Nicholas *Pemb*....................2B **42**
St Owen's Cross *Here*.............3C **51**
St Petrox *Pemb*......................3C **53**
St Thomas *Swan*....................3B **56**
St Twynnells *Pemb*.................3C **53**
St Weonards *Here*..................3B **50**
Salem *Carm*............................3B **46**
Salem *Cdgn*............................3B **28**
Salterswall *Ches W*.................1D **19**
Saltford *Bath*.........................3D **67**
Saltney *Flin*............................1A **18**
Sambrook *Telf*........................2D **27**
**Sandbach** *Ches E*................1D **19**
Sandfields *Neat*......................3C **57**
Sandford *Shrp*........................2A **26**
..........................(nr Oswestry)
Sandford *Shrp*.......................1C **27**
...........................(nr Whitchurch)
Sandford *N Som*.....................3B **66**
Sandiway *Ches W*...................3D **11**
Sandy *Carm*............................2D **55**
Sandycroft *Flin*......................1A **18**
Sandy Cross *Here*...................3D **41**
Sandy Haven *Pemb*.................2B **52**
Sandylane *Swan*.....................1A **62**
Sandyway *Here*......................3B **50**
Sapey Common *Here*..............2D **41**
Sardis *Pemb*...........................2C **53**
....................(nr Milford Haven)
Sardis *Pemb*...........................2A **54**
...........................(nr Tenby)
Sardis *Carm*............................2A **56**
Sarn *B'end*.............................1A **64**
Sarn *Powy*..............................2D **31**
Sarnau *Powy*..........................2B **48**
...........................(nr Brecon)
Sarnau *Powy*..........................3D **25**
...........................(nr Welshpool)
Sarnau *Gwyn*..........................1A **24**
Sarnau *Carm*...........................3D **45**
Sarnau *Cdgn*...........................3C **35**

Sarn Bach *Gwyn*.....................2C **21**
Sarnesfield *Here*......................3A **40**
Sarn Meyllteyrn *Gwyn*.............1B **20**
Sarn Park Service Area *B'end*..1A **64**
Saron *Carm*.............................1B **56**
.........................(nr Ammanford)
Saron *Carm*.............................2C **45**
...............(nr Newcastle Emlyn)
Saron *Gwyn*............................1A **14**
...........................(nr Bethel)
Saron *Gwyn*............................2D **13**
.........................(nr Bontnewydd)
Saughall *Ches W*.....................3A **10**
Saul *Glos*................................2D **61**
Saundersfoot *Pemb*.................2A **54**
Scethrog *Powy*........................3C **49**
School Green *Ches W*...............1D **19**
Scleddau *Pemb*.......................2C **43**
Scolton *Pemb*.........................3C **43**
Scurlage *Swan*........................1A **62**
Seacombe *Mers*.......................1A **10**
Seaforth *Mers*.........................1A **10**
Sealand *Flin*............................1A **18**
Sea Mills *Bris*.........................2C **67**
Sebastopol *Torf*......................3D **59**
Sedbury *Glos*..........................3C **61**
Sefton *Mers*............................1A **10**
Sefton Pk. *Mers*......................2A **10**
Seifton *Shrp*...........................3B **32**
Selattyn *Shrp*.........................1D **25**
Sellack *Here*............................3C **51**
Senghenydd *Cphy*..................3C **59**
Sennybridge *Powy*..................3A **48**
Seven Sisters *Neat*.................2D **57**
Severn Beach *S Glo*................1C **67**
Shakesfield *Glos*.....................2D **51**
Sharpness *Glos*......................2D **61**
Shavington *Ches E*..................2D **19**
Shawbirch *Telf*.......................3D **27**
Shawbury *Shrp*.......................2C **27**
Sheepway *N Som*...................2B **66**
Sheinton *Shrp*........................1D **33**
Shelderton *Shrp*.....................1B **40**
Shell Green *Hal*......................2C **11**
Shelsley Beauchamp *Worc*......2D **41**
Shelsley Walsh *Worc*..............2D **41**
Shelton *Shrp*..........................3B **26**
Shelve *Shrp*...........................2A **32**
Shelwick *Here*........................1C **51**
Shelwick Green *Here*...............1C **51**
Shenmore *Here*.......................2A **50**
Shepperdine *S Glo*..................3D **61**
Shifnal *Shrp*...........................1D **33**
Shipham *Som*.........................3B **66**
Shipton *Shrp*..........................2C **33**
Shirehampton *Bris*..................2C **67**
Shirenewton *Mon*...................3B **60**
Shirl Heath *Here*.....................3B **40**
Shobdon *Here*........................2A **40**
Shocklach *Ches W*..................3B **18**
Shoot Hill *Shrp*.......................3B **26**
Shortwood *S Glo*....................2D **67**
Shoscombe *Bath*.....................3D **67**
**Shotton** *Flin*.......................1A **18**
Shotwick *Ches W*....................3A **10**
Shrawardine *Shrp*...................3B **26**
**Shrewsbury** *Shrp*.....72 (3B **26**)
Shucknall *Here*.......................1C **51**
Sibdon Carwood *Shrp*.............3B **32**
Sidbury *Shrp*..........................3D **33**
Sidcot *N Som*.........................3B **66**
Sigingstone *V Glam*.................2A **64**
Silian *Cdgn*.............................3A **36**
Silvington *Shrp*......................1D **41**
Simm's Cross *Hal*...................2C **11**
Simm's Lane End *Mers*...........1C **11**
Simpson *Pemb*........................1B **52**
Simpson Cross *Pemb*..............1B **52**
Sirhowy *Blae*..........................1C **59**

Siston *S Glo*...........................2D **67**
Six Bells *Blae*.........................2D **59**
Skenfrith *Mon*........................3B **50**
Sketty *Swan*...........................3B **56**
Skewen *Neat*..........................3C **57**
Skyborry Green *Shrp*..............1D **39**
Slade *Swan*............................1A **62**
Sleap *Shrp*.............................2B **26**
Slimbridge *Glos*......................2D **61**
Smithies, The *Shrp*.................2D **33**
Smithy Green *Ches E*..............3D **11**
Snailbeach *Shrp*.....................1A **32**
Snead *Powy*............................2A **32**
Snead Common *Worc*..............2D **41**
Snitton *Shrp*...........................1C **41**
Snodhill *Here*..........................1A **50**
Soar *Powy*..............................2A **48**
Soar *Gwyn*..............................1B **22**
Soar *IOA*..................................3C **5**
Soar *Carm*..............................3B **46**
Sodom *Den*..............................3B **8**
Sollers Dilwyn *Here*................3B **40**
Sollers Hope *Here*...................2D **51**
Solva *Pemb*............................3A **42**
Soudley *Shrp*..........................2B **32**
...................(nr Church Stretton)
Soudley *Shrp*..........................2D **27**
...................(nr Market Drayton)
Soughton *Flin*.........................1D **17**
Sound *Ches E*.........................3D **19**
Soundwell *S Glo*.....................2D **67**
South Cornelly *B'end*..............1D **63**
Southdown *Bath*.....................3D **67**
Southend *Glos*........................3D **61**
Southerndown *V Glam*.............2D **63**
Southgate *Swan*.....................1A **62**
Southgate *Cdgn*......................3A **28**
South Stoke *Bath*...................3D **67**
South Widcombe *Bath*.............3C **67**
Speke *Mers*............................2B **10**
Spital *Mers*.............................2A **10**
Spittal *Pemb*...........................3C **43**
Sproston Green *Ches W*..........1D **19**
Spurstow *Ches E*....................2C **19**
Stableford *Shrp*......................2D **33**
Stackpole *Pemb*......................3C **53**
Stackpole Elidor *Pemb*...........3C **53**
Stafford Pk. *Telf*.....................1D **33**
Stamford Bridge *Ches W*.........1B **18**
Standford Bridge *Telf*.............2D **27**
Stanford Bishop *Here*..............3D **41**
Stanford Bridge *Worc*.............2D **41**
Stanford on Teme *Worc*...........2D **41**
Stanley *Shrp*...........................3D **33**
Stanley Hill *Here*.....................1D **51**
Stanlow *Ches W*.....................3B **10**
Stansbatch *Here*.....................2A **40**
Stanthorne *Ches W*.................1D **19**
Stanton Drew *Bath*.................3C **67**
Stanton Lacy *Shrp*..................1B **40**
Stanton Long *Shrp*..................2C **33**
Stanton Prior *Bath*..................3D **67**
Stanton upon Hine Heath *Shrp*.2C **27**
Stanton Wick *Bath*..................3D **67**
Stanwardine in the Fields
    *Shrp*................................2B **26**
Stanwardine in the Wood
    *Shrp*................................2B **26**
Stapeley *Ches E*.....................3D **19**
Staple Hill *S Glo*....................2D **67**
Stapleton *Bris*........................2D **67**
Stapleton *Here*.......................2A **40**
Stapleton *Shrp*.......................1B **32**
Staplow *Here*.........................1D **51**
Star *Pemb*..............................2B **44**
Staunton *Glos*........................1C **61**
Staunton on Arrow *Here*.........2A **40**
Staunton on Wye *Here*...........1A **50**
Staylittle *Powy*......................2D **29**

Steel Heath *Shrp*....................1C **27**
Steen's Bridge *Here*................3C **41**
Stepaside *Pemb*......................2A **54**
Steynton *Pemb*.......................2C **53**
Stifford's Bridge *Here*.............1D **51**
Stinchcombe *Glos*...................3D **61**
Stiperstones *Shrp*...................1A **32**
Stirchley *Telf*..........................1D **33**
Stoak *Ches W*.........................3B **10**
Stocking *Here*.........................2D **51**
Stockton *Shrp*.........................2D **33**
...........................(nr Bridgnorth)
Stockton *Shrp*........................1D **31**
...........................(nr Chirbury)
Stockton *Here*.........................2C **41**
Stockton Heath *Warr*..............2D **11**
Stockton on Teme *Worc*..........2D **41**
Stockwood *Bris*......................3D **67**
Stoke Bliss *Worc*....................2D **41**
Stoke Cross *Here*....................3D **41**
Stoke Edith *Here*....................1D **51**
Stoke Gifford *S Glo*................2D **67**
Stoke Heath *Shrp*...................2D **27**
Stoke Lacy *Here*.....................1D **51**
Stoke on Tern *Shrp*.................2D **27**
Stoke Prior *Here*.....................3C **41**
Stoke St Milborough *Shrp*.......3C **33**
Stokesay *Shrp*........................3B **32**
Stone *Glos*..............................3D **61**
Stoneacton *Shrp*.....................2C **33**
Stonebridge *N Som*.................3A **66**
Stone-edge Batch *N Som*........2B **66**
Stoneley Green *Ches E*...........2D **19**
Stoney Stretton *Shrp*..............1A **32**
Stony Cross *Here*....................1D **51**
...................(nr Great Malvern)
Stony Cross *Here*....................2C **41**
...........................(nr Leominster)
Storeton *Mers*........................2A **10**
Storridge *Here*........................1D **51**
Stottesdon *Shrp*.....................3D **33**
Stowe *Glos*.............................2C **61**
Stowe *Shrp*.............................1A **40**
Stowey *Bath*...........................3C **67**
Strangford *Here*......................3C **51**
Strata Florida *Cdgn*................2C **37**
Street Dinas *Shrp*...................1A **26**
Strefford *Shrp*........................3B **32**
Stretford *Here*.........................3C **41**
Stretton *Ches W*.....................2B **18**
Stretton *Warr*.........................2D **11**
Stretton Grandison *Here*.........1D **51**
Stretton Heath *Shrp*...............3A **26**
Stretton Sugwas *Here*............1B **50**
Stretton Westwood *Shrp*.........2C **33**
Stroat *Glos*.............................3C **61**
Stryd *IOA*................................2B **4**
Stryt-issa *Wrex*......................3D **17**
Suckley *Worc*..........................3D **41**
Suckley Knowl *Worc*...............3D **41**
Sudbrook *Mon*........................1C **67**
Sugar Loaf Halt (Rail) *Powy*......1D **47**
Sugwas Pool *Here*..................1B **50**
Sully *V Glam*...........................3C **65**
Summerhill *Pemb*....................2A **54**
Sutton *Shrp*...........................3D **33**
...........................(nr Bridgnorth)
Sutton *Shrp*...........................1D **27**
...................(nr Market Drayton)
Sutton *Shrp*...........................2A **26**
...........................(nr Oswestry)
Sutton *Shrp*...........................3C **27**
...........................(nr Shrewsbury)
Sutton *Pemb*..........................1C **53**
Sutton *Worc*...........................2D **41**
Sutton Leach *Mers*.................1C **11**
Sutton Maddock *Shrp*.............1D **33**
Sutton St Michael *Here*...........1C **51**
Sutton St Nicholas *Here*..........1C **51**

Sutton Weaver *Ches W*............3C 11
Swainshill *Here*......................1B 50
Swanbridge *V Glam*.................3C 65
Swan Green *Ches W*................3D 11
**Swansea** *Swan*..............**72** (3B 56)
Swansea Airport *Swan*...........3A 56
Swansea Service Area *Swan*...3B 56
Swanwick Green *Ches E*........3C 19
Sweet Green *Worc*..................2D 41
Swffryd *Blae*...........................3D 59
Swineford *S Glo*.....................3D 67
Swinmore Common *Here*........1D 51
Sworton Heath *Ches E*...........2D 11
Swyddffynnon *Cdgn*................2B 36
Sycharth *Powy*.......................2D 25
Sychdyn *Flin*..........................1D 17
Sychnant *Powy*......................1A 38
Sychtyn *Powy*........................1A 30
Sydney *Ches E*.......................2D 19
Sylen *Carm*............................2A 56
Sylfaen *Powy*.........................1C 31
Symonds Yat *Here*.................1C 61
Synod Inn *Cdgn*......................3D 35

## T

Tadwick *Bath*.........................2D 67
Tafarnaubach *Blae*.................1C 59
Tafarn-y-bwlch *Pemb*.............2D 43
Tafarn-y-Gelyn *Den*...............1C 17
Taff's Well *Rhon*....................1C 65
Tafolwern *Powy*.....................1D 29
Tai-bach *Powy*.......................2C 25
Taibach *Neat*........................1C 63
Tai-Nant *Wrex*.......................3D 17
Tai'n Lon *Gwyn*.....................2D 13
Tairgwaith *Neat*....................1C 57
Talachddu *Powy*....................2B 48
Talacre *Flin*...........................2C 9
Talardd *Gwyn*........................2D 23
Talbenny *Pemb*......................1B 52
Talbot Green *Rhon*.................1B 64
Talerddig *Powy*......................1A 30
Talgarreg *Cdgn*......................3D 35
Talgarth *Powy*.......................2C 49
Tallarn Green *Wrex*...............3B 18
Talley *Carm*...........................2B 46
Talog *Carm*............................3C 45
Talsarn *Carm*.........................3C 47
Talsarn *Cdgn*.........................3A 36
Talsarnau *Gwyn*.....................1B 22
Talwrn *Wrex*..........................3D 17
Talwrn *IOA*............................3D 5
Tal-y-Bont *Cnwy*....................1C 15
Tal-y-bont *Gwyn*.....................3B 6
..............................(nr Bangor)
Tal-y-bont *Gwyn*....................2A 22
.............................(nr Barmouth)
Tal-y-bont *Cdgn*.....................3B 28
Talybont-on-Usk *Powy*............3C 49
Tal-y-cafn *Cnwy*.....................3C 7
Tal-y-coed *Mon*......................1B 60
Tal-y-llyn *Gwyn*......................1C 29
Talyllyn *Powy*........................3C 49
Talysarn *Gwyn*.......................2D 13
Tal-y-waenydd *Gwyn*..............3B 14
Talywain *Torf*.........................2D 59
Tal-y-Wern *Powy*....................1D 29
Tanerdy *Carm*........................3D 45
Tangiers *Pemb*.......................1C 53
Tan-lan *Cnwy*.........................1C 15
Tan-lan *Gwyn*........................3B 14
Tan-y-bwlch *Gwyn*..................3B 14
Tan-y-fron *Cnwy*....................1A 16
Tanyfron *Wrex*.......................2D 17
Tanygrisiau *Gwyn*...................3B 14
Tan-y-groes *Cdgn*..................1B 44
Tan-y-pistyll *Powy*..................2B 24
Tan-yr-allt *Den*.......................2B 8

Tarbock Green *Mers*...............2B 10
Tarporley *Ches W*...................1C 19
Tarrington *Here*......................1D 51
Tarvin *Ches W*........................1B 18
Tasley *Shrp*............................2D 33
Tattenhall *Ches W*..................2B 18
Tavernspite *Pemb*..................1A 54
Taynton *Glos*.........................3D 51
Tedsmore *Shrp*.......................2A 26
Tedstone Delamere *Here*.........3D 41
Tedstone Wafer *Here*..............3D 41
Tegryn *Pemb*.........................2B 44
**Telford** *Telf*......................3D 27
Temple Bar *Carm*...................1A 56
Temple Bar *Cdgn*...................3A 36
Temple Cloud *Bath*.................3D 67
Templeton *Pemb*....................1A 54
Tenbury Wells *Worc*...............2C 41
Tenby *Pemb*...........................2A 54
Terfyn *Cnwy*...........................3A 8
Ternhill *Shrp*..........................1D 27
Tetchill *Shrp*..........................1A 26
Thatto Heath *Mers*.................1C 11
Thelwall *Warr*........................2D 11
Thingwall *Mers*......................2D 9
Thomas Chapel *Pemb*.............2A 54
Thomastown *Rhon*..................1B 64
Thorn *Powy*............................2D 39
**Thornbury** *S Glo*...............3D 61
Thornbury *Here*......................3D 41
Thornhill *Cphy*.......................1C 65
Thornton *Mers*.......................1A 10
Thornton *Pemb*......................2C 53
Thornton Hough *Mers*.............2A 10
Thornton-le-Moors
.... *Ches W*............................3B 10
Threapwood *Ches W*..............3B 18
Three Ashes *Here*...................3C 51
Three Cocks *Powy*..................2C 49
Three Crosses *Swan*...............3A 56
Thruxton *Here*........................2B 50
Thurstaston *Mers*...................2D 9
Tibberton *Telf*........................2D 27
Tickenham *N Som*..................2B 66
Ticklerton *Shrp*......................2B 32
Tidenham *Glos*.......................3C 61
Tiers Cross *Pemb*...................1C 53
Tillers Green *Glos*..................2D 51
Tilley *Shrp*.............................2C 27
Tillington *Here*.......................1B 50
Tillington Common *Here*.........1B 50
Tilstock *Shrp*.........................1C 27
Tilston *Ches W*.......................2B 18
Tilstone Fearnall *Ches W*........1C 19
Timsbury *Bath*.......................3D 67
Tintern *Mon*...........................2C 61
Tircoed Forest Village
.... *Swan*...............................2B 56
Tir-Phil *Cphy*.........................2C 59
Tir-y-dail *Carm*......................1B 56
Titley *Here*.............................3A 40
Tiverton *Ches W*.....................1C 19
Tockington *S Glo*...................1D 67
Todding *Here*.........................1B 40
Ton *Mon*................................3A 60
Tondu *B'end*..........................1D 63
Tonfanau *Gwyn*......................1A 28
Tongwynlais *Card*..................1C 65
Tonmawr *Neat*.......................3D 57
Tonna *Neat*............................3C 57
Tonnau *Neat*..........................3C 57
Ton Pentre *Rhon*....................3A 58
Ton-Teg *Rhon*........................1B 64
Tonypandy *Rhon*....................3A 58
Tonyrefail *Rhon*.....................1B 64
Tortworth *S Glo*.....................3D 61
Tower Hill *Mers*.....................1B 10
Town End *Mers*......................2B 10

Townhill *Swan*........................3B 56
Towyn *Cnwy*..........................3A 8
Toxteth *Mers*.........................2A 10
Trallong *Powy*........................3A 48
Trallwng, Y *Powy*...................1D 31
Tranmere *Mers*......................2A 10
Trapp *Carm*...........................1B 56
Trawscoed *Powy*....................2B 48
Trawsfynydd *Gwyn*.................1C 23
Trawsgoed *Cdgn*....................1B 36
Treaddow *Here*......................3C 51
Trealaw *Rhon*.........................3B 58
Trearddur *IOA*........................3B 4
Trebanog *Rhon*......................3B 58
Trebanos *Neat*.......................2C 57
Trecastle *Powy*......................3D 47
Trecelyn *Cphy*........................3D 59
Trecenydd *Cphy*.....................1C 65
Trecwn *Pemb*.........................2C 43
Trecynon *Rhon*......................2A 58
**Tredegar** *Blae*...................2C 59
Trederwen *Powy*....................3D 25
Tredogan *V Glam*....................3B 64
Tredomen *Powy*.....................2C 49
Tredunnock *Mon*....................3A 60
Tredustan *Powy*......................2C 49
Trefaldwyn *Powy*....................2D 31
Trefasser *Pemb*......................2B 42
Trefdraeth *IOA*........................3D 5
Trefdraeth *Pemb*....................2D 43
Trefecca *Powy*.......................2C 49
Trefechan *Mer T*....................2B 58
Trefeglwys *Powy*....................2A 30
Trefenter *Cdgn*......................2B 36
Treffgarne *Pemb*...................3C 43
Treffynnon *Flin*......................3C 9
Treffynnon *Pemb*...................3B 42
Trefil *Blae*.............................1C 59
Trefilan *Cdgn*.........................3A 36
Trefin *Pemb*...........................2B 42
Treflach *Shrp*.........................2D 25
Trefnant *Den*..........................3B 8
Trefonen *Shrp*.......................2D 25
Trefor *Gwyn*...........................3C 13
Trefor *IOA*.............................2C 5
Treforest *Rhon*.......................1B 64
Trefriw *Cnwy*.........................1C 15
Tref-y-Clawdd *Powy*...............1D 39
Trefynwy *Mon*........................1C 61
Tregare *Mon*...........................1B 60
Tregaron *Cdgn*.......................3B 36
Tregarth *Gwyn*.......................1B 14
Tregeiriog *Wrex*.....................1C 25
Tregele *IOA*............................1C 5
Tregolwyn *V Glam*..................2A 64
Tregoyd *Powy*........................2C 49
Tre-groes *Cdgn*......................1D 45
Tregynon *Powy*......................2B 30
Trehafod *Rhon*.......................3B 58
**Treharris** *Mer T*................3B 58
Treherbert *Rhon*....................3A 58
Trelales *B'end*.......................1D 63
Trelawnyd *Flin*........................3B 8
Trelech *Carm*.........................2B 44
Treleddyd-fawr *Pemb*............3A 42
Trelewis *Mer T*......................3C 59
Trellech *Mon*..........................2C 61
Trelleck Grange *Mon*..............2B 60
Trelogan *Flin*..........................2C 9
Trelystan *Powy*......................1D 31
Tremadog *Gwyn*.....................3A 14
Tremain *Cdgn*........................1B 44
Tremeirchion *Den*....................3B 8
Tremorfa *Card*.......................2D 65
Trench *Telf*............................3D 27
Treoes *V Glam*.......................2A 64
Treorchy *Rhon*.......................3A 58
Treorci *Rhon*.........................3A 58
Tre'r-ddol *Cdgn*......................2B 28

Tre'r llai *Powy*........................1D 31
Tresaith *Cdgn*........................3B 34
Tresigin *V Glam*......................2A 64
Tresimwn *V Glam*...................2B 64
Tre Taliesin *Cdgn*...................2B 28
Trethomas *Cphy*....................1C 65
Tretio *Pemb*...........................3A 42
Tretire *Here*...........................3C 51
Tretower *Powy*.......................3C 49
Treuddyn *Flin*.........................2D 17
Trevalyn *Wrex*.......................2A 18
Trevaughan *Carm*...................3D 45
..............................(nr Carmarthen)
Trevaughan *Carm*...................1A 54
..............................(nr Whitland)
Trevethin *Torf*.......................2D 59
Trevor *Wrex*...........................3D 17
Trevor Uchaf *Den*...................3D 17
Trewern *Powy*........................3D 25
Trewyddel *Pemb*....................1A 44
Trimsaran *Carm*.....................2D 55
Trinant *Cphy*..........................3D 59
Trisant *Cdgn*..........................1C 37
Troedrhiwdalar *Powy*..............3A 38
Troedrhiwfuwch *Cphy*.............2C 59
Troedrhiw-gwair *Blae*.............2C 59
Troedyraur *Cdgn*....................1C 45
Troedyrhiw *Mer T*...................2B 58
Truck Stop *Card*.....................1D 65
Truck Stop *Card*.....................2B 64
Truck Stop *Flin*........................3D 9
Truck Stop *IOA*.......................2B 4
Truck Stop *Carm*....................2A 56
Truck Stop *Powy*....................2D 31
Trumpet *Here*........................2D 51
Tryfil *IOA*...............................2D 5
Tudorville *Here*......................3C 51
Tudweiliog *Gwyn*....................1B 20
Tufton *Pemb*..........................3D 43
Tugford *Shrp*.........................3C 33
Tumble *Carm*.........................1A 56
Tunley *Bath*...........................3D 67
Tupsley *Here*..........................1C 51
Turnastone *Here*....................2A 50
Tutshill *Glos*...........................3C 61
Tweedale *Telf*........................1D 33
Twerton *Bath*.........................3D 67
Twinhoe *Bath*........................3D 67
Twiss Green *Warr*...................1D 11
Twitchen *Shrp*........................1A 40
Two Bridges *Glos*...................2D 61
Twyford Common *Here*...........2C 51
Twynllanan *Carm*...................3C 47
Twyn-y-Sheriff *Mon*................2B 60
Tyberton *Here*........................2A 50
Tycroes *Carm*........................1B 56
Tycrwyn *Powy*.......................3C 25
**Tyddewi** *Pemb*..................3A 42
Ty Issa *Powy*.........................1C 25
**Tyldesley** *G Man*...............1D 11
Tylorstown *Rhon*....................3B 58
Tylwch *Powy*.........................3A 30
Tymbl, Y *Carm*......................1A 56
Ty-nant *Cnwy*........................3A 16
Tynewydd *Rhon*.....................3A 58
Ty'n-y-bryn *Rhon*...................1B 64
Tyn-y-celyn *Wrex*...................1C 25
Tyn-y-cwm *Swan*...................2B 56
Tyn-y-ffridd *Powy*...................1C 25
Tynygongl *IOA*........................2A 6
Tynygraig *Cdgn*......................2B 36
Ty'n-y-groes *Cnwy*..................3C 7
Ty'n-yr-eithin *Cdgn*................2B 36
Tyn-y-rhyd *Powy*....................3B 24
Tyn-y-wern *Powy*...................2B 24
Tythegston *B'end*...................2D 63
Tytherington *S Glo*.................1D 67
Tywyn *Cnwy*..........................3C 7
Tywyn *Gwyn*..........................1A 28

## U

Ubley *Bath*..........................3C **67**
Uckington *Shrp*.................1C **33**
Uffington *Shrp*..................3C **27**
Ullingswick *Here*................3C **41**
Underdale *Shrp*..................3C **27**
Underton *Shrp*...................2D **33**
Underwood *Newp*...............1A **66**
Undy *Mon*..........................1B **66**
Upcott *Here*.......................3A **40**
Uphampton *Here*................2A **40**
Uphill *N Som*......................3A **66**
Upleadon *Glos*...................3D **51**
Upper Affcot *Shrp*.............3B **32**
Upper Bangor *Gwyn*............. 3A **6**
Upper Borth *Cdgn*.............3B **28**
Upper Breinton *Here*...........1B **50**
Upper Brynamman *Carm*......1C **57**
Upper Chapel *Powy* .............1B **48**
Upper Church Village
   *Rhon*............................1B **64**
Upper Coedcae *Torf*............2D **59**
Upper Cound *Shrp*..............1C **33**
Upper Cwmbran *Torf*..........3D **59**
Upper Dinchope *Shrp*.........3B **32**
Upper Framilode *Glos*.........1D **61**
Upper Grove Common
   *Here*............................3C **51**
Upper Hardwick *Here*..........3B **40**
Upper Hayton *Shrp*.............3C **33**
Upper Heath *Shrp*...............3C **33**
Upper Hengoed *Shrp*..........1D **25**
Upper Hergest *Here*............3D **39**
Upper Hill *Here*..................3B **40**
Upper Killay *Swan*..............3A **56**
Upper Langford *N Som*........3B **66**
Upper Longwood *Shrp*..........1D **33**
Upper Lydbrook *Glos*..........1D **61**
Upper Lye *Here*..................2A **40**
Upper Maes-coed *Here*........2A **50**
Upper Millichope *Shrp* ..........3C **33**
Upper Nash *Pemb*...............2D **53**
Upper Netchwood *Shrp*........2D **33**
Upper Rochford *Worc*...........2D **41**
Upper Sapey *Here*...............2D **41**
Upper Soudley *Glos*............1D **61**
Upper Town *N Som* ..............3C **67**
Upper Town *Here*................1C **51**
Uppington *Shrp*..................1D **33**
Upton *Ches W*.....................1B **18**
Upton *Mers*..........................2D **9**
Upton *Pemb*.......................2D **53**
Upton Bishop *Here*..............3D **51**
Upton Cheyney *S Glo*..........3D **67**
Upton Cressett *Shrp*............2D **33**
Upton Crews *Here*...............3D **51**
Upton Heath *Ches W*............1B **18**
Upton Magna *Shrp*..............3C **27**
Urdimarsh *Here* .................1C **51**
Usk *Mon*...........................2A **60**
Utkinton *Ches W*................1C **19**
Uwchmynydd *Gwyn*............2A **20**
Uzmaston *Pemb*..................1C **53**

## V

Valley *IOA*..........................3B **4**
Van *Powy*...........................3A **30**
Varteg *Torf*........................2D **59**
Vauld, The *Here*.................1C **51**
Vaynor *Mer T*.....................1B **58**
Velindre *Powy*....................2C **49**
Vennington *Shrp*.................1A **32**
Venn's Green *Here*..............1C **51**
Vernolds Common *Shrp*...........3B **32**
Viney Hill *Glos*..................2D **61**
Vowchurch *Here*.................2A **50**
Vulcan Village *Mers*.................1C **11**

## W

Waddicar *Mers* ..................1A **10**
Waen *Den*.........................1C **17**
   .............................(nr Llandymog)
Waen *Den*.........................1A **16**
   .................................(nr Nantglyn)
Waen *Powy*.......................2A **30**
Waen Fach *Powy*.................3D **25**
Waen Goleugoed *Den* .............3B **8**
Walcot *Telf*........................3C **27**
Walford *Here*.....................1A **40**
   ........................(nr Leintwardine)
Walford *Here*.....................3C **51**
   .........................(nr Ross-on-Wye)
Walford *Shrp*.....................2B **26**
Walford Heath *Shrp*............3B **26**
Walgherton *Ches E*.............3D **19**
**Walkden** *G Man*.................1D **11**
Walker's Green *Here*..............1C **51**
**Wallasey** *Mers*.....................1D **9**
Wallaston Green *Pemb*............2C **53**
Wallis *Pemb*.......................3D **43**
Wall under Heywood *Shrp*......2C **33**
Walterston *V Glam*..............2B **64**
Walterstone *Here*................3A **50**
Walton *Mers*.......................1A **10**
Walton *Powy*.......................3D **39**
Walton *Telf*........................3C **27**
Walton East *Pemb* ...............3D **43**
Walton in Gordano *N Som*........2B **66**
Walton West *Pemb* ..............1B **52**
Walwyn's Castle *Pemb* ..........1B **52**
Wanswell *Glos*...................2D **61**
Wapley *S Glo*.....................2D **67**
Warburton *G Man*................2D **11**
Wardle *Ches E*....................2D **19**
Warmingham *Ches E*............1D **19**
Warmley *S Glo*....................2D **67**
Warren *Pemb*.....................3C **53**
**Warrington** *Warr*...................2D **11**
Waterloo *Cphy*...................1C **65**
Waterloo *Here*....................1A **50**
Waterloo *Mers*....................1A **10**
Waterloo *Pemb*...................2C **53**
Waterloo *Shrp*.....................1B **26**
Waterston *Pemb*.................2C **53**
Waters Upton *Telf*...............3D **27**
Wattlesborough Heath *Shrp*.....3A **26**
Wattstown *Rhon*.................3B **58**
Wattsville *Cphy*..................3D **59**
Waun *Powy* ........................3D **25**
Waun, Y *Wrex*....................1D **25**
Waunarlwydd *Swan*................3B **56**
Waun Fawr *Cdgn*.................3B **28**
Waunfawr *Gwyn*..................2A **14**
Waungilwen *Carm*..............2C **45**
Waun-Lwyd *Blae* .................2C **59**
Waun y Clyn *Carm*...............2D **55**
Waverton *Ches W*.................1B **18**
Wavertree *Mers*..................2A **10**
Wdig *Pemb*........................2C **43**
Weaverham *Ches W*...............3D **11**
Webton *Here*......................2B **50**
Wellington *Here*.................1B **50**
Wellington *Telf*..................3D **27**
Wellington Heath *Here*...........1D **51**
Wellow *Bath*......................3D **67**
Wells Green *Ches E*.............2D **19**
Welshampton *Shrp*..............1B **26**
Welsh End *Shrp*..................1C **27**
Welsh Frankton *Shrp* ..............1A **26**
Welsh Hook *Pemb* ...............3C **43**
Welsh Newton *Here*.............1B **60**
Welsh Newton Common *Here*..1C **61**
Welshpool *Powy*.................1D **31**
Welsh St Donats *V Glam*..........2B **64**
Wem *Shrp* .........................2C **27**
Wenallt *Gwyn* ....................3A **16**
Wenallt *Cdgn*....................1B **36**
Wentnor *Shrp* ....................2A **32**
Wenvoe *V Glam*..................2C **65**
Weobley *Here*....................3B **40**
Weobley Marsh *Here*............3B **40**
Wern *Powy*.........................1C **59**
   ....................................(nr Brecon)
Wern *Powy*.........................3D **25**
   .................................(nr Guilsfield)
Wern *Powy*.........................3A **24**
   ..............................(nr Llangadfan)
Wern *Powy*.........................2D **25**
   .............................(nr Llanymynech)
Wern *Gwyn*.......................3A **14**
Wernffrwd *Swan*.................3A **56**
Wernyrheolydd *Mon*.................1A **60**
Wervin *Ches W*....................3B **10**
West Aberthaw *V Glam*...........3B **64**
West Bank *Hal*....................2C **11**
Westbrook *Here*..................1D **49**
Westbury *Shrp*....................1A **32**
Westbury-on-Severn *Glos*........1D **61**
Westbury on Trym *Bris* ...........2C **67**
West Cross *Swan*.................1B **62**
West Derby *Mers*.................1A **10**
West End *N Som*..................3B **66**
West End *S Glo*...................1D **67**
Westerleigh *S Glo*................2D **67**
Westfield *Bath*....................1B **26**
West Felton *Shrp*.................2A **26**
West Harptree *Bath* .............3C **67**
West Hewish *N Som*.............3A **66**
Westhide *Here*....................1C **51**
West Hill *N Som*..................2B **66**
Westhope *Here*...................3B **40**
Westhope *Shrp*...................3B **32**
**West Kirby** *Mers*..................2D **9**
Westleigh *G Man* .................1D **11**
Westley *Shrp*......................1A **32**
Weston *Ches E*....................2D **19**
Weston *Shrp*.......................2C **33**
   ...............................(nr Bridgnorth)
Weston *Shrp*.......................1A **40**
   ..................................(nr Knighton)
Weston *Shrp*.......................2C **27**
   .......................................(nr Wem)
Weston *Bath*.......................3D **67**
Weston *Here*.......................3A **40**
Weston *Hal*.........................2C **11**
Weston Beggard *Here*............1C **51**
Westoncommon *Shrp*.............2B **26**
Weston in Gordano *N Som*........2B **66**
Weston Lullingfields *Shrp* ........2B **26**
Weston Rhyn *Shrp*................1D **25**
**Weston-super-Mare**
   *N Som*..........................3A **66**
Weston under Penyard *Here* ....3D **51**
Westra *V Glam*....................2C **65**
West Town *Bath*..................3C **67**
West Town *N Som*................3B **66**
West Wales Airport Aberporth
   *Cdgn* ...........................1B **44**
West Wick *N Som*.................3A **66**
West Williamston *Pemb*...........2D **53**
Wettenhall *Ches E*...............1D **19**
Weythel *Powy*....................3D **39**
Wharton *Ches W*.................1D **19**
Wharton *Here*.....................3C **41**
Whatmore *Shrp*...................1D **41**
Wheathill *Shrp*...................3D **33**
Wheelock *Ches E*.................2D **19**
Wheelock Heath *Ches E*...........2D **19**
Whelston *Flin*......................3D **9**
Whiston *Mers*......................1B **10**
Whitbourne *Here*.................3D **41**
Whitby *Ches W*....................3A **10**
Whitbyheath *Ches W*.............3A **10**
Whitchurch *Bath*..................3D **67**
Whitchurch *Card*..................2C **65**
Whitchurch *Here*..................1C **61**
Whitchurch *Pemb*................3A **42**
Whitchurch *Shrp*.................3C **19**
Whitcot *Shrp*......................2A **32**
Whitcott Keysett *Shrp*.............3D **31**
Whitebrook *Mon*..................2C **61**
Whitechurch *Pemb* ..............2A **44**
Whitecroft *Glos*...................2D **61**
Whitegate *Ches W*................1D **19**
Whitehaven *Shrp*.................2D **25**
White Mill *Carm*..................3D **45**
White Rocks *Here*................3B **50**
White Stone *Here*................1C **51**
Whitfield *S Glo*...................3D **61**
Whitford *Flin*......................3C **9**
Whitland *Carm*...................1B **54**
Whitney-on-Wye *Here*............1D **49**
Whitson *Newp*....................1A **66**
Whittingslow *Shrp*...............3B **32**
Whittington *Shrp*.................1A **26**
Whitton *Powy*.....................2D **39**
Whitton *Shrp*......................1C **41**
Whixall *Shrp*......................1C **27**
Whyle *Here*........................2C **41**
Wibdon *Glos*......................3C **61**
Wick *S Glo*.........................2D **67**
Wick *V Glam*......................2A **64**
Wick St Lawrence *N Som* ........3A **66**
Wickwar *S Glo*....................1D **67**
**Widnes** *Hal*.......................2C **11**
Wigmore *Here*....................2B **40**
Wilcott *Shrp*.......................3A **26**
Wilderspool *Warr*.................2D **11**
Wilkesley *Ches E*.................3D **19**
Willaston *Ches E*.................2D **19**
   .......................................(nr Crewe)
Willaston *Ches W*.................3A **10**
   ....................................(nr Neston)
Willersley *Here*....................1A **50**
Willey *Shrp*........................2D **33**
Willington Corner *Ches W* .......1C **19**
Willoughbridge *Staf*.............3D **19**
Willsbridge *S Glo* ................2D **67**
Wilmington *Bath*..................3D **67**
Wilson *Here*.......................3C **51**
Wimboldsley *Ches W*............1D **19**
Wincham *Ches W*.................3D **11**
Windle Hill *Ches W*...............3A **10**
Winford *N Som*....................3C **67**
Winforton *Here*...................1D **49**
Winnal Common *Here*............2B **50**
Winnington *Ches W*..............3D **11**
Winnington *Staf*..................1D **27**
Winscombe *N Som*...............3B **66**
**Winsford** *Ches W*.................1D **19**
Winsh-wen *Swan*.................3B **56**
Winterbourne *S Glo*..............1D **67**
Winterley *Ches E*.................2D **19**
Winwick *Warr*....................1D **11**
Wirswall *Ches E*...................3C **19**
Wistanstow *Shrp*.................3B **32**
Wistanswick *Shrp*................2D **27**
Wistaston *Ches E*.................2D **19**
Wiston *Pemb*......................1D **53**
Withington *Here*..................1C **51**
Withington *Shrp*..................3C **27**
Withington Marsh *Here*..........1C **51**
Wixhill *Shrp*.......................2C **27**
Wolferlow *Here*...................2D **41**
Wolf's Castle *Pemb*...............3C **43**
Wolfsdale *Pemb*..................3C **43**
Wollaston *Shrp* ..................3A **26**
Wollerton *Shrp*...................1D **27**
Wolverley *Shrp*...................1B **26**
Wolvesnewton *Mon*..............3B **60**
Womaston *Powy*..................2D **39**
Wood *Pemb*.......................3B **42**
Woodbank *Ches W*...............3A **10**
Woodchurch *Mers*................2D **9**
Woodcroft *Glos*...................3C **61**

| | | |
|---|---|---|
| Woodford *Glos*......................3D **61** | Wootton *Shrp*......................2A **26** | Wykey *Shrp*......................2A **26** |
| Woodhill *N Som*......................2B **66** | ......................(nr Oswestry) | Wyndham *B'end*......................3A **58** |
| Woodhill *Shrp*......................3D **33** | Worldsend *Shrp*......................2B **32** | Wyson *Here*......................2C **41** |
| Woodhouses *Ches W*......................3C **11** | Worle *N Som*......................3A **66** | |
| Woodlane *Shrp*......................2D **27** | Worleston *Ches E*......................2D **19** | |
| Woods Eaves *Here*......................1D **49** | Wormbridge *Here*......................2B **50** | |
| Woodseaves *Shrp*......................1D **27** | Wormelow Tump *Here*......................2B **50** | |
| Woodstock Slop *Pemb*......................3D **43** | Wormsley *Here*......................1B **50** | |
| Woofferton *Shrp*......................2C **41** | Worsley *G Man*......................1D **11** | |
| Woolaston *Glos*......................3C **61** | Worthen *Shrp*......................1A **32** | |
| Woolhope *Here*......................2D **51** | Worthenbury *Wrex*......................3B **18** | |
| Woollard *Bath*......................3D **67** | Wotherton *Shrp*......................1D **31** | |
| Woolley *Bath*......................3D **67** | Wraxall *N Som*......................2B **66** | |
| Woolstaston *Shrp*......................2B **32** | **Wrecsam** *Wrex*......................**72** (2A **18**) | |
| Woolston *Shrp*......................3B **32** | Wrenbury *Ches E*......................3C **19** | |
| ......................(nr Church Stretton) | Wrennall *Shrp*......................1B **32** | |
| Woolston *Shrp*......................2A **26** | **Wrexham** *Wrex*......................**72** (2A **18**) | |
| ......................(nr Oswestry) | Wrickton *Shrp*......................3D **33** | |
| Woolston *Warr*......................2D **11** | Wrinehill *Staf*......................3D **19** | |
| Woolton *Mers*......................2B **10** | Wrington *N Som*......................3B **66** | |
| Woonton *Here*......................3A **40** | Wrockwardine *Telf*......................3D **27** | |
| ......................(nr Kington) | Wroxeter *Shrp*......................1C **33** | |
| Woonton *Here*......................2C **41** | Wybunbury *Ches E*......................3D **19** | |
| ......................(nr Leominster) | Wyddgrug, Yr *Flin*......................1D **17** | |
| Woore *Shrp*......................3D **19** | Wyesham *Mon*......................1C **61** | |
| Wootton *Shrp*......................1B **40** | Wyke, The *Shrp*......................1D **33** | |
| ......................(nr Ludlow) | Wyke *Shrp*......................1D **33** | |

## Y

| | | |
|---|---|---|
| Yanley *N Som*......................3C **67** | Ynysmeudwy *Neat*......................2C **57** |
| Yardro *Powy*......................3D **39** | Ynystawe *Swan*......................2B **56** |
| Yarkhill *Here*......................1D **51** | Ynys-wen *Rhon*......................3A **58** |
| Yarpole *Here*......................2B **40** | Ynyswen *Powy*......................1D **57** |
| Yarsop *Here*......................1B **50** | Ynys y Barri *V Glam*......................3C **65** |
| Yate *S Glo*......................1D **67** | Ynysybwl *Rhon*......................3B **58** |
| Yatton *Here*......................2B **40** | Ynysymaerdy *Neat*......................3C **57** |
| ......................(nr Leominster) | Yockleton *Shrp*......................3B **26** |
| Yatton *Here*......................2D **51** | Yorkley *Glos*......................2D **61** |
| ......................(nr Ross-on-Wye) | Yorton *Shrp*......................2C **27** |
| Yatton *N Som*......................3B **66** | Yorton Heath *Shrp*......................2C **27** |
| Yazor *Here*......................1B **50** | Ysbyty Cynfyn *Cdgn*......................1C **37** |
| Yearsett *Here*......................3D **41** | Ysbyty Ifan *Cnwy*......................3D **15** |
| Yeaton *Shrp*......................3B **26** | Ysbyty Ystwyth *Cdgn*......................1C **37** |
| Yerbeston *Pemb*......................2D **53** | Ysceifiog *Flin*......................3C **9** |
| Ynysboeth *Rhon*......................3B **58** | Yspitty *Carm*......................3A **56** |
| Ynysddu *Cphy*......................3C **59** | Ystalyfera *Neat*......................2C **57** |
| Ynysforgan *Swan*......................3B **56** | Ystrad *Rhon*......................3A **58** |
| Ynyshir *Rhon*......................3B **58** | Ystrad Aeron *Cdgn*......................3A **36** |
| Ynyslas *Cdgn*......................2B **28** | Ystradfellte *Powy*......................1A **58** |
| Ynysmaerdy *Rhon*......................1B **64** | Ystradffin *Carm*......................1C **47** |
| | Ystradgynlais *Powy*......................1C **57** |
| | Ystradmeurig *Cdgn*......................2C **37** |
| | Ystrad Mynach *Cphy*......................3C **59** |
| | Ystradowen *V Glam*......................2B **64** |
| | Ystradowen *Carm*......................1C **57** |
| | Ystumtuen *Cdgn*......................1C **37** |

Published by Geographers' A-Z Map Company Limited
An imprint of HarperCollins Publishers
Westerhill Road
Bishopbriggs
Glasgow
G64 2QT

www.az.co.uk
a-z.maps@harpercollins.co.uk

HarperCollinsPublishers
Macken House, 39/40 Mayor Street Upper, Dublin 1, D01 C9W8, Ireland

13th edition 2023